Eye Tracking in Experience Design

Eye Tracking in User Experience Design

Jennifer Romano Bergstrom, Ph.D
Andrew Jonathan Schall

AMSTERDAM • BOSTON • HEIDELBERG • LONDON
NEW YORK • OXFORD • PARIS • SAN DIEGO
SAN FRANCISCO • SINGAPORE • SYDNEY • TOKYO

Morgan Kaufmann is an imprint of Elsevier

Acquiring Editor: *Meg Dunkerley*
Editorial Project Manager: *Heather Scherer*
Project Manager: *Punithavathy Govindaradjane*
Designer: *Alan Studholme*

Morgan Kaufmann is an imprint of Elsevier
225 Wyman Street, Waltham, MA 02451, USA

Library of Congress Cataloging-in-Publication Data
Eye tracking in user experience design / edited by Jennifer Romano Bergstrom and Andrew Jonathan Schall.
    pages cm
  Includes bibliographical references and index.
  ISBN 978-0-12-408138-3 (alk. paper)
  1. Human-computer interaction. 2. Visual perception. 3. Eye–Movements. 4. Eye tracking. 5. User interfaces (Computer systems) I. Bergstrom, Jennifer Romano. II. Schall, Andrew Jonathan.
  QA76.9.H85E974 2014
  004.01'9–dc23

                                                   2013045342

British Library Cataloguing-in-Publication Data
A catalogue record for this book is available from the British Library

ISBN: 978-0-12-408138-3

For information on all MK publications, visit our website at *www.mkp.com*

DEDICATION

To Hadley, for your endless encouragement and inspiration.

-Jen

To Grandma Mollie for helping to instill in me a love of learning and to never be satisfied with just doing "good enough."

-Andrew

CONTENTS

ACKNOWLEDGMENTS

Thank you to Elizabeth Buie for guidance during the book's formation; to Meg Dunkerly, Heather Scherer, and Kaitlin Herbert (Morgan Kaufmann) for editorial assistance; to Brian Griepentrog, Sean Marsh, and Jason Fors (Fors Marsh Group) for support and encouragement, and to Spencer Gerrol (Spark Experience) for being a supporter and passionate advocate for this project. Also a big thanks to Brett Tunick (Spark Experience) for an amazing cover design.

ABOUT THE EDITORS

Andrew Schall has worked with numerous public and private organizations to use eye tracking as part of their user-centered design process including organizations such as Aflac, Fossil, GlaxoSmithKline, NASA, PBS, Rovio, and the U.S. Department of Energy. His eye tracking projects have ranged from understanding how children interact with online multimedia to evaluating advanced search and retrieval systems.

Andrew has pioneered new ways to collect, analyze, and present eye-tracking data. He is currently working on strategies to integrate eye-tracking data with other user research metrics for a more holistic understanding of the user's experience. He was formerly the eye-tracking guru and trainer at Human Factors International and has conducted his Eye Tracking Bootcamp with several organizations including Comcast and GlaxoSmithKline. He is a frequent presenter on eye tracking, speaking at conferences such as Human Computer Interaction International, User Experience Professionals Association, and User Focus.

Andrew has over 10 years of experience as a UX researcher and designer and is currently Vice President of User Experience at SPARK Experience, a UX consulting firm outside Washington, DC. He received his B.S. in Information Technology and New Media from the Rochester Institute of Technology, M.S. in Interaction Design and Information Architecture from the University of Baltimore, and is currently pursuing a Ph.D. in Human-Centered Computing at the University of Maryland, Baltimore County.

After many years of studying human behavior and decision making, studying the user experience comes natural to Jennifer. She views the user experience from a psychological perspective to understand why design influences experience.

At Fors Marsh Group, Jennifer Romano Bergstrom is the UX Project Leader and specializes in experimental design, quantitative analysis, and usability for older users. She frequently leads a variety of user experience studies, including low- medium- and high-fidelity studies with eye tracking on desktop, mobile, and paper. Prior to joining Fors Marsh Group, she studied age-related differences in Internet performance, which led to the improvement of websites and Web-based surveys for all users, including older adults. She completed a post doc at the U.S. Census Bureau where she conducted numerous usability studies, many including eye-tracking analyses. Before joining the Census Bureau, Jennifer studied cognitive aging and lifestyle factors, such as bilingualism and piano playing, which promote healthy cognition in old age.

Jennifer has presented research at numerous national and international conferences and publishes in peer-reviewed journals. She teaches training courses in usability, information architecture, writing for the Web, eye tracking, and survey design. She has peer-reviewed articles in *International Journal of Human-Computer Interaction*, *Journal of Usability Studies*, *Applied Cognitive Psychology*, and *Memory*. She currently serves as the Director of Marketing and Communications for the User Experience Professionals Association (UXPA), and she was previously President of the D.C. Chapter of UXPA and President of the D.C. Chapter of the American Association for Public Opinion Research (AAPOR).

Jennifer received a Ph.D. and M.A. in Applied/Experimental Psychology from The Catholic University of America and a B.A. in Psychology from Central Connecticut State University.

LIST OF CONTRIBUTORS

Mike Bartels
Tobii Technology, Falls Church, VA, USA

Lorenzo Burridge
Red C, Dublin, Ireland

Barbara Chaparro
Wichita State University, Wichita, KS, USA

Nina Chrobot
Tobii Technology, Falls Church, VA, USA

Angela Colter
Electronic Ink, Philadelphia, PA, USA

Soussan Djamasbi
Worcester Polytechnic Institute, Worcester, MA, USA

Sabrina Duda
Users' Delight, Berlin, Germany

Ian Everdell
Mediative, Toronto, ON, Canada

Adrienne Hall-Phillips
Worcester Polytechnic Institute, Worcester, MA, USA

David Hawkins
Fors Marsh Group, Arlington, VA, USA

Jibo He
Wichita State University, Wichita, KS, USA

Temika Holland
US Census Bureau, Washington, D.C., USA

Caroline Jarrett
Effortmark, Leighton Buzzard, UK

Eugene Loos
University of Amsterdam, Amsterdam, The Netherlands

Mike McGill
Pace University, New York, NY, USA

Erica Olmsted-Hawala
US Census Bureau, Washington, D.C., USA

Victor Quach
Human Solutions Inc., Washington, D.C., USA

Jennifer Romano Bergstrom
Fors Marsh Group, Arlington, VA, USA

Andrew Schall
Spark Experience, Bethesda, MD, USA

Christina Siu
Wichita State University, Wichita, KS, USA

Karl Steiner
TandemSeven Inc., Plymouth, MA, USA

Jonathan Strohl
Fors Marsh Group, Arlington, VA, USA

Kathryn Summers
University of Baltimore, Baltimore, MD, USA

Wilkey Wong
Tobii Technology, Falls Church, VA, USA

Veronica Zammitto
Electronic Arts Inc., Burnaby, BC, Canada

FOREWORD

Evaluation of user experience is critical to every domain in which people interact with products and services. Whether intending to make an automobile dashboard easy to interpret, a cereal box on a store shelf attention grabbing, or a new Web page component easily understandable, substantial resources are allocated to evaluating end user performance. This book considers how a data stream of a user's visual gaze points can inform this user experience assessment.

Eye tracking is now accepted as a proven contributor in the arsenal of UX evaluation tools. The frequency of UX activities utilizing eye tracking has recently exploded, largely due to huge improvements in the calibration and usage of eye-tracking hardware and software systems, coupled with cheaper costs. The coming of open source eye-tracking systems will further drive down these costs. This book is the first to clearly demonstrate the breadth of eye tracking's contributions across domains such as commercial websites, social networking, mobile devices, video games, literacy, and physiological interactions. Common threads, like visual hierarchies, areas of interest, and judicious use of heat maps emerge, and form the backbone of a larger body of practical knowledge.

Eye-tracking hardware will soon become a commodity. Many inexpensive, video-based systems, intended for a variety of evaluation and control applications, have recently entered the market. Mobile devices are also starting to include the basic ability to track users' eyes for a variety of purposes. While low-cost eye trackers may have poorer resolution, calibration, accuracy, and frame refresh compared to higher cost systems, they may still be sufficient for many potential UX evaluation applications.

There is a large potential to make eye-tracking analysis software more capable and easier to use by a variety of user experience professionals. Quantitative indicators are needed to quickly compare scanning strategies within and between groups of end users. Areas of interest must be defined automatically for dynamic Web interfaces using methods such as video processing. Additional work is also needed to determine the validity of eye-tracking metrics, relative to more traditional usability measures of efficiency, effectiveness, and satisfaction.

What was once a very specialized field requiring deep knowledge and substantial patience has matured sufficiently, allowing user experience and marketing specialists to easily incorporate gaze analysis into a study. There are, however, many subtle aspects of setup, calibration, recording, analysis, and interpretation that can benefit from guidance provided by this book. Topics such as measurement and calibration standards in usability evaluation are now under discussion. The anecdotes and scenarios in this volume will help to provide a framework for further research in the area. Readers approaching from eye tracking, marketing, website development, and usability evaluation domains will find this material very helpful for setting expectations and guiding studies.

This book covers both the art and practice of eye tracking within the context of UX research for improving user experience and informing development and marketing decisions. It is an important contribution for the promotion of eye tracking and is one of the first works to specifically consider the intersection of eye tracking and user research. I'm certain that this book will help to expand your previous notions for how eye tracking can be applied to measuring user experience.

Joseph H. Goldberg, Ph.D., CPE
Chief Research Scientist, Applications User Experience,
Oracle Corporation

OVERVIEW OF EYE TRACKING AND VISUAL SEARCH

INTRODUCTION TO EYE TRACKING

Andrew Schall[1] and Jennifer Romano Bergstrom[2]

[1]*Spark Experience, Bethesda, MD, USA*
[2]*Fors Marsh Group, Arlington, VA, USA*

WHAT IS EYE TRACKING?

Eye tracking is a methodology that helps researchers understand visual attention. With eye tracking, we can detect where users look at a point in time, how long they look at something, and the path their eyes follow (Figure 1.1). Eye tracking has been applied to numerous fields including human factors, cognitive psychology, marketing, and the broad field of human–computer interaction. In user experience research, eye tracking helps researchers understand the complete user experience, even that which users cannot describe.

HOW EYE TRACKING WORKS

An eye tracker is a tool that allows user experience (UX) researchers to observe the position of the eye to understand where an individual is looking. Most modern eye trackers rely on a method called corneal reflection to detect and track the location of the eye as it moves. Corneal reflection uses a light source to illuminate the eye, which then causes

FIGURE 1.1 Participant using a computer equipped with an eye tracker. (Courtesy of Tobii Technology.)

a reflection that is detected by a high-resolution camera. The image captured by the camera is then used to identify the reflection of the light source on the cornea and in the pupil, as shown in Figure 1.2. Advanced image processing algorithms are then used to establish the point of gaze related to the eye and the stimuli.

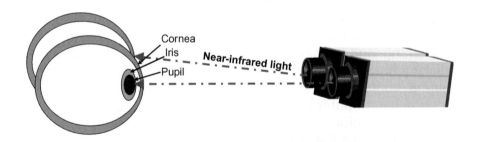

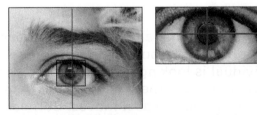

FIGURE 1.2 A conceptual illustration of how eye-tracking technology works.

The same eye-tracking methodology applies no matter what the individual is looking at. Even though our vision appears extremely stable, the eye is constantly moving around to help construct a complete picture of what we are looking at.

This process is divided into fixation and saccades. A fixation is the pause of the eye movement on a specific area of the visual field. These pauses are often extremely brief, as the eye continually performs saccades. Saccades are rapid movements of the eye from one fixation to another to help the eye piece together a complete scene of what an individual looks at. You might assume that fixations and saccades give us a clear picture of what an individual perceives, but this is not the whole story.

Fixations take place in our foveal vision, which accounts for nearly half of the visual information sent to our brain (see Figure 1.3). This part of our vision is highly detailed and provides complete clarity about what we are looking at. Our primary attention is usually focused on what we register in our foveal vision. Eye trackers only track what is registered in an individual's foveal vision. Unfortunately, this only accounts for less than 8% of our visual field (Tobii Technology, 2010).

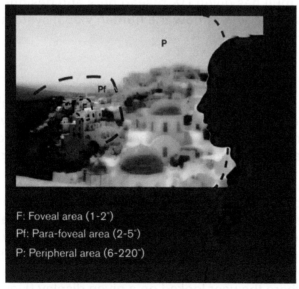

F: Foveal area (1-2°)
Pf: Para-foveal area (2-5°)
P: Peripheral area (6-220°)

FIGURE 1.3 Representation of the human visual field. (Courtesy of Tobii Inc.)

The rest of our vision is composed of parafoveal and peripheral vision. These regions surround our foveal vision and help us to gain a sense of what is happening around us. These types of vision are almost certainly the result of evolution where our ancestors needed to worry about potential predators out of the corner of their eye. Stimuli registered in either parafoveal or peripheral vision tend to be things that involve a lot of movement (again, think about human evolution). The stimuli detected are low resolution and only give us a sense of an object's general color, shape, and motion (Rayner, 1998).

While we cannot detect the details of objects in these regions of our vision, our brain is pretty good about theorizing what the object could be. This is an extremely powerful capability that provides us with the ability to scan a website and get the lay of the land within a few moments without carefully reading all of the content. Our mind can compose a high-level understanding of a scene within seconds.

This makes it tricky to analyze eye-tracking data. Just because a user did not specifically fixate an image does not mean that they are not aware that it is there. They might even be able to identify page elements without fixating them for any detectable period of time.

Eye tracking's unique ability to detect and follow the eye as it looks at stimuli has given UX researchers and designers a much better understanding of how the human visual system works.

WHAT EYE TRACKERS CAN AND CANNOT TELL US

An eye tracker can be a powerful tool that gives us a highly accurate representation and understanding of an individual's eye movement behavior. The three attributes of *location*, *duration*, and *movement* form the basis for this understanding.

Location

The location of a user's eye gaze at a particular moment in time (i.e., a fixation) provides the most basic unit of analysis for understanding visual attention. Fixations are extremely short and typically only last between 100 and 600 milliseconds. Fixations can be mapped to specific *x* and *y* coordinates on a grid that help pinpoint where the user looked on a given display (Figure 1.4).

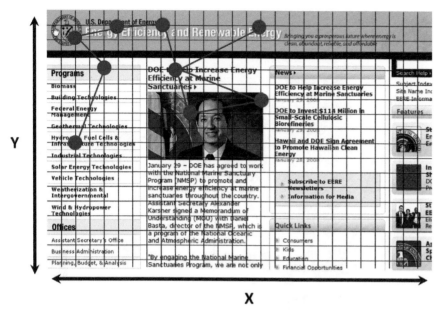

FIGURE 1.4   Fixations are mapped to *x* and *y* coordinates on a grid.

The challenges with interpreting mapped fixations lie in the fact that just because a fixation was registered does not necessarily mean that the user really *saw* it or that it registered cognitively in their brain. This is often the case with orphan fixations where the eye may have momentarily rested in a random area of the screen but did not intentionally look at it, such as when users complete forms that require created answers, as discussed in Chapter 5. In these cases, users look at the screen, but their attention is elsewhere, and thus the eye-tracking data are not useful.

The clustering of a number of fixations in a particular region can provide more evidence that the user deliberately looked at something, and significantly increases the likelihood that the brain processed it. However, eye trackers are not mind-reading devices, and they can only tell us *what* the person looked at but not *why*.

Duration

The length of time that a user fixates a particular area on the screen (as shown in a gaze plot diagram in Figure 1.5) helps us to understand whether he/she is paying particular attention to a specific visual element. The duration of fixations is often extremely short and is typically represented in milliseconds.

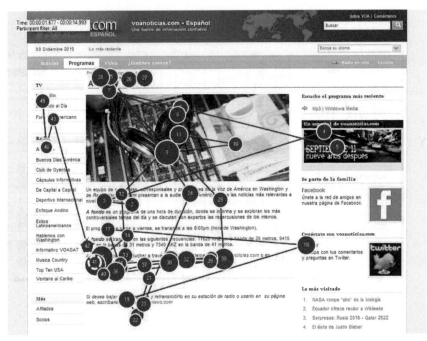

FIGURE 1.5 Eye trackers can detect the length of a given fixation, and can represent longer and shorter durations by increasing and decreasing the relative size of the dots in a gaze plot visualization.

Unfortunately, duration is a particularly difficult measurement to interpret. There are many possible reasons why a user fixates for a relatively short or long period of time on a particular area. Are they confused by this element? Do they find it engaging? In order to understand these measurements we need to look at the data in context with other research methods. This will be discussed extensively in Chapter 3.

Movement
The movement of a user's eyes is based on saccades from one fixation to another and establishes the eye-gaze pattern that reflects how the user interprets a particular visual stimulus. This pattern provides the basis for understanding the visual hierarchy of a scene. Visual hierarchy refers to the sequence in which a user views visual elements in a particular scene. For example, on a website, a user might first notice a large graphic in the center of the page, then look at the primary navigation, then look at the search box, and so on. Eye tracking is particularly good at revealing the effectiveness of how gestalt principles of design influence the order of elements the user looks at.

EYE TRACKING PAST AND PRESENT

Our ability to understand the human mind has remained relatively primitive since the earliest days of measuring cognitive and physiological functions. Only in the last half-century have we made significant technological advancements that have allowed us to capture and visualize cognitive processes and to accurately observe visual perception.

A combination of various physiological instruments (discussed further in Chapter 4), including eye trackers, has helped us understand how the brain functions in response to various stimuli. Researchers have now gained a sophisticated understanding of how the human visual system works and how our minds process visual feedback.

Medieval Torture Devices and Early Eye Trackers

Early attempts at tracking the movements of the eye started in the late 1800s and were not at all pleasant for study participants. Some of the earliest devices relied on putting a plaster of Paris covering over the eye with sticks attached pointing outward. The sticks indicated the position of the eye relative to what the participant was looking at. Later eye trackers still used eye coverings but utilized devices similar to today's contact lenses. (Duchowski, 2007)

Early eye-tracking studies were reserved for understanding the most basic hypotheses of how the brain and visual system worked together (Figure 1.6). The studies were often highly academic and too complicated and expensive to be applied for commercial uses.

By the 1940s, systems had been developed that used film recordings of the eye to track movement. In 1947, Paul Fitts and his colleagues began using cameras to study the movements of pilots' eyes as they used cockpit controls and instruments to land an airplane (Figure 1.7). This was one of the earliest eye-tracking usability studies; its goal was to systematically study users interacting with an interface to improve the system's design (Jacob & Karn, 2003).

The evolution of the video-based eye tracker in the 1960s and 1970s gave birth to a new generation of eye trackers and opened up possibilities for additional uses for eye tracking (Figure 1.8). Unfortunately, while the technology became more accessible

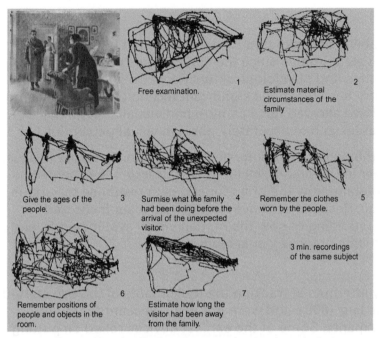

FIGURE 1.6   Eye tracking visualizations demonstrating that the task given to a person has a strong influence on his or her eye movements. (From Lucs-kho at en.wikipedia [Public domain], via Wikimedia Commons.)

FIGURE 1.7   Cockpit designs were one of the earliest interfaces studied in human factors research and also some of the earliest practical applications of eye tracking. (From Forward (Fg Off), Royal Air Force official photographer [Public domain], via Wikimedia Commons.)

FIGURE 1.8   An early remote eye tracker. (Courtesy of ASL Inc.)

to researchers, participants still suffered from a highly intrusive device that required a head restraint and bite bar. These still primitive eye trackers, shown in Figure 1.9, obviously made it impossible to simulate a comfortable and realistic environment for users of a system.

The late 1990s brought about the modern day eye tracker that many researchers in the UX industry use today. New breakthroughs in both hardware and software design allowed the eye tracker to leave the academic arena and be incorporated into commercial user experience labs.

Maturity of Eye Tracking into a User Experience Research Tool

We are at the beginning of a golden age for eye tracking in user experience research. Many major academic and commercial labs have an eye tracker or plan to purchase one in the near future. The technology has been available for over 50 years, so why is eye tracking now becoming such a popular tool?

In the past, eye tracking had only been accessible to those with a highly advanced understanding of human physiology,

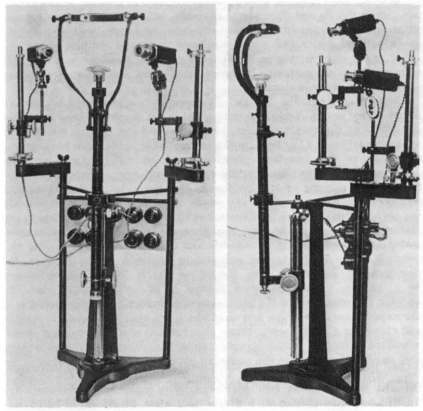

The apparatus used in recording eye movements.

FIGURE 1.9 Early eye trackers required participants to be extremely still during operation and often used uncomfortable bite bars or chin rests to keep the head stationary. (From Yarbus, A. L. [GFDL (http://www.gnu.org/copyleft/fdl.html) or CC-BY-SA-3.0 (http://creativecommons.org/licenses/by-sa/3.0)], via Wikimedia Commons.)

engineering, and computer science. Users of these systems had to have extensive training in order to properly operate the equipment. Making sense of the data (Figure 1.10) was extremely cumbersome and time-consuming, requiring researchers to conduct analyses by hand. The outcome from eye-tracking research was often too complex for laymen to understand and did not easily contribute to design recommendations.

Fast-forward to the twenty-first century and we find ourselves with both hardware and software that are both researcher and participant friendly. No longer are we slaves to the technology; instead researchers can seamlessly integrate eye

Timestamp	Number	GazePointXLeft	GazePointYLeft	CamXLeft	CamYLeft	DistanceLeft	PupilLeft	ValidityLeft	GazePointXRight	GazePointYRight	CamXRight	CamYRight	DistanceRight	PupilRight
95														
117	0	400.617	261.2175	0.7513002	0.6374704	648.1887	3.773164	0	400.9024	291.1999	0.5961173	0.6521371	636.4001	3.661853
133	1	398.393	264.065	0.7516774	0.6375161	648.2229	3.636122	0	418.6002	298.9395	0.5564873	0.6516686	636.5583	3.64993
150	2	396.2955	273.9963	0.7518954	0.6374961	647.8473	3.77234	0	393.907	301.2133	0.5968071	0.6517037	636.8112	3.675694
167	3	402.125	265.7434	0.7523934	0.6374515	648.0519	3.798369	0	399.3078	284.1953	0.5971763	0.6513929	636.6243	3.675363
183	4	414.2168	251.4495	0.7526376	0.6372757	648.2616	3.804291	0	430.813	272.5971	0.5972641	0.6511323	636.9761	3.629609
200	5	423.9691	255.5654	0.7527026	0.6372469	648.3549	3.810735	0	440.9816	264.9081	0.597554	0.6508659	636.6008	3.630603
216	6	423.9865	245.771	0.7531195	0.6373391	648.2988	3.817439	0	425.7016	274.3857	0.5979909	0.6507218	636.7742	3.65217
233	7	428.22	254.2387	0.7534257	0.6373549	648.2095	3.75736	0	426.7341	262.5856	0.5983127	0.6505361	637.0329	3.608105
250	8	427.502	235.5433	0.7537678	0.6372594	648.4797	3.747369	0	430.5081	257.4155	0.5986091	0.6503124	636.6136	3.607276
266	9	435.1046	242.4257	0.7539775	0.6371354	648.0962	3.729671	0	442.2343	254.1302	0.5980012	0.6500827	637.0001	3.587219
283	10	423.2355	261.5889	0.7541669	0.6370122	648.5149	3.7557	0	423.743	269.3259	0.5989991	0.6499335	636.6981	3.627686
300	11	433.2017	254.9062	0.7542553	0.6368436	648.4265	3.748498	0	421.653	262.9049	0.5990345	0.6497296	636.5421	3.588275
316	12	419.2951	253.153	0.7542648	0.6367035	648.2444	3.760934	0	423.6463	278.318	0.5990194	0.6495155	636.5270	3.576233
333	13	434.8374	248.5142	0.7542472	0.6363882	648.1369	3.736739	0	426.3913	273.6594	0.5989965	0.6492424	636.5372	3.573587
350	14	422.3765	290.4351	0.7540954	0.6367216	647.9878	3.742778	0	429.8147	309.0193	0.5990117	0.6495135	636.341	3.581557
366	15	418.8178	377.8113	0.753844	0.6371815	647.6741	3.709197	0	421.1444	391.3314	0.5930075	0.6500124	636.3063	3.590075
383	16	423.7291	365.6831	0.7537999	0.6366101	647.6413	3.717006	0	412.6543	375.5868	0.5986618	0.6496465	636.2298	3.577973
400	17	417.3529	375.5489	0.7536264	0.6365598	647.4268	3.708932	0	415.1166	374.7775	0.5884939	0.6496119	636.0198	3.570415
416	18	409.0291	369.9335	0.7534955	0.6363221	647.1501	3.723507	0	423.0877	365.2895	0.5982617	0.6494093	635.5084	3.535283
433	19	418.0613	366.2758	0.7534091	0.636264	647.0584	3.723622	0	417.2631	361.453	0.5981212	0.6494185	635.6729	3.55276
450	20	420.4647	372.5575	0.7533571	0.6362619	646.9561	3.710567	0	412.9641	375.7278	0.5980012	0.6496475	635.6643	3.553964
466	21	418.5887	366.1826	0.7533312	0.6367543	646.6282	3.744848	0	417.0449	370.9076	0.5989514	0.6495544	645.9091	3.641268
500	22	448.1517	426.7739	0.7534814	0.6373926	646.251	3.728294	0	425.8824	357.3699	0.5980556	0.6505944	634.8905	3.526945
516	23	425.5454	366.0304	0.7536324	0.6375493	646.0896	3.677925	0	424.6074	420.3143	0.5981955	0.6506779	634.8333	3.661961
533	24	407.2442	382.1878	0.7539406	0.6376214	646.032	3.724641	0	362.4293	368.4	0.5989246	0.6505076	634.8312	3.545217
550	25	382.0437	376.847	0.7543042	0.6372561	645.8999	3.731122	0	346.7462	378.2516	0.5996398	0.6500002	634.6049	3.559673
566	26	370.777	371.6201	0.7546104	0.637073	645.6644	3.765136	0	326.4905	386.1813	0.5997646	0.6495686	634.5554	3.610301
583	27	365.62	362.2698	0.7550178	0.6368808	645.6926	3.770904	0	345.1357	379.1794	0.6001299	0.6490359	634.3461	3.595069
600	28	371.8418	361.1357	0.7553933	0.636552	645.5532	3.794081	0	333.3998	378.8482	0.6004177	0.6485349	634.0366	3.58077
616	29	352.739	377.1207	0.7557038	0.6364896	645.5298	3.792601	0	327.5732	374.5496	0.6007668	0.6482773	634.3557	3.644621
633	30	364.7997	376.6232	0.7559024	0.6365534	645.5516	3.8125	0	331.7	389.1884	0.6010663	0.6481025	634.0649	3.648695
650	31	353.9612	370.7149	0.7562348	0.6367001	645.4138	3.871641	0	348.1435	390.4786	0.6013653	0.640073	633.7674	3.663214
666	32	358.9431	359.4175	0.7565079	0.6369652	645.5173	3.876763	0	337.5291	386.1313	0.6016595	0.6480598	634.0899	3.68345
683	33	353.6521	389.5632	0.7568166	0.6370529	645.5229	3.863897	0	343.4176	391.1053	0.6019519	0.6480272	633.6667	3.694201
700	34	353.5806	366.2641	0.7569903	0.6370781	645.5316	3.89461	0	346.4277	378.5706	0.6021655	0.6477951	634.028	3.689347
716	35	357.2749	368.0299	0.7571286	0.6369992	645.3062	3.907702	0	336.7175	406.1323	0.6023462	0.6476824	633.6699	3.730237
733	36	353.7257	374.9613	0.7573475	0.6370668	645.4896	3.919348	0	330.6878	388.4258	0.6024563	0.6477064	633.4849	3.735837
750	37	352.9518	379.0769	0.7575161	0.637355	645.4871	3.929201	0	340.0563	371.7014	0.6026729	0.6479211	634.0341	3.73941
766	38	351.5531	366.0008	0.7575135	0.6377777	645.552	3.9787	0	360.0238	400.5162	0.602391	0.6483828	633.5637	3.778778
783	39	448.1368	350.5203	0.7569316	0.6383128	645.7051	3.990263	0	490.351	386.9582	0.601163	0.6489347	633.8975	3.786376
800	40	476.1451	336.3235	0.7566356	0.6389554	645.7972	3.981491	0	503.899	390.9497	0.6012101	0.6494787	634.3527	3.814618
816	41	482.7939	350.1748	0.7566625	0.6394892	645.7811	3.990834	0	487.9269	396.0833	0.6013622	0.6496792	634.0419	3.818946

FIGURE 1.10   Sample of raw data output from eye tracker.

tracking into their user-centered design practices with minimal accommodation.

Hardware Designed for Quick and Easy Data Capture

Advancements in remote eye-tracker technology now make it possible to calibrate the participant's eyes in a matter of seconds. Eye trackers today are extremely accurate, can track diverse populations (see Chapters 12 and 13), and retain their calibrations for long periods of time (Figure 1.11). The operation

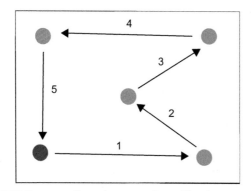

FIGURE 1.11   Example eye tracker calibration sequence.

of eye trackers today requires minimal training and does not require a dedicated technician during use.

Participant Friendly

Gone are the days of clamping down participants' heads into a vice and sticking a bite bar into their mouths. Today's eye-tracking technology has been miniaturized and integrated into computer monitors or as standalone devices that are no longer physically connected to the participant (Figure 1.12). The technology is so covert that participants often have no indication that they are being tracked except for the brief calibration that takes place at the beginning of the study session. As researchers, we want the eye tracker to be completely unobtrusive; we want participants to forget that it is even there.

Analysis Software Designed for User Experience Researchers

The eye trackers that UX professionals use today come with software suites (as shown in Figure 1.13) that instantaneously produce visualizations of the eye-tracking data and automate a significant amount of tasks that previously took weeks to analyze manually.

The output from these software packages help to highlight where the user looked, the length of time they looked there, and the gaze pattern their eyes followed. Some of the most

FIGURE 1.13   SMI's BeGaze eye tracking analysis software. (Courtesy of SensoMotoric Instruments Inc.)

commonly used visualizations include the heat map and gaze plot (Figure 1.14).

A heatmap is a visualization that uses different colors to show the amount of fixations participants made or for how long they fixated areas. Heat maps are color coded: red is typically used to indicate a relatively high number of fixations or duration and green the least, with varying levels in between. An area with no color on a heat map signifies that the participants may not have fixated on the area. This does not necessarily mean they did not *see* anything—they may have looked there for a short period or may have only registered peripherally, but it may have not been detectable by the eye tracker (Figure 1.15).

Gaze plots are a visual representation of fixations and saccades for a particular time frame. In most software applications, fixations are represented by dots, and saccades are lines connecting the dots (Figure 1.16). Fixations are typically numbered to show the order of the fixations and can vary in size to illustrate the duration of the fixation.

FIGURE 1.14 A heat map based on fixation count.

FIGURE 1.15 A heat map based on fixation duration for the same group of participants as shown in Figure 1.14.

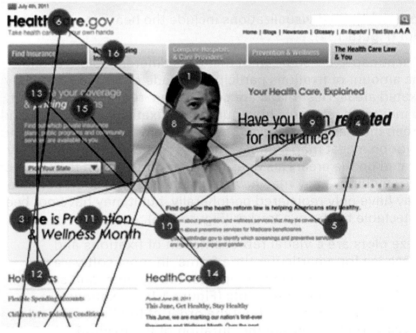

FIGURE 1.16 Example of a gaze plot diagram representing fixations from one individual participant.

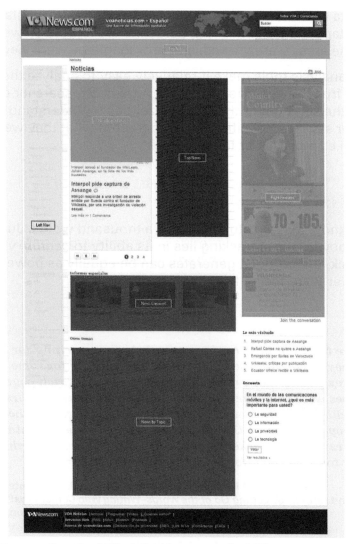

FIGURE 1.17   Example of AOIs defined for an analysis of different components of a web page.

Areas of interest (AOIs) help researchers analyze the various components of a visual scene (Figure 1.17). Researchers can categorize regions of a display into geometric shapes that correspond to elements on the screen. For example, in analyzing the various components of a website, the researcher may want to create AOIs for the primary and secondary navigation, search box, graphical, and textual elements.

The data from AOIs can be aggregated across participants to understand the order in which particular areas were viewed, how often the areas were viewed, and how long they were viewed.

These analysis tools make it relatively easy to analyze the results from an eye-tracking study. A trained researcher can adjust the settings for these visualizations to understand what the user saw at a specific time in context of what they were doing (i.e., a particular task).

EYE TRACKING CAN EMPOWER YOUR DESIGN TEAM

We all know that a picture is worth a thousand words. Just as the power of eye tracking lies in its ability to *capture* visual feedback, the *output* it generates can be equally as powerful to empower your design team.

I use eye tracking pictures in my workshops on writing for the web. They make the case immediately and visually for some of my key points. The typical F pattern for content rich pages convinces workshop participants to put the key message first. An eye-tracking picture from the test of a landing page convinces workshop participants that people don't focus on large pictures or congratulatory marketing messages when they are moving quickly towards the information they need.

Janice (Ginny) Redish, President of Redish & Associates, Inc. and author of *Letting Go of the Words–Writing Web Content that Works,* **2nd edition, 2012**

As user-centered design advocates, we are always seeking ways to encourage the design team to observe user research sessions. The eye tracker's ability to produce real-time eye-gaze output has helped to captivate team members and has been a key motivator in getting them to attend sessions. Beyond simply the "cool factor," the team can immediately "see" if users are looking where they expected users to look.

UX designers are often shocked when interface elements that they have spent months on receive barely a glance by

Eye tracking makes it clear very quickly, exactly what users are and aren't looking at. None of our other research methods such as gathering analytics, A/B testing designs or even non-eye tracking usability tests give us such clear and decisive data on where the users are focused and what they are missing. I feel more well equipped to speak to teams with confidence about what our users saw and didn't see.

Carri Craver, Fossil, Inc., USA

users. Observing eye tracking in real time can be a humbling experience for designers and yet often results in them being an advocate for using the technology for future research studies.

Visualizations generated from eye-tracking software can be used to tell a story about the findings to the user experience team and executive management. Gaze plots can help non-researchers quickly understand the visual hierarchy of an interface and make informed decisions about how to optimize the placement of screen elements.

Eye tracking is often used to further emphasize findings. For example, to illustrate the cause of a task failure in a usability test, a heat map can show "cold" regions indicating that users were not looking at an element that would have helped them. It can also exemplify "hot" screen elements that distracted users from completing their tasks more efficiently.

Data from eye tracking can be very useful in supporting other evidence from a usability test. In one study, we were concerned about the placement of an important link on the home page. In the scenario where that link would have been appropriate, no one chose it. While I could have intuited that placement was the problem, having gaze plots to confirm that people just didn't look at that part of the screen when trying to do the task certainly helped convince the client to move the link.

Janice (Ginny) Redish, President of Redish & Associates, Inc. author of *Letting Go of the Words–Writing Web Content that Works,* **2nd edition, 2012.**

Gaining Insights from Eye Gaze

In nearly all cases, the user experience of digital interfaces is driven by visual output. These days, user experience designers are creating visual content for everything from wall-mounted displays to laptops to mobile devices.

Our visual field is constantly being bombarded by many concurrent stimuli (as shown in the example in Figure 1.18). We are overloaded and overwhelmed by visual information, and we constantly resort to prioritizing what we pay attention to. To measure the effectiveness of content, researchers need to determine what users are looking at and what they choose or do not choose to engage with.

See Where People Looked, Not Where They Think They Looked

In trying to understand what users pay attention to, we cannot always rely on the participants to accurately tell us. Participants are terrible at self-reporting where they looked. For the most part, this is due to our eyes often moving involuntarily and the limits of our short-term memory. Guan et al. (2006) measured the extent to which participants did not discuss elements that they in fact visually attended to. They labeled these as omissions. Participants had omissions 47% of the time, meaning that almost half of the time they did not mention elements that they looked at.

Omissions may occur because participants forget about seeing the elements, or perhaps simply because they just do not think or care to mention them (Albert & Tedesco, 2010). It should go without saying that a researcher cannot simply ask a participant if they noticed a certain on-screen element. This action draws the participant's attention directly toward something that they may or may not have originally seen. This inherently and irreversibly biases the participant, and no confident answer can be obtained. Eye tracking provides an objective running commentary of where the individual looks without any need for participants to verbalize what they have seen.

Determining the Effectiveness of a Visual Hierarchy

As mentioned earlier, the visual hierarchy of an interface dictates what a user will pay attention to and when. A well-designed interface directs the user's attention to specific areas that the designer intended (as shown in the example in

FIGURE 1.18   Many visual elements on the Finish Line website compete for attention.

FIGURE 1.19   This user quickly noticed and fixated the current promotions at Macy's. Macy's goal of getting its website visitors to notice promotions is easily validated through the use of eye tracking. Combined with web analytics, these data offer a clear understanding of what visitors initially notice, what holds their attention, and ultimately whether by looking at an element they decide to click or not.

Figure 1.19). An interface that lacks a clear visual hierarchy (as shown in the example in Figure 1.20) will often result in erratic scan patterns and does not effectively guide the user to any specific content. This sequence of visualizations can be critical for both the usability of a system and consumption of content.

As most UX designers already know, users will spend very little time on a web page. Jakob Nielsen's (2011) guidance on this is that "to gain several minutes of user attention, you must clearly communicate your value proposition within 10 seconds."

FIGURE 1.20   Ralph Lauren's temporary homepage related to the 2012 Summer Olympics centers on a portrait of the U.S. Olympic team. The brightly colored and centrally located flag is immediately noticed by all participants and receives the highest amount of fixations. However, only one participant read the statement under the flag that explains that Ralph Lauren designed all of the team's uniforms.

FIGURE 1.21 Within about 10 seconds, users unfamiliar with Ben Gurion University quickly identified the organization and its key initiatives. First time visitors to the Ben Gurion University website often know very little about the organization. Eye tracking revealed that most users fixated the university logo first and then scanned over the current key initiatives, events, and eventually down to the area about the organization within the first 10 seconds.

This is absolutely critical if this is a user's first visit to your website (as demonstrated in Figure 1.21). Within a few seconds, the user needs to answer the following questions:

- Whose website is this?
- What is it about?
- What can I do here?
- Do I want to continue exploring it?

The visual hierarchy of the site is critical to quickly guiding the user's eyes to these key pieces of information.

CONCLUSION

Eye tracking has come a very long way from its earliest years of being highly invasive for users and extremely complex to use, to a nearly unobtrusive and researcher-friendly technology. The last 10 years have been a golden age for eye tracking in user research.

Eye trackers are now being widely used to understand how users interact with a variety of devices and software from websites to video games (discussed further in Chapter 11). They can also be used to gain deeper insights into how certain audience groups view and interact with interfaces differently, and help researchers identify and address issues that affect the usability of their products.

The chapters that follow provide a more in-depth exploration of how eye tracking is used in the UX field at large. The fundamental capabilities of eye-tracking hardware and software are the same and provide a highly accurate, objective understanding of the patterns of eye movement and what grabs and sustains the user's attention.

ACKNOWLEDGMENTS

Thank you to Chris Lankford (Eyetellect) and Jon West (LC Technologies) for helpful feedback on an earlier version of this chapter.

REFERENCES

Albert, W., Tedesco, D., 2010. Reliability of self-reported awareness measures based on eye tracking. Journal of Usability Studies 5 (2), 50–64.

Duchowski, A.T., 2007. Eye Tracking Methodology: Theory & Practice, second ed. Springer-Verlag, London.

Guan, Z., Lee, S., Cuddihy, E., Ramey, J., 2006. The validity of the stimulated retrospective think-aloud method as measured by eye tracking. In: Grinter, R., Rodden, T., Aoki, P., Cutrell, E., Jeffries, R., Olson, G. (Eds.), Proceedings of the SIGCHI Conference on Human Factors in Computing Systems. ACM Press, New York, pp. 1253–1262.

Jacob, R.J.K., Karn, K.S., 2003. Eye Tracking in human-computer interaction and usability research: ready to deliver the promises. In: Radach, R., Hyona, J., Deubel, H. (Eds.), The mind's eye: Cognitive and Applied Aspects of eye Movement Research. North-Holland/Elsevier, Boston, pp. 573–605.

Nielsen, J., 2011. How long do users stay on web pages? Alertbox. [blog], September 12, 2011. Available at: http://www.nngroup.com/articles/how-long-do-users-stay-on-web-pages (Accessed: 1 July 2013).

Rayner, K., 1998. Eye movements in reading and information processing: 20 years of research. Psychol. Bull. 124 (3), 372.

Tobii Technology, 2010. An Introduction to Eye Tracking and Tobii Eye Trackers, Whitepaper.

VISUAL SEARCH

Soussan Djamasbi and Adrienne Hall-Phillips

Worcester Polytechnic Institute, Worcester, MA, USA

INTRODUCTION

Paying attention to how users look for information on websites is becoming increasingly important in designing positive user experiences. Users are no longer impressed with the basic utility of a website and are now more demanding for websites that have superb user experiences.

More and more research shows that paying attention to how users visually search web pages can be very helpful in designing satisfying user experiences. Eye tracking is an invaluable tool for studying how people search web pages because it allows us to "see" exactly what users look for on web pages.

In this chapter, we look at eye-tracking studies that examine how people visually search sites for information. We will discuss research that examines why and when people turn a blind eye to information that looks like advertisements. Finally, we provide a list of take away points for designing positive visual search experiences.

HOW DO WE VISUALLY SEARCH FOR INFORMATION ON WEB PAGES?

Paying attention to how users view web pages can provide a wealth of information for designing successful websites. Better yet, understanding why people inspect web pages the way they do can help predict users' reactions to particular web page designs. For example, the theory of visual hierarchy (Faraday, 2000) helps us predict a user's fixation behavior by explaining that users search a web page through a two-phase cognitive process. During the first phase, or scanning phase, a user skims through the page to find an entry point to the page. Once an entry point is found, the user starts the second phase or inspection phase, during which the user looks around the entry point for information. Essentially, a user inspects a page by going through a chain of entry points, each of which, like an anchor, allows the user to scan for information (Figure 2.1).

Eye tracking can provide unique insight into visual search tasks. Researchers often ask participants to think out loud and describe what they're doing, but there are two potential downsides to this approach: 1), the participant can become distracted from the task, 2) the participant may not report everything that he or she sees, either as an omission or because the information is not observed at a conscious level. Eye tracking provides an objective measurement of participants' visual patterns that allows us to determine what aspects of our designs draw attention first and most.

For websites like ours, this is particularly valuable when educating a user on a complex topic, making it clear what the next step in a process is, or driving users towards a call to action.

Tom Tullis, VP, User Experience Research, Fidelity Investments, United States

Both of these phases are influenced by the characteristics of the objects on the web page. Whether an object on a page can act as an effective entry point depends on a number of characteristics, such as location, size, color, text style, and type (e.g., whether it is textual or image based). By manipulating these characteristics, we can entice users to pay special attention to

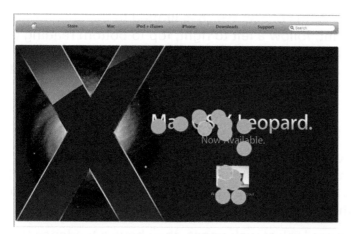

FIGURE 2.1   A user's gaze, demonstrating scanning and inspection behavior. Yellow circles represent entry points. Green circles represent inspecting fixations around the entry point.

an object. For example, increasing the size of an object on a web page is a good way to convey to a user that this object is important and therefore encourages the user to pay attention to that object before (or more often than) other smaller objects on the same page.

The location of an object can impact the order in which a user views it. In most cultures, top locations typically cue importance, and top left locations are typically attended to because that is typically where reading begins (Faraday, 2000). We are accustomed to reading from top to bottom and from left to right, so we tend to view objects on top left locations on a page before or more frequently than other objects located on the right side of the page or in lower locations.

As with the scanning phase, the inspecting phase (the second phase, which starts right after an entry point is found) is also influenced by the characteristics of the objects. The way objects are arranged on a page is an important factor in this phase. We tend to limit our visual search in this phase to the area that encloses the entry point and items that seem to be related to it. For example, we tend to perceive items around the entry point with the same background as being related to each other.

Proximity is also important—items that are close to each other signal that they have a relationship. Eye tracking shows that fixations in this phase, which is limited to the area around an entry point, follow a left to right, top to bottom reading order for text and bulleted points. We do not use the left-right, top-bottom pattern of fixations when we are looking at images or links around the entry points (Faraday, 2001).

WHAT DOES VISUAL SEARCH LOOK LIKE?

When we search a web page, we can only pay attention to one object at a time. This means that our search behavior naturally creates a hierarchy or sequence. Eye tracking is a helpful tool to show this behavior.

When users look at web pages, they have a tendency to look at the top and left portions of the page (Faraday, 2000). This pattern of visual search has also been called the golden triangle or F-shaped pattern of viewing. The frequently reported F-shaped pattern (Buscher et al., 2009; Nielsen, 2006) tells us that when we scan a website, we tend to miss some very important information that is placed on the right portion of the page (Figure 2.2).

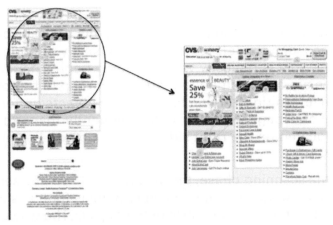

FIGURE 2.2   An example of a user's typical viewing sequence when searching a website. (From Djamasbi et al., 2011b.)

Users are also less likely to look at information that is "below the fold" of a web page, which requires scrolling. Eye-tracking research shows that fixations on a web page decrease as users scroll down a page (for further reading, see Djamasbi et al., 2010, 2011a; Granka et al., 2004; Shrestha & Owens, 2008).

However, favoring the top rather than the bottom of the page seems to be more pronounced in younger users. For example, in one study, when comparing the fixation behavior of professional employees of a company, Generation Y participants (ages 18–34) paid far less attention to areas below the fold, compared to their Baby Boomer colleagues (ages 47–65; Djamasbi et al., 2011a). In that same study, cluttered pages were less appealing to both generations, but the younger users had significantly less tolerance for clutter (Figure 2.3). Clutter often results in a "flat" visual design, where there seems to be little or no difference in relative importance of objects on a page. Clutter makes it harder for users to find entry points on a page. The viewing behavior

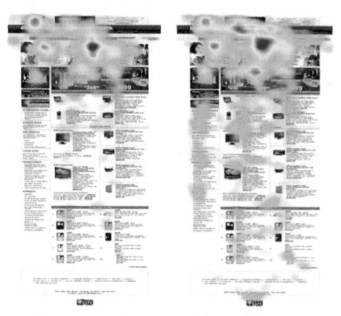

FIGURE 2.3   Heat maps comparing younger and older participants' viewing pattern for a cluttered page (Djamasbi et al., 2011a). Younger participants (left) exhibited far less patience when they explored a cluttered web page, compared to older participants (right) who examined the same page more carefully. On these pages, the areas covered by fixations (colored areas on the heat maps) were significantly smaller for younger participants than older participants. Fewer areas on the page received intense fixations (red areas on the heat map) by younger participants compared to older participants.

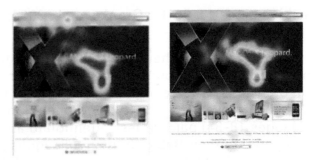

FIGURE 2.4 Heat maps comparing younger (left) and older (right) participants' viewing pattern for an uncluttered page. Both generations exhibited a similar pattern of viewing on pages that were not cluttered.

of the two generations is quite similar for pages that are not cluttered. Uncluttered pages entice both generations to view them thoroughly (Figure 2.4).

The tendency of users to favor only a portion of the page coupled with the fact that web pages have limited screen real estate makes it quite challenging to design an effective communication experience. A good design encourages users to look at the entire page, not just the top left portion that they typically favor. This means that as user experience designers, we have to find out what type of design could possibly change the natural viewing bias of users. For example, would the natural viewing bias change if a website uses an image-based design rather than a text-based design? What about the arrangement of textual information—would it change the way we search for information on a web page?

The answer to both questions is yes. Research shows that when we search image-based pages, our F-shaped pattern of viewing is no longer apparent, although we still favor above the fold (Shrestha & Lenz, 2007). Also, when textual information is arranged in two columns, we change our search behavior. While we still favor above the fold, we tend to look at the right side and the bottom of the page more when text is displayed in two columns rather than in one column. Basically, users search web pages more thoroughly when the textual information on the page is arranged in various distinct sections and placed in multiple columns, as shown in Figure 2.5 (Djamasbi et al., 2011c).

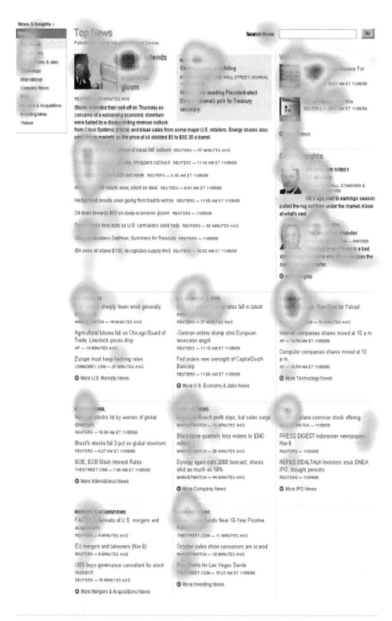

FIGURE 2.5 Example of dispersed viewing pattern (Djamasbi et al., 2011c). The dispersed pattern of fixations spanning the entire page shows that users inspected the page thoroughly, even below the fold, looking almost at every link and title on the page. Links and titles are particularly important in effective visual communication because they summarize key textual information.

Eye tracking makes the invisible visible. We often employ eye tracking when we observe an unexpected behavior using a different methodology, such as a quantitative online study. Eye tracking is one way we can understand what is actually happening in those instances.

With eye tracking, we've found that the subtlest design modifications can drive large differences in user behavior. Seemingly small changes such as background color, placement, and labeling can drive large differences in users' scan patterns. Ultimately, this can be the tipping point between a successful call to action and a failure.

Marisa Siegel, Principal User Researcher, User Experience Research, Fidelity Investments, United States

ARE THERE DIFFERENT TYPES OF VISUAL SEARCH?

Visual search is a combination of two different types of behavior: goal-directed and exploratory search behavior, each using a different part of our brain. In goal-directed search, we actively search for information following a specific strategy or plan. In exploratory search, we just monitor the environment, and we usually do not have a search plan in mind. Exploratory search is our default behavior because whenever we are not actively involved in looking up information, our visual system keeps screening the environment. (From Posner & Petersen, 1990; Janiszewski, 1998.)

In both types of visual search behavior, our fixations are influenced by how objects are laid out on a web page. Objects on a web page compete with each other to win our attention. The intensity of this competition can be numerically calculated as a function of the number of objects on the viewable screen, their size, and their proximity to each other. The competition for attention theory (Janiszewski, 1998) tells us that the race for attention between the objects in our field of view affects how we screen the environment (exploratory search) and how we actively search for a piece of information (goal-directed search). Therefore, when we examine search behavior, we should carefully look at how objects compete for attention (Janiszewski, 1998).

Let's look at this competition in practice. Consider a retail shopping website. Some sites display their products in a list format, while others display their products in a matrix format. Displaying products in a list format creates a more competitive environment for attracting user attention than displaying products in a matrix format (Hong et al., 2005). This suggests that visual search behavior on search engine results pages (SERPs), which typically have a list format, is influenced by a visually demanding environment.

VISUAL SEARCH BEHAVIOR OF SERPS

Visual search behavior of SERPs is becoming increasingly important as more and more users use search engines daily. Among the top four search engines (Google, Yahoo!, Bing, and Ask Network), Google is by far the most popular and has the largest growth (Figure 2.6).

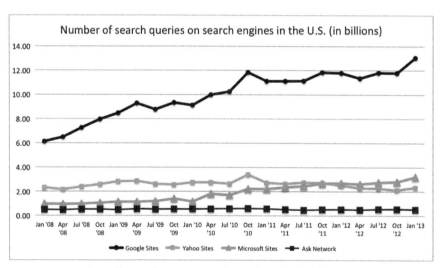

FIGURE 2.6   Search query frequency: top 4 search engines (U.S., from Jan 2008 to Jan 2013). (From comScore, 2013.)

Eye-tracking data have demonstrated that people look at Google SERPs longer than they look at Bing SERPs (Figure 2.7; UserCentric, 2011). Longer fixations do not

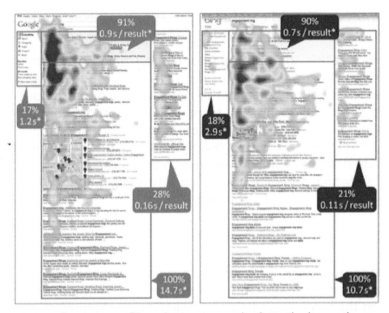

FIGURE 2.7 Google versus Bing: a heat map example of attention in gaze time. Users look at the Google search results longer than the Bing results. Heatmaps showing the aggregate gaze time of all 24 participants on Google (left) and Bing (right) for one of the transactional tasks. The red color indicates areas that received the most total gaze time (4.5 seconds and above). Each callout includes the percentage of participants who looked at the area and the time (in seconds) they spent looking there. The numerical data are an average across all four tasks. Asterisks indicate values that were significantly different between Google and Bing at alpha = .1. (UserCentric, 2011).

necessarily mean that a web page has a more engaging experience; it may also mean that users are confused or they cannot locate what they are looking for quickly. While eye tracking is a valuable tool for revealing attention, sometimes the eye-tracking data by itself may not be sufficient in helping to determine the cause of a behavior.

Using the competition for attention point of view, a recent eye-tracking study ($N = 11$) examined search behavior on Google SERPs. Results confirmed the competition for attention theory: areas other than the search results section, which was the focus of the task in the study, also received attention (Djamasbi et al., 2013a). Within the search results area, the competition for attention was among the top five entries as the attention on the rest of the entries was negligible. This schematic is shown in Figure 2.8. This is consistent with what we learned from the theory of visual

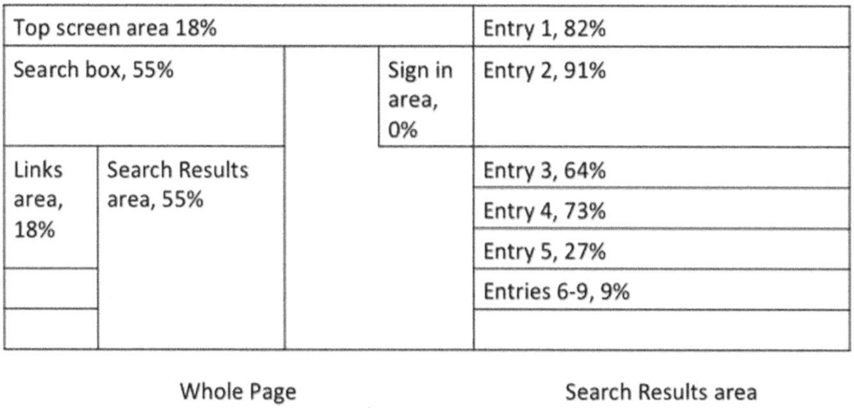

Top screen area 18%			Entry 1, 82%
Search box, 55%		Sign in area, 0%	Entry 2, 91%
Links area, 18%	Search Results area, 55%		Entry 3, 64%
			Entry 4, 73%
			Entry 5, 27%
			Entries 6-9, 9%

Whole Page   Search Results area

FIGURE 2.8 Percentage of viewers for SERP objects (Djamasbi et al., 2013a). While all participants attended to the search results area, 55% of users also looked at the search box area, and 18% of users looked at the links and top screen areas (left side). On the right side, Entry 5, which was lowest on the top five entry list, attracted the least number of viewers, and the top two entries attracted the most number of viewers.

hierarchy, which tells us that top locations attract more attention than lower locations.

CAN IMAGES OF FACES IMPACT OUR SEARCH BEHAVIOR MORE THAN OTHER TYPES OF IMAGES?

When it comes to competing for attention, a recent study showed that images of faces may be more effective than other types of images in attracting our gaze. For this reason, including faces on web pages may not always be helpful for users searching for information (Djamasbi et al., 2012b). Grounded in neuropsychology and evolutionary psychology, paying attention to faces has played a significant role in human evolution; thus, we are naturally drawn to faces. Using the theory of visual hierarchy and competition for attention theory, a group of researchers speculated that this natural tendency to look at faces, while useful in attracting attention, might also have the unintended consequence of diverting us from the task at hand. Eye-tracking results demonstrate that faces indeed divert attention from textual information adjacent to faces. Faces, compared to non-face images, tend to attract more fixations. Textual information, particularly titles, tends to receive less intense fixations when placed next to faces (Figure 2.9).

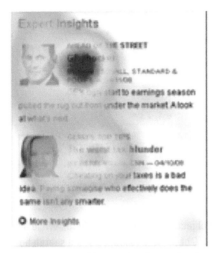

FIGURE 2.9   Heat maps shows that faces (left side) diverted attention from the textual information while logos did not have a similar effect (right side). (From Djamasbi et al., 2012b.)

A distinct part of our brain is dedicated for processing the visual characteristics of faces. We are able to distinguish between faces as early as two months after birth. This ability is crucial in survival of infants who need to distinguish their mothers from other individuals. Faces are also invaluable sources of information for social communication. For example, people with Asperger's syndrome often have trouble understanding subtle non-verbal communication because they tend not to look at faces and when they do look at faces, they often have trouble interpreting subtle facial expressions.

The effect of faces on performance is more complex. When faces are above the fold, they affect performance negatively; it takes people significantly longer to locate desired information that is placed next to faces. When faces are below the fold, however, performance improves. This behavior suggests that the location of faces is an important factor in their impact on the level of attention they demand (Djamasbi et al., 2012b).

WHAT IS BANNER BLINDNESS, AND WHY IS IT IMPORTANT?

We exhibit banner blindness when we intentionally attempt to avoid looking at advertisements on a web page. This is even true when we are presented with advertisements that are placed on top of the page, with images, and it can sometimes be triggered by fancy formatting (Nielsen, 2007). Banner blindness presents UX designers with a tricky challenge. As you may remember from an earlier discussion in this chapter, the very design elements that can help users find entry points to a web page (e.g., images, formatting) can also cue users to ignore a message.

Banner blindness has a significant impact on the return on investment of companies that count on online search traffic for reaching consumers. Online search provides a lucrative venue for marketers. In 2012, 76% of the $36.6 billion of Internet advertising revenues was generated from advertisements in search, web page banners, and mobile ads (IAB, 2013). Unfortunately for marketers, despite this push in revenues, up 15% from 2011, consumers are still skipping ads.

Banner blindness can effectively be detected by tracking where people look as they interact with websites and search results. For example, banner blindness was detected in an eye-tracking study that examined differences in viewing behavior between males and females (Djamasbi et al., 2007). As shown in Figure 2.10, there was a small window on the web page that

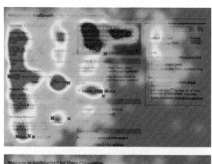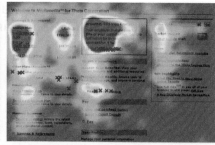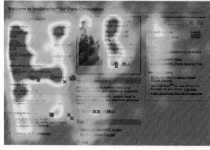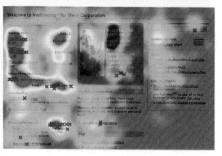

FIGURE 2.10   The bricklet with the light background color and no image received the most attention and clicks (top right). The "red x" denotes a click. "Banner blindness" is particularly noticeable for the bricklets in the two bottom panels, which have images. Of the four designs, the bricklets with images received the least amount of attention. (From Djamasbi et al., 2011b.)

assisted with navigation (a "bricklet"). While no differences in viewing behavior were found between genders, the bricklet with the simplest design (i.e., lacking pictures and color) grabbed the most attention of both men and women. This behavior was attributed to the banner blindness—the more complex design caused users intentionally to ignore it, even though the web pages were designed to have advertisement-free content, and bricklets were obviously not ads. The graphics and background color made the bricklets stand out. This likely gave users the impression that bricklets were ads, and therefore they paid less attention to them.

Another study showed that the contrasting background color of bricklets had a significant impact on how quickly they were noticed (Djamasbi et al., 2012a). Bricklets with a contrasting background color, even when the contrast followed the color style of the page, caused participants to have a slower reaction time (Figure 2.11). The contrasting color makes a bricklet more salient or more "ad-like." The result is that they become a low priority in users' eyes.

When considering advertisements on a web page, it is wise to remember that not just graphic-based ads can cause banner blindness—people are also blind to textual ads (Figure 2.12). Users pay less attention to text in ads compared to text in

FIGURE 2.11   The time to first fixation on the right bricklet (circled) was significantly longer than the time to first fixation on the left bricklet (circled), which lacked contrast. (From Djamasbi et al., 2012a.)

FIGURE 2.12   Textual ad (left) and graphical ad (right).

editorial content on a web page (Hervet et al., 2011). Users also tend to avoid text banners on the right side of the web page more than they avoid text banners at the top of the page (Owens & Chaparro, 2011). This behavior suggests that ads do not change our natural tendency to favor the top and left locations on a web page. As we learned earlier from the theory of visual hierarchy, people tend to view top locations on a page and somewhat ignore the information that is on the right side of the page.

Banner blindness is particularly important on SERPs, which are often used by companies and marketers to reach consumers; however, banner blindness may not be as pronounced on SERPs, particularly on mobile devices (Djamasbi et al., 2013b). For example, a recent eye-tracking study shows that the majority of users pay attention to ads both on desktop and mobile SERPs with mobile ads receiving relatively more attention than desktop ads. More mobile users, compared to desktop users, view SERP ads. Mobile users also tend to spend a greater portion of their total viewing time looking at ads (Figure 2.13). While this is good news for marketing on SERPs particularly on mobile phones, more research is needed to find out the factors that can increase or decrease the visibility of ads on SERPs (Djamasbi et al., 2013b).

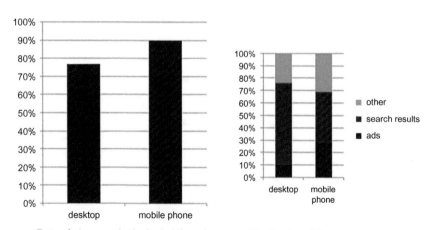

Rate of viewers who looked at the ads   Distribution of fixations

FIGURE 2.13   Ad attention on SERPs on desktop versus mobile phone. Seventy-seven percent of desktop users and 90% of mobile users looked at ads on SERPs. On a desktop computer, SERP ads attracted 10% of total attention (total fixation on the screen). On a mobile phone, attention to SERP ads increased to 28% of total attention. (From Djamasbi et al., 2013b.)

THE ROAD AHEAD FOR DESIGNING VISUAL SEARCH EXPERIENCES

The bottom line—designing positive search experiences matters. Creating pleasant and effective search experiences will continue to be a major topic in UX design. Our on-the-go lifestyle will increase our need to use mobile devices to search for information. The upward trend in mobile device usage (Figure 2.14) puts a great emphasis on the importance of designing successful mobile search experiences. This in turn impacts what we expect from websites and how we search them. Eye tracking will continue to be a great tool for understanding a user's search experience whether they are searching on a desktop or on a mobile device.

Visual design used to be purely about the emotion you got from something. You try to put your best foot forward and make an educated guess about how people would search your website. With eye tracking, now we can put more science behind it.

Dan McAuliffe, User Experience Manager, Dyn Inc., United States

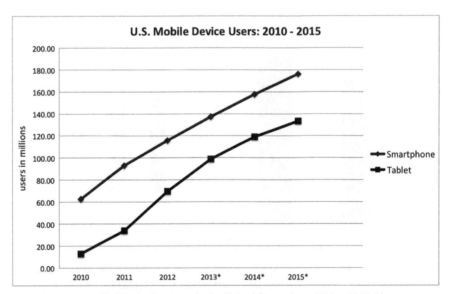

FIGURE 2.14   Mobile device users in the United States from 2010 to 2015; *denotes forecasted values. (From eMarketer 2012, 2013.)

Visual design has a significant impact on visual search behavior. It affects how effectively a web page communicates with its intended audience, and eye tracking is a valuable tool for assessing a user's search behavior. Some key things to remember about search:

- UX testing is a crucial part of designing positive search experiences. Eye tracking can aid in testing the effectiveness of visual communication and a user's visual search behavior.
- Banner blindness can easily and clearly be detected by eye-tracking heat maps or by the amount of time it takes a user to notice an ad on a page.
- Testing for banner blindness is important because the very design elements that prove to be effective in attracting attention can backfire and make a design look like an ad. Even subtle contrasting colors can cue banner blindness.
- A good visual design encourages users to inspect a page thoroughly. This can be detected by fixations that are dispersed throughout the page covering important information.
- On heat maps, look for fixations on titles and links; they suggest effective visual communication.
- Be careful when using faces on web pages. Faces can be effective in drawing attention; however, at times they can be distracting and divert fixations from key information.
- Pages with a clear visual hierarchy provide a pleasant search experience because they help users find entry points to the page easily. Note the emphasis here is on "clear visual hierarchy." A page where everything in it stands out is "hierarchically flat."

REFERENCES

Buscher, G., Cutrell, E., Morris, M.R., 2009. What do you see when you're surfing? Using eye tracking to predict salient regions of web pages. In: Proceedings of the SIGCHI Conference on Human Factors in Computing Systems. ACM, Boston, MA, pp. 21–30.

comScore, 2013. Comscore Releases March 2013 U.S. Search Engine Rankings. Retrieved May 4, 2013, from, http://www.comscore.com/Insights/Press_Releases/2013/4/comScore_Releases_March_2013_U.S._Search_Engine_Rankings.

Djamasbi, S., Hall-Phillips, A., Yang, R., 2013a. Search results pages and competition for attention theory: an exploratory eye-tracking study. In: Yamamoto, S. (Ed.), Human interface and the management of information. Information and interaction design, vol. 8016. Springer, Berlin, pp. 576–583.

Djamasbi, S., Hall-Phillips, A., Yang, R., 2013b. Serps and ads on mobile devices: an eye tracking study for Generation Y. In: Stephanidis, C., Antona, M. (Eds.), Universal access in human-computer interaction. User and context diversity, vol. 8010. Springer, Berlin, pp. 259–268.

Djamasbi, S., Siegel, M., Skorinko, J., Tullis, T., 2011a. Online viewing and aesthetic preferences of Generation Y and the Baby Boom generation: testing user web site experience through eye tracking. Int. J. Electron. Commerce 15 (4), 121–158.

Djamasbi, S., Siegel, M., Tullis, T., 2010. Generation Y, web design, and eye tracking. Int. J. Hum. Comput. Stud. 68 (5), 307–323.

Djamasbi, S., Siegel, M., Tullis, T., 2011b. Seeing Through Users Eyes: Examining User Experience Through Eye Tracking. Paper presented at the NeuroIS Symposium at the Hawaii International Conference on System Sciences, Kauai, Hawaii.

Djamasbi, S., Siegel, M., Tullis, T., 2011c. Visual hierarchy and viewing behavior: an eye tracking study. In: Human-Computer Interaction, Design and Development Approaches. Lecture Notes in Computer Science, vol. 6761, pp. 331–340.

Djamasbi, S., Siegel, M., Tullis, T., 2012a. Designing noticeable bricklets by tracking users' eye movements. In: Proceedings from the 45th Hawaii International Conference on System Science (HICSS).

Djamasbi, S., Siegel, M., Tullis, T., 2012b. Faces and viewing behavior: an exploratory investigation. AIS Trans. Hum. Comput. Interact. 4 (3), 190–211.

Djamasbi, S., Tullis, T., Hsu, J., Mazuera, E., Osberg, K., Bosch, J., 2007. Gender preferences in web design: usability testing through eye tracking. In: Proceedings of the 13th Americas Conference on Information Systems, Keystone, Colorado, August, pp. 1–8.

eMarketer, 2012. Ipad use to Nearly Double This Year. Retrieved May 6, 2013, from, http://www.emarketer.com/Article/iPad-Use-Nearly-Double-This-Year/1009106.

eMarketer, 2013. Smartphones Continue to Gain Share as Us Mobile Usage Plateaus. Retrieved May 6, 2013, from, http://www.emarketer.com/Article/Smartphones-Continue-Gain-Share-US-Mobile-Usage-Plateaus/1008958.

Faraday, P., 2000. Visually critiquing web pages. In: Multimedia `89: Proceedings of the Eurographics Workshop in Milano, Italy, September 7–8, 1999. Springer Vienna, pp. 155–166.

Faraday, P., 2001. Attending to web pages. In: Proceedings from the CHI'01 Extended Abstracts on Human Factors in Computing Systems.

Granka, L.A., Joachims, T., Gay, G., 2004. Eye-Tracking Analysis of User Behavior in www Search. Paper presented at the 27th Annual International Conference on Research and Development in Information Retrieval–SIGIR '04, New York, http://portal.acm.org/citation.cfm?doid=1008992.1009079.

Hervet, G., Guérard, K., Tremblay, S., Chtourou, M.S., 2011. Is banner blindness genuine? Eye tracking internet text advertising. Appl. Cogn. Psychol. 25 (5), 708–716.

Hong, W., Thong, J.Y., Tam, K.Y., 2005. The effects of information format and shopping task on consumers' online shopping behavior: a cognitive fit perspective. J. Manag. Inform. Syst. 21 (3), 149–184.

IAB, 2013. Internet Advertising Revenue Report 2012. Internet Advertising Bureau. Retrieved April 2013 from, http://www.iab.net/media/file/IAB_Internet_Advertising_Revenue_Report_FY_2012_rev.pdf (accessed 06.05.13.).

Janiszewski, C., 1998. The influence of display characteristics on visual exploratory search behavior. J. Consum. Res. 25 (3), 290–301.

Nielsen, J., 2006. F-Shaped Pattern for Reading Web Content. Alertbox: Current Issues in Web Usability. Retrieved January 18, 2007, from, http://www.nngroup.com/articles/f-shaped-pattern-reading-web-content/.

Nielsen, J., 2007. Fancy Formatting, Fancy Words = Looks Like a Promotion = Ignored. Retrieved May 16, 2013 from, http://www.nngroup.com/articles/fancy-formatting-looks-like-an-ad/.

Owens, J.W., Chaparro, B.S., 2011. Text advertising blindness: the new banner blindness? JUS 6 (3), 172–197.

Posner, M.I., Petersen, S.E., 1990. The attention system of the human brain. Annu. Rev. Neurosci. 13 (1), 25–42.

Shrestha, S., Lenz, K., 2007. Eye gaze patterns while searching vs. browsing a website. Usability News 9 (1).

Shrestha, S., Owens, J.W., 2008. Eye movement patterns on single and dual-column web pages. Usability News 10 (1).

UserCentric, 2011. Eye Tracking Bing vs. Google: A Second Look. UserCentric. Retrived from, http://www.usercentric.com/news/2011/01/26/eye-tracking-bing-vs-google-second-look (accessed 03.06.13.).

EVALUATING THE
USER EXPERIENCE

3

USABILITY TESTING

Erica Olmsted-Hawala[1], Temika Holland[1], and Victor Quach[2]
[1]*US Census Bureau, Washington, D.C., USA*
[2]*Human Solutions Inc., Washington, D.C., USA*

INTRODUCTION

Usability testing is a technique in user-centered design used to evaluate a product by testing it with actual users. It enables us to obtain direct feedback on how real users work with a product. We can measure how well they perform with respect to accuracy or efficiency and note if they meet preset goals. Users can often surprise us; they do the unexpected. To create a design that works, it is helpful for developers to see what real people do and look at as they interact with a product.

The International Organization for Standardization (ISO) defines usability as "the extent to which a product can be used by specified users to achieve specified goals with effectiveness, efficiency, and satisfaction in a specified context of use (ISO 9241-11, 1998)." In a typical usability study, a test administrator observes the user performing a task or using a product while thinking aloud (i.e., giving a running verbal commentary about his/her experiences using the product). With this information and users' performance measures of accuracy, efficiency, and subjective satisfaction, the user experience (UX) team can better understand the issues that users have with the product and can suggest improvements to the design.

In recent years, eye tracking has been combined with usability testing as another method to measure the user experience. Eye-tracking data has emerged as a useful way to inform the emerging design of a user interface. Within usability, eye tracking is a methodology to study eye movements with the premise that the data provide information on the human–computer interaction. Knowing where participants look can help developers of a website know which features are being attended to and which features are being overlooked.

It is possible to combine eye-tracking data with existing usability metrics (i.e., accuracy, efficiency, satisfaction) to learn something that we would not know without it. When determining the placement of links, navigational tools, written content, input fields, link labels, images, slogans, and other features, usability practitioners often wonder: "Do users notice this feature? Do users understand what they need to do to accomplish their goals?" Eye-tracking results are useful when answering these questions. Eye-tracking data can help the UX team make recommendations based on a deeper understanding of the problem. This can lead to more effective decisions about the design of the user interface.

I am working on a project titled "How should online health information be provided to older cancer patients?" and we focused on how we can visually present cancer-related information to them. In some studies, we argue that illustrations that supplement written text may improve recall of information. However, this implies that people actively look at and pay attention to these illustrations. Therefore, we used eye tracking to explore whether people look at the illustrations on a web page with written information plus illustrations and whether paying attention to text and illustrations would increase recall of the information. We learned that some people do not pay attention to illustrations or other specific parts of the website at all (parts we usually assume). The eye-tracking measures (e.g., fixation duration) provided us with a more pure measurement of attention and processing of information on a health-related website.

Nadine Bol, PhD candidate in Amsterdam School of Communication Research, University of Amsterdam, Netherlands

In this chapter, we explore how eye tracking is used with usability testing to evaluate and inform decisions on websites using real-world examples from recent usability studies. We examine the following:

- Incorporating eye tracking in usability testing
- How eye-tracking data provide a comprehensive picture of users' experiences with an interface and helps inform the design
- How eye tracking aids in communicating results more effectively with clients
- Other considerations and drawbacks researchers should be aware of when using eye tracking with usability studies.

INCORPORATING EYE TRACKING IN USABILITY TESTING

Eye tracking has been used to supplement usability testing of websites and web-based surveys (see Chapter 5 for more about surveys). Eye tracking fits well with usability studies because it is often non-invasive (i.e., if using an eye tracker that does not require a chin rest or head piece), which makes it easier for participants to concentrate on the assigned tasks. With technological advancements, most eye trackers use infrared cameras to track participants' eyes and interaction with an application. A simple calibration of the participants' eyes is all that is needed before starting a usability test. However, depending on the eye-tracking hardware, the calibration of the participant's eyes can sometimes prove challenging, resulting in the loss of data.

Calibration continues to be the bane of an eye-tracking researcher's existence. Losing calibration in the middle of a study because the participant stood up or moved her head in a fashion you didn't expect continues to be our biggest source of frustration, and even the high-end, dual Purkinje eye trackers we've used continue to waste time and resources because of calibration loss.

Tharon Howard, Director of the Clemson University
Usability Testing Facility, USA

It is good practice to remind participants to stay in the position they were calibrated in without too much movement. A fixed chair is also ideal so that movement is minimized while capture rate is maximized.

It is important to review the capture rate and not include anyone in the analysis whose eye-tracking data falls below a certain threshold. A good rule of thumb is to review sessions where the sample rate percentage drops below 75% (Romano Bergstrom et al., under review) and to recalibrate during the session or conduct fixation checks during data collection (for more details, see Hornof & Halverson, 2002; Poole & Ball, 2005).

The use of an eye tracker can also limit interactions between the moderator and participant. Handing objects to the participant, sitting next to him/her, and asking probing questions could all disrupt eye tracking and lead to a lower capture rate (Pernice & Nielsen, 2009). These techniques should be kept to a minimum when using eye tracking during usability tests.

Eye tracking can be used at any stage of the usability testing cycle, depending on what stage in the visual design the product is at and for different purposes. When working with low-fidelity prototypes that do not have a finished visual design, such as wireframes viewed on a computer screen (Figure 3.1), eye tracking can be used to get a general feel for how the wireframe works. For example, eye tracking can be used to answer the question of whether users notice link labels or placements of objects on the page.

 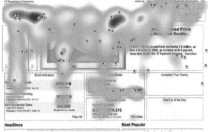

FIGURE 3.1   Screen shot of a low-fidelity wireframe prototype (left) that was usability tested using eye tracking (right). Some of the boxes do not have content and are merely placeholders for future content. The client wanted feedback primarily on the top navigation labels. Usability testing showed that users noticed and clicked on (denoted in red and white icons) some of the top navigation labels/links.

> *Eye tracking can be used on low-, medium-, and high-fidelity usability tests.*
>
> - *Low fidelity: Non-functional interfaces, can be html wireframes or paper mock-ups*
> - *Medium fidelity: Partially functional clickable interfaces, not all links or buttons work*
> - *High fidelity: Fully functional interface*

With a slightly higher fidelity interface, where the visual design is more complete with some of the links working, eye tracking can be used to get a better sense of how the different elements work together on the page, where people attend, and where they do not. Eye tracking with paper prototypes and different interfaces, such as mobile devices (see Chapter 10), can be informative, though it is good to remember that it can change a user's interaction with the prototype or device. For example, eye tracking often requires users to interact with a mobile device on a fixed mount instead of in the more natural position of holding it in their hands. As such, the inclusion of eye tracking can change how usability study participants interact with a device. See Figures 3.2 and 3.3 for examples of eye trackers used in typical usability testing environments.

Data obtained by eye tracking requires additional time to analyze, interpret, and convey to clients, but it often makes for

FIGURE 3.2 Easy to use desktop eye tracker that is built into the monitor.

FIGURE 3.3   Mobile eye tracker mounted on a laptop.

well-rounded feedback on the product being tested. There are a variety of data outputs by most eye-tracking software that a UX team can look at/analyze. For example, heat maps and gaze plots can be used to visualize where participants spend most of their time looking. The UX team may also identify areas of interest (AOIs) and then identify how long participants looked at those areas (fixation duration), how often (fixation frequency), and where the participant looked next (order of fixations).

At the National Cancer Institute, we have conducted over 70 usability studies using eye-tracking technology in the areas of web design, digital content, and social media. Eye tracking has allowed us to understand the needs of the 72 million cancer patients and survivors, clinicians, researchers, and Spanish-speakers that visit our sites each year. Our original intent was to identify and interpret design and usability problems across platforms. For example, we were able to determine the best placement and design for Spanish website language toggles, identify banner blindness issues, and design easy to read templates for online versions of publications.

Silvia Inéz Salazar, User-Informatics Lab Manager,
National Cancer Institute, USA

EYE-TRACKING DATA PROVIDES A COMPREHENSIVE PICTURE OF USERS' EXPERIENCE AND CAN HELP INFORM THE DESIGN

When testing a product, the UX team often shares information with the client about users' actions and verbalizations uttered while they worked on tasks, as well as typical usability measures, such as:

- Task accuracy (whether participants completed the task correctly)
- Task efficiency (how long it took participants to complete the task)
- How satisfied the participants were with the user interface

The additional data obtained from eye tracking can give a broader understanding of participants' behavior when they experience issues during product use. Interpretations cannot be understood in a vacuum, but they should be guided by the context of the session: what the test objectives are, tasks and the goals associated with them, what participants said and did, and where they were looking. For example, looking back and forth at some point on an interface could indicate a participant was confused or simply double checking before moving on (Goldberg and Kotval, 1999; Mitzner et al., 2010). This eye-movement analysis needs to be informed by everything else that occurs within the usability session (e.g., specific task and user verbalizations). A number of resources are available to understand what the different eye-tracking data can mean for usability testing. See Table 3.1 for a brief overview and Ehmke & Wilson (2007) for an extensive summary.

Table 3.1 Interpretations of Eye-Tracking Data

Eye-Tracking Measure	Description/Interpretation
How long it took users to first fixate an AOI	If not seen immediately, not visually obvious Longer fixations indicate interest or confusion
How long it took users from making their first fixation on where they will click to actually making the mouse click	If a longer time from first fixating to making the click, link label was not clear, link was not obvious, or there were other distractors on page
Where users looked during an initial interaction	What stimuli attracted the users' attention What users are first attracted to
Number of times users looked at a link before clicking on it	Confusion over the purpose of a link User wants to make sure it is the correct link for their task
Whether and how often participants had to recheck the content they were seeking	Difficulty understanding content User attraction to the area

To be honest, by itself the data provided by eye-tracking alone is of limited value because it doesn't tell you *why* a user was looking in a particular area of the screen. It only lets you know that users looked at a region. But when you triangulate that data with data collected through think-aloud protocols or through a stimulated retrospective think-aloud protocol where you show the user a video of his or her eye tracking immediately after they complete a task and ask them to describe what they were thinking, then you have a much more compelling dataset, which can lead to actionable findings and recommendations.

Tharon Howard, Director of the Clemson University Usability Testing Facility, USA

Fixations and Saccades

Eye movements may reflect emotional states and cognitive processes, thereby capturing another dimension of the user's experience with an interface. Common measurements captured from eye tracking are fixations (where a user looks) and saccades (rapid eye movements between fixations).

A fixation is an instant where the eyes are relatively still (Poole & Ball, 2005), and they can be measured by frequency and length of time looking at content. Depending on context, fixations can be interpreted in multiple ways. Some evidence suggests that during an encoding task, such as looking at a web page, a higher number of fixations indicates the need for processing time or greater difficulty identifying the target object (Poole & Ball, 2005). If participants spend a long time looking at a specific area before making an action, depending on the context of the task and what the participant might have verbalized, the UX researcher might be able to draw some conclusions about whether participants found the examined area confusing.

Alternatively, longer fixation duration (or clusters of fixations) may indicate greater interest and engagement with the target (Poole & Ball, 2005). For example, in examining whether time spent looking at definitions in a survey varied depending on level of effort required to access the definitions, Galesic et al. (2008) found that the more time respondents fixated a definition, the more it seemed to impact their answers.

(See Chapter 5 for more about eye tracking for surveys and forms.) When comparing two different designs, eye-tracking data (e.g., the number of fixations) can be another measure to determine whether a design is more efficient (Bojko, 2006).

Regressive saccades, where a user's eye movements are backtracked, could be indicative of confusion in higher level processing of content (Mitzner et al., 2010; Olmsted-Hawala, Romano Bergstrom & Rogers, 2013). Additionally, regression can be used to measure recognition in that the more salient the text or content, the fewer regressions there will be (Poole & Ball, 2005).

> *Eye tracking is valuable because it shows both conscious and unconscious processes of people looking at, e.g., websites. During debriefing, you may ask people what they looked at and why, but this might not cover everything they looked at. Not only because they don't want to tell, but also because they might have forgotten it already. With eye tracking, you can see what people do online and, in addition, during a debriefing after eye tracking, you can kind of look into someone's head to understand why certain choices were made while searching the web, etc. I think that eye tracking is a very valuable tool for usability testing and should be conducted before launching any website to your broader target audience.*
>
> **Nadine Bol, PhD candidate in Amsterdam School of Communication Research, University of Amsterdam, Netherlands**

Areas of Interest (AOIs)

AOIs are specific areas or content of the user interface that interests the UX team. AOIs can be defined at the beginning or end of a usability study as a way to single out components of the interface so that further analyses can be performed. Depending on the goals of the study, it may be important to know where participants looked first on the page, how long they looked, and whether they focused on the content or quickly moved on to another area of the screen.

Eye tracking can help UX researchers understand how users interact with navigational tools on an interface. For example, in a medium-fidelity usability study on the geography pop-up window of the American FactFinder website, eye tracking

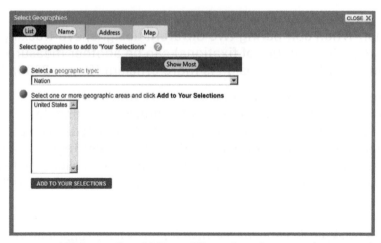

FIGURE 3.4 AOIs in a medium-fidelity usability study on the geography pop-up window of the American FactFinder website. (From Olmsted-Hawala & Quach, 2012.)

allowed the UX team to see how participants interacted with a drop-down box (Figure 3.4; Olmsted-Hawala & Quach, 2012). By specifying the drop-down box as an AOI, the UX team examined:

- How many people looked at the dropdown box
- How long it took before participants looked at the dropdown box
- How long the drop-down box was examined
- How long before participants actually clicked on the dropdown box

As can be seen in Table 3.2, participants took longer to fixate the "Show Most" dropdown box compared to other areas of the page. They also spent the least amount of time fixating it. Eight out of ten users saw the "Show Most" dropdown box; however, only six out of ten actually clicked it. Two of those six participants commented during debriefing that the "Show Most" dropdown box did not have any meaning. It took those six participants 20 seconds, on average, before they made their first click. With this information, the team concluded that, within the context of this task, it was not immediately obvious to users what they need to do to find their geography (Olmsted-Hawala & Quach, 2012).

Using the quantitative eye-tracking results as justification, the UX team recommended that the developers remove the

Table 3.2 Across all Participants, Sum of Total Fixation Duration, Mean Time Elapsed to First Look at AOI, and Mean Time to First Mouse Click

Geography Overlay: Most Requested Geographies versus all Geographies	
	Time (in seconds)
Total Fixation Duration	
List	16.46
Name	8.37
Address	6.38
Map	16.90
"Show Most"	4.42
Time Elapsed to First Look at AOI	
List	0.31
Name	0.58
Address	0.65
Map	1.99
"Show Most"	5.84
Time to First Mouse Click	
List	0
Name	0
Address	0
Map	24.05
"Show Most"	20.85

dropdown box and expose the options on the screen. The client took these recommendations and opted to expose both geography display options on the screen with radio-button functionality, rather than hide them behind a dropdown box (Figure 3.5; Olmsted-Hawala & Quach, 2012).

FIGURE 3.5 Geography pop-up window: old design (left); new design (right). (From Olmsted-Hawala & Quach, 2012.)

Sometimes UX researchers are not sure if participants see a link and do not click on it or if they do not see the link at all. Eye tracking can be used to understand whether the issue is with the placement and design of the link or with the label name itself. For example, in a usability study of a medium-fidelity prototype of the American FactFinder website, the UX team had the impression that people did not see a link (see Figure 3.6) since it was not often used (Romano et al., 2007).

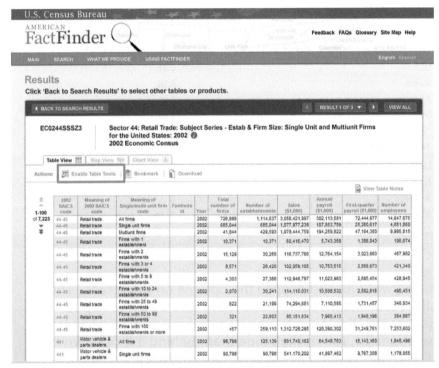

FIGURE 3.6   Early prototype with the AOI of a key link "Enable Table Tools" circled. Eye tracking demonstrated that most participants had many fixations on the link even though they did not click it. (From Romano et al., 2007.)

To verify this hunch, the team turned to eye-tracking data and learned the following:

- It took participants, on average, 36 seconds before they first looked at the "Enable Table Tools" link.
- Participants fixated the "Enable Table Tools" link, on average, 35 times during the study.
- Five of 13 participants never clicked on the "Enable Table Tools" link; of those five, they either never looked at the "Enable Table Tools" link or only looked at it once or twice.

The UX team concluded that the participants who saw the link were confused by the link label name. However, in the case of the few participants who missed the "Enable Table Tools" link entirely, the UX team concluded that it did not attract their attention. These data led to a recommendation to change the link label name and modify the design to draw more attention to the link. In the end, the client changed the link label from "Enable Table Tools" to a more intuitive "Modify Table" (Romano et al., 2007).

This example illustrates that the initial assumption the UX team had was incorrect (i.e., that participants did not see the link because, in fact, many users did see the link). It was only after reviewing the eye-tracking data that the team had a better understanding of what was going on (i.e., participants mostly saw the link, but were confused by the label).

Gaze Opacity and Heat Maps

Additional eye-tracking visualizations of the user experience that can aid in understanding users' interaction with an application are the gaze-opacity and heat map images. As discussed in Chapter 1, these images (based on fixation counts) show the areas where most participants did and did not look (i.e., fixate). This can be useful information to relay to clients who may not realize that users overlook critical areas of the screen. As well, these visual displays can be easier for clients to understand than raw numbers or percentages.

These types of maps offer a useful visual image when trying to understand areas of the user interface that participants saw and missed, including important text entry fields, instructions, or key content on a page, such as "Next" when moving forward in a survey.

Eye-tracking results were used to diagnosis a log-in issue observed during usability testing on the American Community Survey (ACS), shown in Figure 3.7. To successfully log in to complete the web-based survey, users needed to enter the Household ID and PIN found on the address label of mailing materials that had been sent to their household. Early rounds of usability tests showed that participants had difficulty locating the Household ID and PIN on the mailing materials. Rather than entering the numbers that appeared on their mailing materials, participants frequently entered numbers that appeared on the example image on the main log-in screen. Note in Figure 3.7

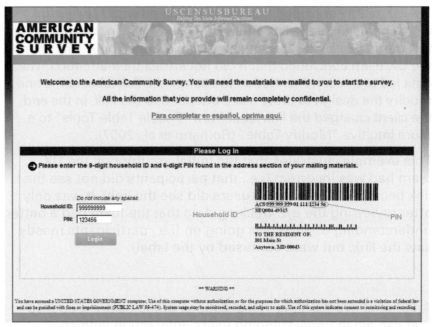

FIGURE 3.7 Eye-tracking results were used to diagnose a log-in issue observed during usability testing on the ACS. Participants had difficulty locating the Household ID and PIN on the mailing materials and typed in the numbers on the example barcode. (From Ashenfelter et al., 2012.)

that the barcode image on the right has real numbers—participants frequently typed those exact numbers into the spaces provided instead of locating the numbers on their personal mailing materials (Ashenfelter et al., 2012).

To determine what participants were looking at while interacting with the web-based survey, AOIs were defined as the instructions on the page and parts of the example image. The UX team examined what areas of the screen participants focused on before entering their log-in numbers. Eye tracking shown in Figure 3.8 revealed that participants skimmed over text that instructed them where to find the Household ID and PIN; instead they fixated the log-in fields and example images. As a result, participants often entered the numbers shown on the example image. Using gaze opacity and heat map images, the UX team was able to show the client that users were not reading the instructions (Ashenfelter et al., 2012). The ACS log-in page went through several revisions influenced by eye-tracking analysis, user behavior, and verbalizations, and the end result is shown in Figure 3.9.

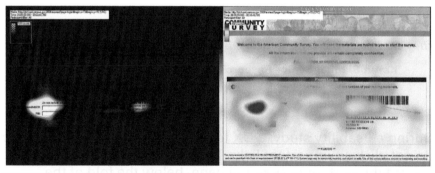

FIGURE 3.8　Gaze opacity map (left) and heat map (right) showing that the majority of fixations were on the log-in section and the example Household ID, not on the instruction text. (From Ashenfelter et al., 2012.)

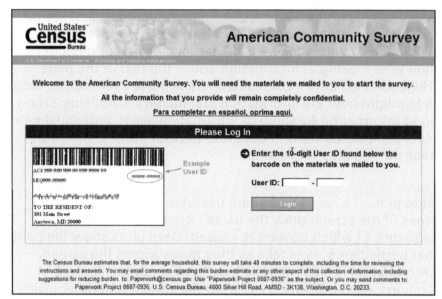

FIGURE 3.9　The final ACS log-in page after many rounds of usability testing with eye tracking. Changes include: log-in instructions and log-in fields were swapped with the example image to dissuade the user from jumping immediately to the log-in field, the instructions were shortened and text-wrapped to accommodate users' reading behavior, the example image on the screen was modified to indicate it was an example, and pound signs (£) were used to make it more difficult for users to enter into the input field. Last, to reduce jargon and simplify the task, the two terms Household ID and PIN were changed to one term: User ID. (From Ashenfelter et al., 2013.)

Eye tracking can show the reality: the respondents mentioned they had read the instructions, but actually, they hadn't.

Karen Blanke, Senior Researcher, Statistisches Destatis, Germany

During a usability study, a UX team may notice that participants do not click on important links. For example, if a link is located toward the bottom right of the page, below the fold of the screen, it could be missed. Participants would be required to scroll all the way down the page and hunt for keywords, following a good information "scent" (Spool et al., 2004).

As discussed in Chapter 7, if the scent is not strong, a user may miss the link, click without confidence, scroll up and down, or take the "wrong" path. If a UX team notices this behavior while capturing eye-tracking data, they may opt to use the visual appeal of the heat map to highlight for the client the fact that participants missed key links below the fold of the page. As demonstrated in Figure 3.10, participants spent most of their time looking at information above the fold of the page (Holland et al., 2014). UX researchers can use eye-tracking data to highlight how the information architecture is not supporting good information foraging or information scent. Individual gaze plots can also be used to understand what parts of the web page participants focused on.

Gaze Plots

Gaze plots (i.e., scan paths) are useful to understand which areas of the screen draw the users' attention and the order/ sequence in which content is viewed. Gaze plots show the path that participants' eyes take as they move across the screen. Each fixation is illustrated by a dot and a number. Longer fixations are represented by larger dots and the number inside the dot shows the sequence of where they looked, such that "1" represents the first place a user looked, "2" represents the second place, and so on. In this way, the gaze plot can be used to help identify more and less efficient scanning of a page (Goldberg et al., 2002).

An example of a participant's gaze plot is shown in Figure 3.11. During the session, this participant appeared frustrated and said, "I'm dumbfounded. If I had an hour to work (on this)...

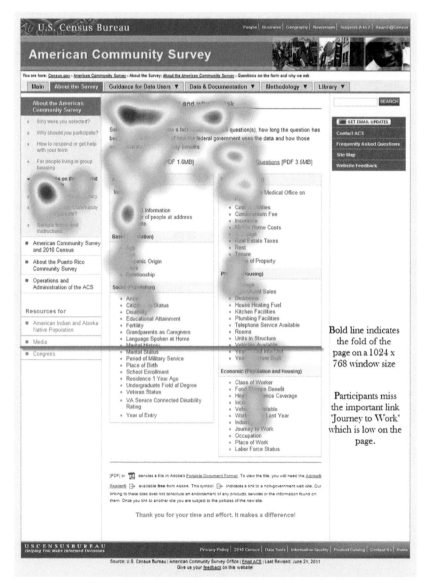

FIGURE 3.10 Heat map of the "ACS Questions on the Form and Why We Ask" web page during the first 10 seconds of task ($n=4$). The heat map can be used to discern patterns of user behavior, such as participants missing the link "Journey to Work," which would have led to a successful completion of the task. Another obvious pattern is that the participants spent most of their time looking at information above the fold of the page. (From Holland et al., 2014.)

I'd just answer the question [rather than look for why a survey question existed]." The gaze plot, showing fixations and saccades, supports this participant's commentary. He scans back and forth over the webpage looking for content. There are

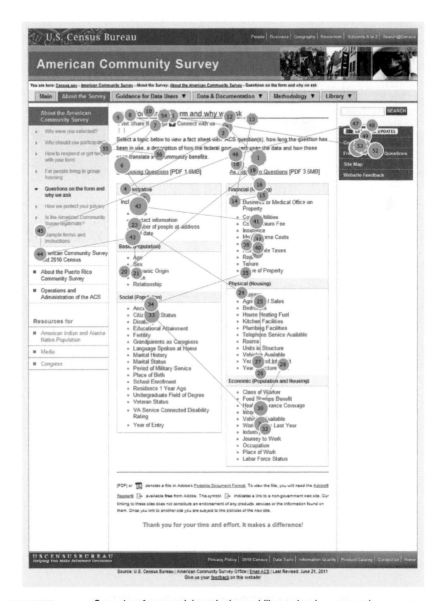

FIGURE 3.11   Gaze plot of one participant in the usability study who came to the correct target page, but failed to see the information he was looking for. (From Holland et al., 2014.)

lengthier fixations in certain areas of the page where he may have been expecting to locate the information (Holland et al., 2014).

In examining response order effects in web-based surveys (i.e., how users worked through long and short listings of response options), Galesic et al. (2008) demonstrated what researchers had long thought occurs, but had not been shown visually: users spend more time fixating the first few response options in a list of available response options than those presented later in the list. Gaze plots of individual users illustrated the path they took while responding to survey questions. This finding provided support to observed trends in survey research, where users were more likely to select options presented first regardless of content. Prior to eye-tracking analyses, this finding was based on users' overt behaviors during survey interviews (e.g., reported responses, response times, and mouse movements). With this study, eye tracking provided a direct way to understand what users attend to as they respond to survey items rather than relying on indirect measures.

Measures, such as numbers of fixations, saccades, and gaze plots, in conjunction with user commentary (think aloud) and behavior (e.g., user shrugs and sighs in frustration) provide insight into the cause of usability problems. From the eye-tracking visuals and user behaviors, the UX team can infer that, for example, important links located toward the bottom of a screen are missed or not attended to. Then the UX team can make recommendations to the client, such as to shorten a page so that important content is visible, or to make the information scent stronger and more salient.

COMMUNICATING USABILITY RESULTS MORE EFFECTIVELY WITH CLIENTS

Eye-tracking analyses allow for an understanding of the user's visual experience. With eye-tracking data, the UX team has an opportunity to present findings that can be both intuitive and appealing to clients. Clients can observe the eye-tracking sessions in real time from a separate observation room. This is helpful as the client too can see where the participant's eyes move as they complete a task. They can see areas of the screen that participants pay attention to and areas that are ignored. Watching the visual eye movements on the screen helps the entire team get an understanding for how users interact with the interface. This capability engages the observer or client and often increases their interest in the sessions, their understanding of the results, and their drive to implement recommendations that result from the sessions.

One of the unique benefits is the live viewer function that has proven instrumental in bringing together observers representing different disciplines by collectively observing gaze plots and fixations. More specifically, designers, developers, and managers jointly observe participants in real time and note how participants respond to stimuli. The observers then work together with user experience researchers to identify usability needs and propose solutions. As a result, observers have a better understanding of the unique needs of each audience type. The live viewer function serves as a tool to quickly determine usability needs and facilitate collaboration.

**Silvia Inéz Salazar, User-Informatics Lab Manager,
National Cancer Institute, USA**

The quantitative data obtained from eye tracking (e.g., number of mouse clicks, fixation duration) add an additional measure of the user experience that is not easily obtained from usability sessions. Visual images obtained from eye tracking make the quantitative information easier to interpret. While conventional usability testing techniques allow one to understand participants' overt behaviors, eye tracking provides in-depth insight about the users' visual behavior and how they interact with an application (Nudelman, 2011).

The beauty of eye tracking is the live-time observation of eye movements. This helps the cognitive interviewer afterwards during the debriefing with what happened during the completion of the survey. It gives additional information on the issues that need to be discussed.

Karen Blanke, Senior Researcher, Statistisches Destatis, Germany

Eye Tracking Can Convince Clients to Make Design Changes to Improve Usability

Traditional usability measures may not always convince clients about usability issues. Eye-tracking data is unique in that it can be rendered on a visual map and can be used to present a convincing argument to clients. For example, take the usability issue of users ignoring important text on a website, as in Figure 3.12. The purpose and importance of the PIN when completing the survey is the focus of this screen. However,

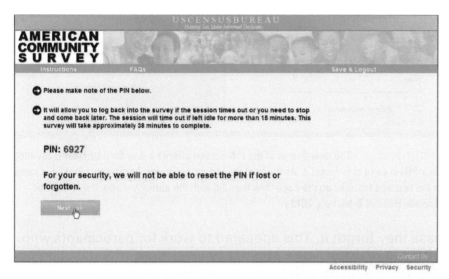

FIGURE 3.12 ACS PIN screen. The purpose and importance of the PIN when completing the survey is the focus of this screen. However, participants failed to understand the importance of the PIN and how they could use it to log back in. (From Ashenfelter et al., 2013.)

usability testing highlighted that when participants were required to log back in to the survey using a provided PIN, they failed to understand the importance of the PIN and how they could use it to log back in (Ashenfelter et al., 2013). While this information was on the initial PIN screen, users did not read it. When asked during the debriefing after the session about the purpose of the PIN, many participants could not recall the information. The gaze opacity map convinced the client that the layout of text on the screen did not highlight the importance and necessity of the PIN (Figure 3.13). The new design of the PIN screen offered a way for participants to reset their PIN in

FIGURE 3.13 Gaze opacity image of users failing to notice relevant content about the use of a PIN on a Census Bureau online survey ($n = 18$). (From Ashenfelter, et al., 2013.)

FIGURE 3.14   The new design of the PIN screen offered a way for participants to reset their PIN in case they forgot it. As the heat map (right) indicates, participants looked at more of the text and features on the page than they did with the earlier version. (From Olmsted-Hawala, Holland & Nichols, 2013.)

case they forgot it. This appeared to work for participants who, after the revision, were asked to answer a security question before moving onto the next page. Figure 3.14 displays a heat map that demonstrates that participants looked at more of the text and features on the page than they did with the earlier version. Even if the participants did not understand the purpose of the PIN, the extra step of setting up a security question reinforced that they would need information (e.g., the PIN or the answer to the security question) to gain access back into the survey (Olmsted-Hawala, Holland & Nichols, 2013).

Eye tracking can help to highlight where participants fixated, and the UX team can visually depict how participants miss areas of the screen where essential text is located. As shown in Figure 3.13, the starkness of a gaze opacity image or heat map can more effectively demonstrate participants' lack of attention to an area of the screen than words alone.

You can show your clients (subject matter experts) by heat maps and scan paths where the users look and how they look and read. Only then does the client understand that we need to adapt the questionnaire design.

Karen Blanke, Senior Researcher, Statistisches Destatis, Germany

Eye-Tracking Visuals Can Aid in the Effort for User-Centered Design

When developing a user interface intended for a specific audience, it can happen that the design may fail, and eye tracking could lend insight as to why. For example, a tool being developed on the American FactFinder Website included a fatal error for novice users (Olmsted-Hawala & Quach, 2012). Specifically, the third step of the path appeared to require users to choose something (e.g., a "dataset" or a "program") that was pure jargon and had no meaning for them.

It was a classic usability issue: The client wanted to include "dataset" as a prominent step on the path, yet the UX team strongly suspected that having "dataset" as a separate step would cause problems for the users. While the UX team knew from the outset that the dataset step would cause confusion, they were initially unable to convince the client. Eye tracking shown in Figure 3.15 helped show the client, in a very visual way, how the tool was leading users to make a key mistake. The eye-tracking data showed how most participants did not read important instruction text that told them to skip this section. Participants instead chose a dataset before moving forward to the next step, frequently selecting an item that did *not* contain the information they needed. During debriefing, some

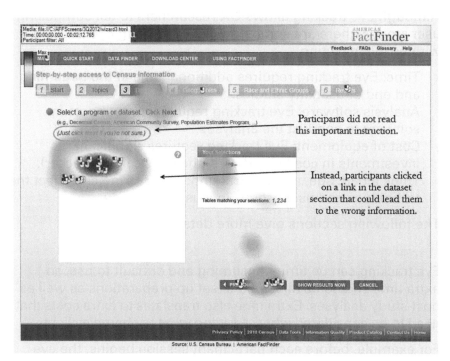

FIGURE 3.15   Eye-tracking heat map shows how most participants do not read important instruction text that tells them to skip this section. (From Olmsted-Hawala & Quach, 2012.)

participants commented that they did not read the instruction. The eye-tracking heat map confirmed users did not read the instruction to *"Just click Next if you are not sure"* (Olmsted-Hawala & Quach, 2012).

In the report, the UX team may opt to include:

- Participant comments (e.g., participants said, "I have no idea what a dataset is!")
- Warnings (e.g., if users begin to think the tool is too complex, it may lead them to give up)
- Visual heat maps of participant fixations with an explanation (e.g., participants missed instruction to skip this step)

When dealing with a skeptical client, a convincing argument should use eye tracking and other user feedback to encourage change. Heat maps, gaze plots, and charts with fixation counts are effective presentations for demonstrating design issues.

CONSIDERATIONS AND DRAWBACKS WITH EYE TRACKING IN USABILITY STUDIES

Although eye tracking allows UX researchers to tell compelling user stories, there are some drawbacks to using eye tracking with usability testing.

- Time: Eye tracking requires additional time at the beginning and end of usability studies.
- Analysis software: Eye tracking requires investments in software to conduct the analyses.
- Cost of equipment: Eye tracking requires significant investments in costly hardware (the physical eye tracker).
- Think aloud, age, and eye tracking: Eye tracking can affect the techniques and user groups in a usability study.

The following sections give more details on these issues.

Time

Eye tracking can be time-consuming and difficult to use, so extra time should be allocated to set up preparations as well as post-study analyses. Extra time also translates to extra costs that need to be considered when deciding what to charge a client.

For example, before each participant session begins, the eye tracker must be calibrated to each participant, adding minutes to a session. The type of web page, dynamic content, page linking, and the amount of time a user is exposed to the page affects the time needed for a thorough eye-tracking analysis. The first exposure to a web page may result in different fixation and gaze patterns than secondary exposures where users have learned that sections of a website are irrelevant to their task. The usability practitioner needs to be aware of this and take such things into consideration when adding in eye-tracking analysis to usability testing.

> *The challenge is the demanding and burdensome procedure to process eye-tracking data from pure life-video clips to AOIs, fixations rates, heatmaps and so on. The software needs improvement. Furthermore, you cannot analyze the data without having supplementary information from the probes and by a cognitive interview. If you don't take into account respondent's thinking, you may end up with wrong conclusions.*
>
> **Karen Blanke, Senior Researcher, Statistisches Destatis, Germany**

Analysis Software

Different eye-tracking software allows UX researchers to conduct different analyses. It can be frustrating when eye-tracking software does not work well with the type of site being tested. Static and dynamic web pages that open links in different URLs offer the quickest analyses since eye-tracking software can generate heat maps and gaze plots from eye-tracking data grouped by unique URLs. However, dynamic web pages that open new pop-up windows without a separate URL (as shown in Figure 3.16) will combine the eye-tracking data for the same URL placing responsibility on the UX team to interpret the data based on their observation and recordings. Depending on the eye-tracking software used, the UX team might have to manually figure out fixation data by observations and timing. This is not as precise and introduces the possibility of human error as the team could attribute the fixations on the screen incorrectly if they do not note exactly where on the screen and at what time a user interacted with the pop-up window.

Other dynamic sites, such as mapping or flash websites, often also require manual time-based analysis. This may mean that each recording will need to be examined separately, increasing the cost and time taken to include specific eye-tracking details

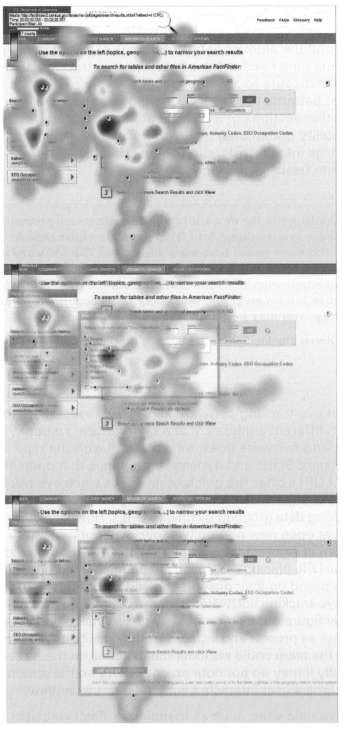

FIGURE 3.16 Screen shot of website with pop-up windows. In this screen shot, it is not clear if the fixations are on the page without any pop up window (top), on the Topics pop-up window (middle), or on the Geography pop-up window (bottom). All three modes could have been used during the task.

into the report. It is important to consider the design of the website and which analyses can be quickly completed (e.g., fixed elements, such as top navigation) and which will require more time (e.g., dynamically loaded content) when planning a usability study with eye tracking.

Think Aloud, Age, and Eye Tracking

An often used technique when conducting usability tests is to have the participant think aloud while completing a task (Dumas & Redish, 1999; Ericsson & Simon, 1996). However, whether usability participants should think aloud while working on a task (e.g., concurrent think aloud [CTA]) and having their eyes tracked is still under discussion. Some have advocated doing retrospective think aloud (RTA) with eye tracking because of the interference that CTA may have on where people look and fixate (Eger et al., 2007; Guan et al., 2006; Maughan et al., 2003). Others have found that CTA combined with eye tracking produces useful feedback about the site tested (Elling et al., 2012) and that for young adult participants, it makes no difference to the eye-tracking data (e.g., fixation counts) whether they use CTA or RTA (Romano Bergstrom & Olmsted-Hawala, 2012a; Romano Bergstrom & Olmsted-Hawala, 2012b). However, the same cannot be said for older adults—the dual task of thinking aloud while working on a website task impacts older adults' performance (Figure 3.17). See Chapter 12 for more about older adults and eye tracking.

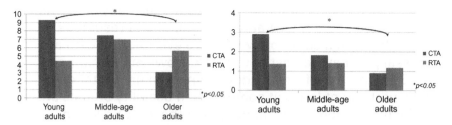

FIGURE 3.17 Mean number of fixations for left navigation (left) and top navigation (right) during usability task. Concurrent think aloud (orange); retrospective think aloud (gray). When age was not a factor, there appeared to be no differences in the number of eye fixations on the website between CTA and RTA. When age was taken into account, older adults had fewer fixations than young adults did in CTA only (Romano Bergstrom & Olmsted-Hawala, 2012a; Romano Bergstrom & Olmsted-Hawala, 2012b). In this study, the moderator sat in the control room, opposite a one-way mirror, and also used non-intrusive probes such as with a traditional or speech communication think-aloud protocol. (For more on traditional or speech communication think-aloud protocols see Boren & Ramey, 2000; Olmsted-Hawala et al., 2010).

While it is still unclear whether verbal think-aloud protocols affect fixation data, we do know that CTA is particularly problematic if the moderator sits next to the participant. There is an increased temptation of the participant (i.e., the speaker) to turn and look at the test administrator (i.e., the listener) while talking and working on the task (Bavelas et al., 2000). Communication between two people includes what is called a "gaze window," when a speaker looks at the listener to make a point (Bavelas et al., 2006). When the participant looks away from the computer screen, there is a loss of eye-tracking data.

RTA combined with eye tracking is typically done while the participant watches a video replay of their task, with the eye movements visible on the video replay. Some UX researchers that advocate using RTA with eye tracking do not find that participants are distracted by seeing the movements of their eyes across the screen (e.g., Guan et al., 2006; Hyrskykari et al., 2008). However, others have noticed that replaying the captured eye movements distracts participants (Freeman, 2011; Olmsted-Hawala & Romano Bergstrom, 2012). Instead of describing what they had been thinking as they had made certain actions or looked at certain areas of the screen, in a moment by moment recall, participants may say such things as, "Wow, was I looking there?" or " I didn't look there!" or "Oh this is neat! That's what my eyes were doing?" This type of verbalization may continue even after redirection probes by the test administrator of "What were you thinking then?"

We believe it is best practice to conduct a usability study that has a combination of CTA and RTA, if time and resources are available. In a situation when pure eye-tracking data are necessary, it may be best to use RTA. However, as happens with CTA, there is often an added benefit of understanding why a participant looks at something. If usability studies are conducted in silence, we do not get at the *why*. So when aiming to understand why something is happening, the user verbalization combined with the eye-tracking data often gives a better understanding of the issues. And CTA should be used. Live eye-tracking data may be used to perfect the CTA probes a UX researcher might make during a usability session (Freeman, 2011). The bottom line is that the triangulation of the think-aloud data (CTA or RTA) with the eye-tracking data and the observed behavior makes for a better understanding of the issues.

CONCLUSION

As we have shared throughout the chapter, eye tracking to supplement usability testing is beneficial and can be essential to understanding the totality of users' experiences. Eye tracking not only supports usability findings and metrics (e.g., accuracy, efficiency, subjective satisfaction), but the analytics add information on such things as where users look before making their first and subsequent clicks on an interface, and how long users look at an area of the screen. Eye tracking highlights information not attainable with traditional user experience techniques.

Eye tracking broadens our understanding of the problems with the design or content of an interface. It can be useful not only to a UX team trying to understand what users are doing as they interact with the interface being tested, but also for the clients to get a visual impression of what users see and do not see on their designs. Convincing the client that there are issues with areas of the screen is an effective first step toward a solution.

But there are certain drawbacks when using eye tracking in usability testing, including additional time, increasing costs, challenges with analysis, or the combining of eye tracking with other usability methods. However, eye tracking adds a crucial dimension to usability testing that is often guessed at without it. Eye tracking creates the possibility of asking new and different questions, and as such, there are many opportunities for empirical research in the field.

The benefits of eye tracking in usability testing include:

- Learning which areas of the screen draw users' attention and which do not
- Understanding whether link labels and instruction text are attended to
- Gathering user data on specific AOIs for the UX team and/or the client
- Creating effective visuals to convince clients
- Providing a triangulation of data with eye tracking visuals, user verbalizations, and overt observed behavior
- Gaining new insight and perspective that can lead to better design recommendations

ACKNOWLEDGMENTS

Thank you to Rachel Horwitz (U.S. Census Bureau) for helpful feedback on an earlier version of this chapter.

REFERENCES

Ashenfelter, K., Holland, T., Quach, V., Nichols, E., 2013. Final Report for the Usability Evaluation of American Community Survey 2011 Online Instrument: Rounds 4a and 4b. https://www.census.gov/srd/papers/pdf/ssm2013-04.pdf.

Ashenfelter, K., Holland, T., Quach, V., Nichols, E., Lakhe, S., 2012. (SSM2012/01). In: Ashenfelter, K.T., Holland, T., Quach, V., Nichols, E.M., Lakhe, S. (Eds.), ACS Internet 2011 Project: Report for Rounds 1 and 2 of ACS Wireframe Usability Testing and Round 1 of ACS Internet Experiment. http://www.census.gov/srd/papers/pdf/ssm2012–01.pdf.

Bavelas, J., Coates, L., Johnson, T., 2000. Listeners as co-narrators. J. Pers. Soc. Psychol. 79 (6), 941–952.

Bavelas, J., Coates, L., Johnson, T., 2006. Listener responses as collaborative process: the role of gaze. J. Commun. 52 (3), 566–580.

Bojko, A., 2006. Using eye tracking to compare web page designs: a case study. JUS 3 (1), 112–120.

Boren, T., Ramey, J., 2000. Thinking aloud: reconciling theory and practice. IEEE Trans. Prof. Comm. 43 (3), 261–278.

Dumas, J., Redish, J., 1999. A practical guide to usability testing. Intellect Press, Portland, OR.

Eger, N., Ball, L.J., Stevens, R., Dodd, J., 2007. Cueing retrospective verbal reports in usability testing through eye-movement replay. In: Proceedings of the 21st British HCI Group Annual Conference on People and Computers: HCI...but not as we know it–Volume 1, BCS-HCI '07. UK British Computer Society, Swinton, UK, pp. 129–137.

Ehmke, C., Wilson, S., 2007. Identifying web usability problems from eye-tracking data. In: Proceedings of the 21st British HCI Group Annual Conference on People and Computers: HCI...but not as we know it–Volume 1, BCS-HCI '07. UK British Computer Society, Swinton, UK, pp. 119–128.

Elling, S., Lentz, L., de Jong, M., 2012. Combining concurrent think-aloud protocols and eye-tracking observations: an analysis of verbalizations and silences. IEEE T. Prof. Commun. 55 (3), 206–220.

Ericsson, K.A., Simon, H.A., 1996. Protocol analysis: verbal reports as data, Revised ed. MIT Press, Cambridge, MA.

Freeman, B., 2011. Triggered think-aloud protocol: using eye tracking to improve usability test moderation. In: Proceedings of the SIGCHI Conference on Human Factors in Computing Systems, CHI '11, pp. 1171–1174.

Galesic, M., Tourangeau, R., Couper, M.P., Conrad, F.G., 2008. New insights on response order effects and other cognitive shortcuts in survey responding. Public Opin. Q. 72 (5), 892–913.

Goldberg, J.H., Kotval, X.P., 1999. Computer interface evaluation using eye movements: methods and constructs. Int. J. Ind. Ergon. 24 (6), 631–645.

Goldberg, J.H., Stimson, M.J., Lewenstein, M., Scott, N., Wichansky, A.M., 2002. Eye tracking in web search tasks: design implications. In: Proceedings of the Eye Tracking Research and Applications Symposium 2002. ACM Press, New York, pp. 51–58.

Guan, Z., Lee, S., Cuddihy, E., Ramey, J., 2006. The validity of the stimulated retrospective think-aloud method as measured by eye tracking. In: Proceedings of the SIGCHI Conference on Human Factors in Computing Systems, CHI '06. ACM Press, New York, pp. 1253–1262.

Holland, T., Olmsted-Hawala, E., Gareau, M., 2014. A Follow-Up Usability Evaluation of the American Community Survey Website with Novice Users. Center for Survey Measurement Study. Series, US Census Bureau.

Hornof, A., Halverson, T., 2002. Cleaning up systematic error in eye-tracking data by using required fixation locations. Behav. Res. Methods Instrum. Comput. 34 (4), 592–604.

Hyrskykari, A., Ovaska, S., Majaranta, P., Raiha, K., Lehtinen, M., 2008. Gaze path stimulation in retrospective think aloud. J. Eye Mov. Res. 2 (4), 5, 1–18.

International Organization for Standardization (ISO) 9241-11, 1998. Ergonomic Requirements for Office Work with Visual Display Terminals (VDTs)—Part 11: Guidance on Usability.

Maughan, L., Dodd, J., Walters, R., 2003. Video replay of eye tracking as a cue in retrospective protocol… don't make me think aloud!. In: Scandinavian Workshop of Applied Eye Tracking, 2003.

Mitzner, T.L., Touron, D.R., Rogers, W.A., Hertzog, C., 2010. Checking it twice: age-related differences in double checking during visual search. In: Proceedings of the Human Factors and Ergonomics Society Annual Meeting, vol. 54. pp. 1326–1330 (18).

Nudelman, G., 2011. Designing Search: UX Strategies for Ecommerce Success. John Wiley & Sons, Indianapolis.

Olmsted-Hawala, E., Holland, T., Nichols, E., 2013. Usability evaluation of the 2013 American Community Survey (ACS) Online Instrument. In: Internal Census Bureau Human Factors & Usability Research short report.

Olmsted-Hawala, E., Murphy, E., Hawala, S.M, Ashenfelter, K., 2010. Think-Aloud protocols: a comparison of three think-aloud protocols for use in testing data dissemination web sites for usability. In: Proceedings of CHI 2010, ACM Conference on Human Factors in Computing Systems. ACM Press, pp. 2381–2390.

Olmsted-Hawala, E., Quach, V., 2012. 3Q2012 Cycle 1 usability results with eye-tracking analysis. In: Internal Census Bureau Human Factors & Usability Research short report.

Olmsted-Hawala, E., Romano Bergstrom, J., 2012. Think-aloud protocols: does age make a difference? In: Proceedings of Society for Technical Communication (STC) Summit, Chicago, IL, May 2012.

Olmsted-Hawala, E., Romano Bergstrom, J., Rogers, W., 2013. Age-related differences in search strategy and performance when using a data-rich web site. In: Proceedings from HCII 2013, Lecture Notes in Computer Science.

Pernice, K., Nielsen, J., 2009. How to Conduct Eyetracking Studies. Nielsen Norman Group. Available at: http://www.useit.com/eyetracking/methodology.

Poole, A., Ball, L.J., 2005. Eye tracking in human-computer interaction and usability research: current status and future prospects. In: Ghaoui, C. (Ed.), Encyclopedia of Human Computer Interaction. Idea Group, Hershey, PA, pp. 211–219.

Romano Bergstrom, J., Olmsted-Hawala, E., 2012a. Effects of age and Think-Aloud Protocol on eye-Tracking Data and Usability Measures, Poster Presentation at the Usability Professionals Association, Las Vegas, NV, June 2012.

Romano Bergstrom, J., Olmsted-Hawala, E., 2012b. Effects of age and think-aloud protocol on eye-tracking data and usability measures, Presentation at the EyeTrackUX, Las Vegas, NV, June 2012.

Romano Bergstrom, J., Olmsted-Hawala, E., Bergstrom, H., (In review). Older adults fail to see the periphery during web site navigation.

Romano, J., Chen, J., Olmsted-Hawala, E., Murphy, E., 2007. A Medium-Fidelity Usability and Eye-Tracking Evaluation of Iteration 2.0 And Iteration 2.5 Of the New American FactFinder Web Site: Capabilities and Functions. Statistical Research Division Study Series Survey Methodology # 2010-07. US Census Bureau. Available at: http://www.census.gov/srd/www/abstract/ssm2010-07.html.

Spool, J., Perfetti, C., Brittan, D., Spool, J., Perfetti, C., Brittan, D., 2004. Designing for the Scent of Information. User Interface Engineering. Available at: http://www.uis.edu/webservices/wp-content/uploads/sites/8/2013/02/Designing_for_Scent.pdf.

4

PHYSIOLOGICAL RESPONSE MEASUREMENTS

Jennifer Romano Bergstrom[1], Sabrina Duda[2], David Hawkins[1], and Mike McGill[3]

[1]Fors Marsh Group, Arlington, VA, USA
[2]Users' Delight, Berlin, Germany
[3]Pace University, New York, NY, USA

INTRODUCTION

Peering into the mind of a user is of high value to both market and user experience (UX) researchers. What are users thinking? What are they feeling? Why are they doing that? Are they thinking something we are not seeing? Some methods, such as interviews, surveys, and think-aloud protocols, attempt to gather this information by simply asking the user, while observational methods rely on viewing user behavior. But what about directly observing what is going on in the user's mind?

UX research is often limited to overt observable behavior. Through the use of interviews, questionnaires or think-aloud protocols, researchers must rely on a participant's memory and subjective judgments as a means of gaining insight into inner cognitive processes and emotional states. A common finding within cognitive neuroscience is that a person's subjective perception of their own behavior does not always correspond with their underlying neural activity (Kretschmar et al., 2013). Simply put, people do not always know what is going on inside their own heads.

This point can be illustrated with research on eye tracking during reading. Eye-tracking studies, which provide objective real-time quantitative measure of eye movements, reveal longer fixation times for reading text with transposed letters compared to reading normal text (Liversedge & Blythe, 2007). However, sentences with transposed letters are subjectively easier for users to read, indicating that the cost of reading such texts, as revealed by the objective analysis of eye movements, does not seem to be accessible to users' conscious judgment of the experience. Similarly, electroencephalography (EEG)-based research of language processing has shown that phrases that are judged as easy to understand and highly acceptable are often accompanied by larger processing effort (e.g., Demiral et al., 2008).

So while we have learned that visual attention and engagement are not necessarily linked to perceptions of experiences, we also struggle to find the best methods to allow us to understand more about users' unconscious desires as they look at certain elements. New biometric devices for measuring physiological responses, which are practical, reasonably priced, and suitable for UX and market research, have evoked enthusiasm. We are now in a place where we can actually measure emotions and implicit reactions and thus at last, are at the beginning stages where we can peer into the mind of the user.

I have used eye tracking with EEG, EDA, and other psychophysical measures for a variety of research projects that aimed to understand user engagement with: video games, design compositions, and different search engine result pages (SERPs). We decided to pair eye-tracking data with the biometric data to learn not only how the users physically reacted to the stimulus but also where on the screen they were looking at the time. In addition to pairing the data with the biometrics, we always looked at the eye-tracking data to understand if users were looking at advertisements in the game or to determine their typical gaze patterns when interacting with the SERPs or design comps.

Dan Berlin, Mad*Pow, USA

Biometric measurements allow us to collect physiological data in ways that were not previously possible. While task performance (e.g., accuracy, efficiency) measures user behavior, physiology (e.g., electrodermal activity, EDA) provides a functional signal of emotional response. While an eye gaze pattern is a measure of behavior, EEG provides a measure of brain activity and lends insight into underlying cognitive processes as the user interacts with a product.

In general, UX researchers can apply biometrics when they are interested in understanding the user's emotional reaction at a certain point in time (e.g., when a specific stimulus is introduced or displayed) or to catch the overall emotional reaction over a longer period of time (i.e., during the entire interaction with the product). In this chapter, we provide an overview of physiological methods that are now applicable within UX research and share some concrete examples of physiological measures coupled with eye tracking that have led to a better understanding of the user experience.

DIMENSIONS OF PHYSIOLOGICAL RESPONSE MEASURES

Most UX methods can be classified according to various dimensions. While the goals of the project largely dictate the methods that will be used, clients and researchers are often interested in knowing what else they can get that is within budget. Here we focus on four main dimensions that UX researchers must consider when introducing physiological metrics into UX projects:

1. Subjective versus Objective
2. Real Time versus Delayed
3. Natural Context versus Artificial Lab
4. Invasive versus Non-invasive

Subjective versus Objective

Typical UX research methods include asking users to rate their experience. For example, UX study participants are often asked to rate their overall satisfaction or perceived difficulty in completing tasks using a Likert scale (e.g., scale of 1 to 5, where 1=not difficult at all and 5=extremely difficult). These measures are purely subjective, and while they are easy to collect, they are susceptible to bias. Because working memory capacity is finite, participants may not completely remember their recent

Satisfaction Questionnaire   Facial Recognition   Pupil Dilation   EDA   EEG

FIGURE 4.1   Objectiveness scale of physiological response measurements. The more objective a measurement is, the better.

interactions with a product. They may unknowingly base their judgments on an incomplete subset of memories (Wiswede et al., 2007). Additionally, participants may not feel comfortable telling the researcher what they really think and feel—perhaps what they feel is socially inappropriate, or as is often the case with older adults, they may feel that they, rather than the interface, are the problem, and so they will rate their satisfaction high even when they cannot complete tasks.

Objective measures of performance do not rely on the user's assessment. Rather, UX researchers can record and measure time on task, number of steps to complete tasks and steps taken, errors, and completion rates.

Physiological response measurements allow researchers to further collect objective measures of performance. For example, rather than asking participants if tasks were difficult or if they were surprised when a stimulus appeared on the screen, we can measure their skin conductance (also known as galvanic skin response, but more on this later) throughout the session or at various points in time (e.g., following the introduction of a stimulus). Skin conductance can be easily measured with electrodes non-invasively placed on the fingertips, wrist, or palm.

Figure 4.2 displays the subjective assessment of emotions and objective skin conductance data, coupled with eye tracking (red crosses in the images) while a participant viewed a very graphic anti-tobacco advertisement. The participant had little variability when subjectively rating her experience, and the low ratings (1's and 2) suggest that the participant was unaffected by the ad. However, the objective skin conductance data combined with the eye-tracking data tell a different story—that she experienced emotional arousal when she saw certain parts of the ad.

Although participants may subjectively rate that they did not feel amused, angry, disgusted, or interested, physiological response data can reveal that at various points during ad viewing, implicit emotional responses occurred. From subjective ratings and

Question: Please indicate how much you experienced each of the following while viewing the advertisement.
Response options: Not at all / A little bit / Moderately / Quite a bit / Extremely (5-pt scale)

	Amused, fun-loving, or silly	Angry, irritated, or annoyed	Disgust, distaste, or revulsion	Guilty, repentant, or blameworthy	Inspired, uplifted, or elevated
P1	1	1	2	1	1
	Interested, alert, or curious	Joyful, glad, or happy	Sad, downhearted, or unhappy	Scared, fearful, or afraid	Sympathy, concern, or compassion
P1	1	1	1	1	1

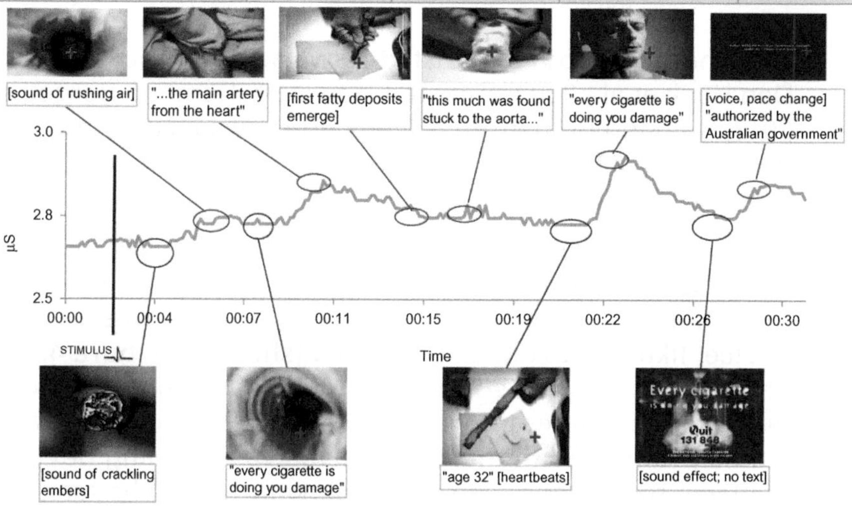

FIGURE 4.2   Subjective Likert-scale data and objective EDA data during a very graphic anti-tobacco advertisement viewing.

debriefing interviews, we can learn that the parts of the ad that cause the greatest arousal are, for example, the parts that participants find to be the most disgusting. It is important to note that the arousal data alone cannot tell us the direction of arousal; for example, if the emotional arousal meant the user liked or hated what they saw. Thus, combining subjective assessments and physiological measures enable us to tell a more complete and accurate story than relying on one measure alone.

Real Time versus Delayed

Another important element for UX researchers to consider is whether they need data in real time or if obtaining data upon completion of a task or session is acceptable (Figure 4.3). Often we rely on the think-aloud method to understand participants' thoughts as they work on a task (for more on the think-aloud method, see Chapter 3). However, UX researchers sometimes opt to not use the think-aloud method because it may interfere with other metrics, like eye tracking (Kim et al., 2007;

Satisfaction Questionnaire   Facial Recognition   Pupil Dilation   EDA   EEG

FIGURE 4.3   Real-time scale of physiological response measurements. The more real-time a measurement is, the better.

Romano Bergstrom & Olmsted-Hawala, 2012), accuracy (Van Den Haak et al., 2003; Olmsted-Hawala & Romano Bergstrom, 2012; Romano Bergstrom & Olmsted-Hawala, 2012), and time on task (Capra, 2002; Van Den Haak et al., 2003; Olmsted-Hawala & Romano Bergstrom, 2012).

Using physiological response measurements, UX researchers can obtain real-time feedback without interrupting data collection. For example, incorporating a non-invasive device, like an EDA tracking device (shown in Figure 4.4) or facial recognition software, allows researchers to see fluctuations in attention and emotion while users interact with a product. With these non-invasive recording devices in place, researchers can then follow up when the task or session is complete to ask what people were thinking at various times during the session (although these measures, as discussed before, are susceptible to error due to reliance upon retrospective memory).

FIGURE 4.4   The participant is wearing a non-invasive EDA device on his left wrist while he participates in a usability study.

Natural Context versus Artificial Lab

In the beginning of the Internet, many devices (e.g., computers and phones) were quite similar. Inviting users to participate in a lab-based study was therefore justifiable. Today, many devices exist differing in size and interaction techniques, and people use them in different situations. As the context of use (e.g., in the subway, bus stop, cafeteria, sofa) can affect the user experience, it may be important to study users in real context, with their own device.

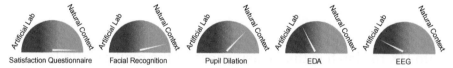

Satisfaction Questionnaire   Facial Recognition   Pupil Dilation   EDA   EEG

FIGURE 4.5   Natural context scale of physiological response measurements. The more natural context a measurement is, the better.

While much user experience research has been conducted in labs, research today increasingly involves observations of users in natural settings, such as in their home, work place, or in other public places. Modern portable eye trackers allow researchers to conduct studies outside the lab (see Chapter 10 for examples of portable eye trackers, which are frequently used in mobile UX research). This is important as user experience researchers may not be able to detect the day-to-day problems and natural needs of users in the lab.

Knowing when to test in the lab or in the user's natural environment depends on the project and the needs of the client. If your client wants to know how restaurant patrons view their social media ads, testing in the lab may lack the realism and generalizability the client desires. However, if the client is interested in task completion times and error rates for an e-commerce interface, you may be justified in setting up an experimental protocol in the lab.

When working in the lab, it is important to create a test situation as natural and realistic as possible, in order to get valid results from UX research. Few modern physiological response measurement devices (such as a wrist-worn EDA device) can be taken outside the lab; thus, many are still limited to use in the lab. While UX researchers may lose the rich natural context in which devices are normally used, lab-based research gives researchers experimental control. For example, in the lab, researchers do not need to worry about extraneous events that can disrupt the project and data. Polluting factors, such as sounds or other people in the environment, can disrupt a study and add undue variability to data.

Researchers must make decisions based on the needs of their clients and on the questions being asked in the study to determine what is more important: experimental control or the distractions that come with interactions in a natural environment.

Invasive versus Non-Invasive

An important consideration when incorporating biometrics into UX research is the invasiveness of the method. While university and medical labs may be able to use more invasive techniques that require participants to lie down in scanners (e.g., functional magnetic resonance imaging, fMRI), inject radioactive isotopes into the bloodstream (e.g., positron emission tomography, PET), or record magnetic fields produced by electrical activity in the brain (magnetoencephalography, MEG; shown in Figure 4.6), the typical UX researcher does not have such luxuries. These techniques are important in terms of localizing brain activity (spatial resolution) and determining precisely when something occurs (temporal resolution); however, these measures are often not feasible for the average UX project (Figure 4.7).

Luckily, UX researchers have tools for understanding brain activity that are far less invasive than PET or fMRI. While EEG may not have optimal spatial resolution, the temporal precision (i.e., knowing when activity occurs in time) is excellent and better than all other existing neuroimaging techniques. This allows for real-time monitoring of brain activity while the participant interacts with a product. More importantly, for UX researchers, EEG and other modern physiological measurement devices are non-invasive, do not require a thorough laboratory, are less expensive, and are thus more practical. We will discuss some of these devices in detail later in this chapter.

FIGURE 4.6

Participant in an MEG study.

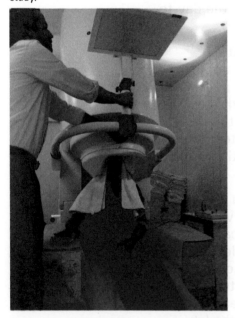

Satisfaction Questionnaire   Facial Recognition   Pupil Dilation   EDA   EEG

FIGURE 4.7   Invasiveness scale of physiological response measurements. The less invasive a measurement is, the better.

PRACTICALITY OF INCORPORATING BIOMETRICS

Two important factors that cannot be disregarded when considering incorporating biometrics into your study include: (1) the budget available for the project and (2) the available time. Buying a new EEG device, investing in learning a new method, handling longer and more complex data analyses, which may require the help of more researchers, all need careful consideration. Is the effort justified by the results? What results are needed, and how much detail is important? Is a simple user observation with think aloud sufficient for optimizing a website or is detailed emotional feedback necessary before making a very important design decision? It is likely that new devices will become more affordable in the near future and that the data evaluation process will become increasingly easy and effortless—the same trend that has already occurred with eye-tracking techniques. But as with eye tracking, the study objectives must be carefully considered before deciding that incorporating biometrics is necessary.

PHYSIOLOGICAL RESPONSE MEASUREMENT IN UX

Once you have decided that biometrics are in fact necessary, it is important to carefully consider the available options. Each method yields different data, so depending on the information you are seeking, you may choose to use one or more of the following (Figure 4.8).

Pupil Dilation

Pupillometry, the measurement of changes in pupil diameter, is a relatively older method for inferring different types of activity in the brain. Pupil dilation is an autonomic sympathetic nervous system response that can provide indices of attention, interest, or emotion and is correlated with mental workload and arousal

Evaluating the User Experience (UX) with Multimodal Data

	Evaluation	Goals	Pros	Cons
Objective	Task Performance (e.g., accuracy, efficiency)	• Assess whether participants can complete intended tasks	• Objective measure of usability	• Does not reveal complete experience (e.g., few errors, but bad experience) • Does not inform the source of the issue • Answers 'what' not 'why'
Subjective	Subjective Reactions (e.g., satisfaction survey, think aloud, debriefing interview)	• Understand participants' thoughts about product	• Real-time insight into users' thoughts (e.g., think aloud) • Quantitative measure of subjective experience (e.g., satisfaction survey)	• Lacks insight into user's experience as they work with the interface (e.g., satisfaction measure at end) • Memory is fallible (debriefing and satisfaction measures at end) • Biases • Social desirability
Subjective	Real-time participant feedback (e.g., button presses)	• Understand users' emotional reactions to product	• Real-time insight into emotions	• Social desirability
Objective	Eye Tracking (e.g., fixations, pupil dilation)	• Assess where users look, how long, how often, order of fixations • Assess excitement, engagement	• Can assess if items are distracting, attracting, confusing • Can assess search strategy • Can assess fear, anxiety response, which is difficult to describe or people may not describe due to social desirability • Assess workload (hand-eye movement) • Non-invasive (modern equipment) • Well understood and used in UX research	• Expensive • Some participants do not track well
Objective	Emotion Recognition (e.g., facial or audio)	• Understand unconscious emotions	• Real-time tracking of expressions • Non-invasive (built-in monitor camera)	• Not well studied in UX research
Objective	Skin Conductance	• Assess excitement	• Real-time measure of sympathetic nervous system through the skin • Correlated with stress, excitement, engagement, frustration, anger • Syncs with eye-tracking data	• Moderately correlated with palm • Not well studied in UX research
Objective	Neuroimaging (e.g., EEG)	• Understand where in the brain excitement is taking place	• Better understanding of what user is experiencing (e.g., fear) • Precision (varies among options)	• Long set-up time • Long analysis time • Need complex lab space • Expensive • Invasive

Data Analysis Complexity (label on left side, vertical)

FIGURE 4.8 Evaluating the UX with physiological response measurements.

(Iqbal et al., 2004; Tullis & Albert, 2008). Thus it is quite obvious that including pupil dilation data with more typical eye-tracking data can provide great insight into the user's experience.

> *Most eye trackers collect pupil dilation data, but software can make it difficult to actually get to this data. If you are in the market for an eye tracker, and pupil dilation data is important to you, be sure to ask the eye tracker companies how to obtain the pupil dilation data.*

How Does Pupil Dilation Measure Emotion?

Pupils respond to more than just light, and collecting this objective data may be a useful alternative or addition to subjective measures. Some cognitive and emotional events occur outside of our conscious control and can cause pupils to constrict and expand. UX researchers can record data from these events to detect fear, anxiety, mental strain, or task difficulty (Ahern & Beatty, 1979). Additionally, because it is nearly impossible to mask implicit cognitive responses, biases such as social desirability that

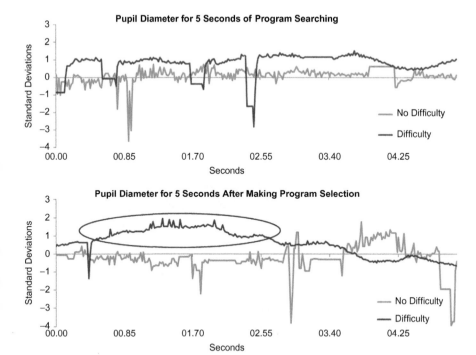

FIGURE 4.9   Pupil dilation data from two participants who interacted with a web-based TV diary tool: one had difficulty accessing the search function (shown in red), and the other had no difficulty (shown in blue). Difficulty using the tool is demonstrated by greater pupil dilation.

prevent people from accurately telling researchers about their experience are of little concern during the analysis of pupil data.

As shown in Figure 4.9, pupil dilation can be used to measure task difficulty. Participants interacted with a web-based TV diary tool: one had difficulty accessing the search function (shown in red), and the other had no difficulty (shown in blue). The participant who had difficulty had greater pupil dilation during the program searching process in some sections (top). Once they selected a program, they selected the time they viewed the program. The participant who had difficulty was surprised while selecting the program time because all her entry data was lost. This is shown by the pupil dilation (circled in red, bottom).

In one recent study, Jósza (2010) used pupillometry in a website usability study. Tasks were designed such that mental effort increased by task. He found that pupil diameter did not change with increased mental effort or with task failure, as was expected. However, Jósza found that with task success, pupil constriction

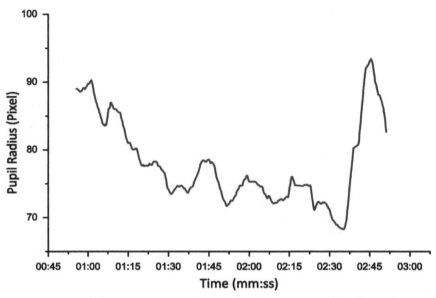

FIGURE 4.10 When the participant thought of a solution to the problem (at 2 minutes, 35 seconds), pupil size increased. (From Józsa, 2010.)

It has been hypothesized that increased blinking is associated with negative feelings and on the contrary, decreases with pleasant psychological states.

Andreassi (2000).

occurred (right side of Figure 4.10). This constriction occurred when the participant gave the right solution, finished the task, or had a new idea how to solve the task. He inferred this as a sign of relief. Therefore, a physiological index of relief can be detected through pupil size change.

Pupil dilation has been used to assess a number of cognitive functions, including fatigue, racial biases, and depression; however, it is impossible to tell what changes in pupil size mean without considering the context in which these changes occur (Powell & Schirillo, 2011). Jagdish Sheth, a marketing professor at Emory University, explains: "There [is] no scientific way to establish whether [pupil dilation] measured interest or anxiety" (Fong, 2012). Therefore, caution must be made when interpreting the results of pupil dilation data.

As with other UX research methods, it is important to combine metrics with pupil dilation. It would be bad practice to only use pupil dilation to make inferences about cognitive processes and user experience, as the story is incomplete. However, considering the ease with which we can collect this data, UX researchers should consider the opportunity.

Facial Emotion Recognition

Non-verbal gestures play a significant role in the communication process and can provide critical insight into one's experience while interacting with websites and other products. Emotion is recognized from facial expression by all humans, regardless of cultural background: happiness, surprise, fear, anger, contempt, disgust, and sadness (plus or minus two; Ekman & Friesen, 1976).

Facial gestures are the primary evidence of affect (Hackney, 1974), and unlike subjective questionnaire measures, facial expressions are more difficult to control. Facial emotion data may tell UX researchers quite a bit about the user experience above and beyond what users are able and/or willing to tell us.

> *Everyone knows that grief involves a gloomy and joy a cheerful countenance. There are characteristic facial expressions which are observed to accompany anger, fear, erotic excitement, and all the other passions.*
>
> **J. Russell, 1994, quoting Aristotle: nd/1913, pp. 805, 808).**

How Does Facial Emotion Recognition Software Measure Emotion?

Terzis et al. (2010) researched real-time and continuous tracking of facial expressions. They distinguished happy, angry, sad, surprised, scared, disgusted, and neutral and reached an overall accuracy of 87%. Two researchers recorded the facial emotion results, and their own estimation of the student's emotions, and results were compared. There was high agreement for neutral, happy, scared, surprised, and sad emotions. However, agreement was lower for disgust and angry emotions. Nevertheless, there was high agreement overall between the emotions measured.

They used FaceReader by Noldus Information Technology, a program for facial analysis (Loijens & Krips, 2013). The program detects the presence of a face, and then the face is modeled using an algorithm based on a database of images describing over 500 key points in the face. The software also detects the position of aspects of the face, such as eyes, mouth open or closed, and brows raised or lowered. As users interact

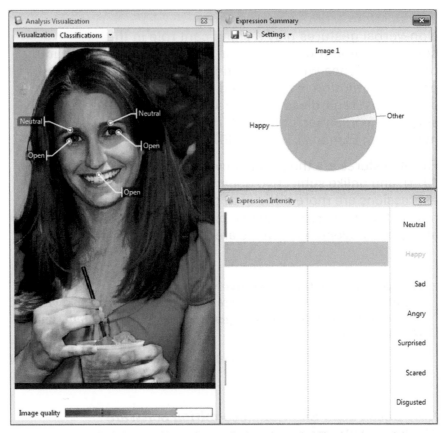

FIGURE 4.11 Facial recognition software displays the probability that the participant is expressing specific emotions. The software detects that she is primarily happy, but it also detects a bit of fear. Source: Noldus Information Technology.

with products and are, for example, frustrated, amused, or surprised, the facial recognition software codes the expression (Figures 4.11 and 4.12). This method can be extremely valuable when working with products that participants may not be comfortable discussing—the facial recognition software can tell researchers what emotions users experience.

But recording facial emotions in UX research has its limitations as well. Emotions can occur without facial expressions, and facial expressions can occur without emotions (Russell, 1995). Additionally, people may experience emotions differently, and thus, the software may not accurately read people's emotions. Thus it seems that while facial emotion recognition has strong potential for measuring the user experience, we are not quite

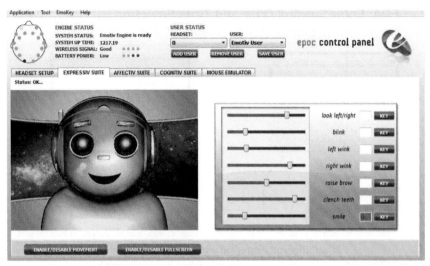

FIGURE 4.12   This suite records and mimics facial expressions in real time. It includes Blink, Smile, Clench Teeth, and Laugh. Source: Emotive.

there yet. As with most methods, facial recognition software should not be used in isolation—it should be coupled with other methods that together explain the complete user experience.

Skin Conductance

Skin conductance, (a.k.a. EDA or galvanic skin response, GSR) is frequently used as a psychophysiological method, because it is easy to use and largely non-intrusive for the participant. EDA and GSR largely assess activity of the "fight-or-flight response," which is controlled by the sympathetic nervous system. The fight-or-flight response is activated in response to emotionally charged stimuli. The extent to which this response is activated can be measured by the secretion of sweat; more sweat is released during a strong emotional response compared to a weak one. The hands have a high density of sweat glands that are sensitive to changes to external stimuli (e.g., temperature) as well as internal stimuli (e.g., emotions changes). EDA data can be collected from the finger (Figure 4.13), wrist, or palm.

EDA is associated with stress, excitement, engagement, frustration, and anger and correlates with self-report measures of arousal (Lang et al., 1993). Attention-grabbing stimuli and attention-demanding tasks increase the frequency and magnitude of GSRs.

FIGURE 4.13
Participants can wear EDA devices on their finger while they participate in user experience studies.

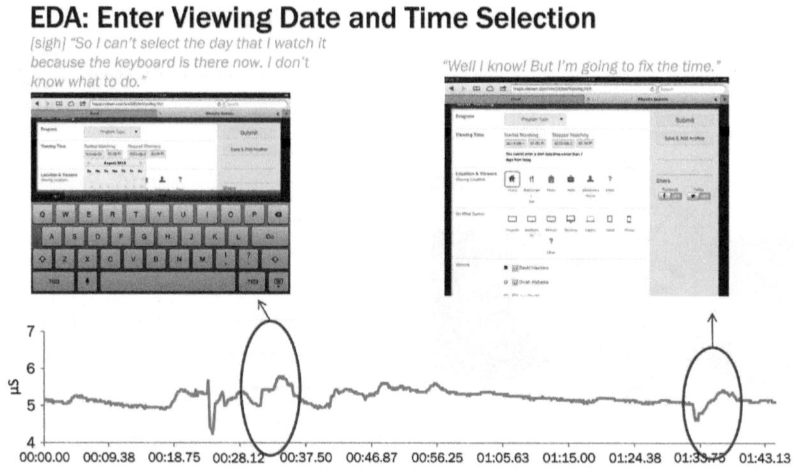

EDA: Enter Viewing Date and Time Selection

FIGURE 4.14   The participant interacted with a tablet app while wearing an EDA device and while her eyes were tracked. EDA increased when the participant had difficulties using the app.

EDA is often used in decision making and emotion research. A recent study assessed EDA during interactions with an online poker game, where numerous and fast decisions were necessary (Palomäki et al., 2013). Poker hand strength was associated with EDA response, and thus, EDA was useful in indicating the anticipated utility of poker game decisions.

Figure 4.14 displays EDA data from a participant who interacted with a tablet application. When she experienced difficulties using the app, her arousal increased. Her verbalizations of frustration (first, that the keyboard covered part of the screen and then later, when she got an error message) were consistent with the points of EDA arousal. EDA allowed us to learn the precise points of frustration and in an objective manner. In this case, the arousal was consistent with the verbalizations, but in other cases, such as when participants do not verbalize frustrations, EDA can be extremely useful in understanding the user experience.

How Does Skin Conductance Measure Emotion?

EDA is composed of tonic and phasic activity. Tonic changes in arousal occur slowly and are measured over a long period of time. Tonic level of emotional arousal can be measured, for example, at the onset and offset of an advertisement and are in essence a "baseline" level of arousal. Phasic activity, however, is composed of rapid secretions of sweat in response to a discrete stimulus. While change in tonic levels of arousal are measured over time, phasic activity occurs quickly in response to stimuli that are startling, surprising, funny, or disgusting.

Researchers are interested in measuring both the tonic and phasic activity in their participants, but accurate measurement can be problematic. While EDA data are useful, dynamic analysis of tonic and phasic activity is complex and requires trained experts (Lajante et al., 2012).

A general problem in consumer neuroscience is that clearly specified threshold values are often left out of reports. Researchers often ignore the fact that activity overlaps, but it is inevitable because the rise time of a skin conductance response (SCR) is shorter than the recovery time, and this information may be important when analyzing results.

When researchers are interested in how emotional arousal changes over time, they often use methods that compare only the tonic levels of skin conductance (SC). These methods are questionable because they ignore the phasic activity and only tell half the story. In other situations, when researchers want to measure phasic activity, they may use a method that compares just the mean change score before and during stimulus onset. Unfortunately this method is considered arbitrary and not entirely correct.

Using the sum of amplitudes of the SCR is the most common method in consumer neuroscience, but it too is still not entirely accurate. For the analysis of SCR data to be fully correct, it needs to incorporate information about the amplitude *and* duration of an SCR. One such correct method (discussed in Lajante et al., 2012), calculates the integrated SCR (ISCR). Calculating the ISCR will more accurately describe an SCR in your users and will help you to make comparisons between user groups. Many UX researchers will sacrifice best practices and proper analytic techniques in favor of easier, yet incorrect analyses. This is bad practice and should be avoided.

Those more interested in how to properly assess and interpret EDA data are encouraged to examine the research of Lajante et al. (2012).

As with other physiological response measures, EDA (GSR) show the intensity of arousal, but not the valence. Therefore it is important to couple SCR measurements with other explicit measures so we can know if users have a positive or negative experience. Similar to the facial emotion recognition, EDA has strong potential for measuring the user experience, but more research is certainly needed. UX researchers should continue to use the method and share their work so we can continue to learn from each other and move the technique forward in the field.

Neuroimaging: EEG

There are various ways to measure brain activity, including fMRI, MEG, and EEG, and each is useful in different situations. In this section, we will focus on EEG as a technique to understanding users' mental states.

EEG enables researchers to monitor users' emotional states in real time. Although still restricted to a lab environment, EEG is far less invasive than other neuroimaging methods, and modern devices are available at a reasonable cost. These modern EEG devices are less time-consuming than previous devices, making EEG a viable solution for UX researchers.

To record EEG data, up to 256 electrodes are placed on the scalp, and they capture cortical activity from underlying regions. The electrical output and frequencies are then mathematically analyzed to derive insight into mental processes, such as excitement or frustration.

While historically, neuroimaging techniques were exclusively used in universities, medical institutions, or other well-funded organizations, recent advances in technology have significantly reduced costs and increased usability (in terms of both mobility and ease of use) for UX practitioners. The private sector has produced EEG devices that have a significantly lower cost by eliminating features that are not typically necessary for the consumer market (e.g., 14 sensors for consumers vs. 128 sensors for medical researchers; Figure 4.15). In addition, these new devices were designed for ease of use and mobility to suit the needs of a wide array of consumers, such as UX practitioners, market researchers, and gamers. Modern mobile EEG software applications automatically process certain key emotions at a temporal resolution comparable with eye tracking (i.e., it is real time).

FIGURE 4.15   Participant interacting with a website while she wears the Emotiv EPOC headset with 14 sensors (http://www.emotiv.com).

Modern wireless EEG devices include high-resolution neuro-headsets that record user's brain activity via electrodes that are placed on the scalp. Brain activity is translated into various aspects of emotion. Modern systems often come with preprogrammed features, which offer detection of different emotional states and various facial expressions that often mirror a person's inner feelings. EEG can help evaluate user satisfaction and user experience by enabling researchers to detect user feelings, thoughts, and expressions in a test situation. It can be applied to a variety of testing situations, including website and mobile research (Figure 4.16).

FIGURE 4.16
Woman wearing the Neurosky EEG headset with 1 sensor.

EEG can show if a user is frustrated when they experience usability problems (Figures 4.17–4.20) and also when they really like a product (Figure 4.21). For example, during online shopping, brain activity can be measured with an EEG, and participants can comment about their experiences in a debriefing interview. EEG data can confirm areas where users had difficulties using the website (e.g., issues with registration and in completing forms).

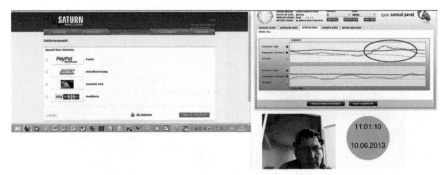

FIGURE 4.17   Participant having trouble filling in his address in the registration process; he gets an error message (shown on left) and the EEG data show a rise in his excitement (circled in red).

FIGURE 4.18   As the PayPal logo could not be clicked on immediately during "payment methods," this caused new stress for this participant (shown on upper right).

FIGURE 4.19   The participant is trying to put a pair of shoes into the shopping basket, but a pop-up blocker will not allow her to do so. Cortical activity correlated with excitement rises (shown on right).

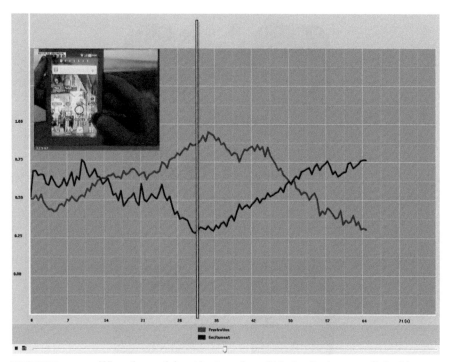

FIGURE 4.20 When the participant is struggling within the display menu (left of the vertical line), frustration (red) increases and excitement (blue) decreases.

FIGURE 4.21 Larger increases in activity related to excitement appear when participants like something very much; this participant was quite fond of the cosmetic bag.

EEG can also be used to assess emotional engagement during interaction with products. For example, in a recent study, the emotional effects of two smartphones were compared, the Google Nexus and the Apple iPhone 4G, and EEG enabled researchers to identify parts of the interface that led to high emotional engagement. As shown in Figure 4.22, the iPhone

FIGURE 4.22 Participants experience a higher level of emotional engagement with the iPhone, and specifically with the main button. Top and middle: EEG data; bottom: eye-tracking data. (From eye square.)

(right) had higher overall emotional engagement compared to the Google Nexus (left). The quantified EEG results (middle) were consistent with the visualization data (top). For the iPhone, people experienced high engagement with the one main button, but for Google Nexus, people experienced low emotional engagement likely due to the unpopular hard keys. Further, the eye-tracking data (bottom) demonstrated the areas where participants looked, and these data were consistent with the EEG data as well. The researchers were able to use the EEG data in combination with the eye-tracking data to provide evidence for parts of the interfaces that were looked at and that were emotionally engaging.

> *Pairing eye tracking with biometric data gives researchers the opportunity to collect unbiased, behavioral, quantitative data. It is unbiased because we are relying on how users physically react, not on what is coming out of their mouths. The qualitative data that UX researchers typically rely upon is filtered through the users' cognition—they are thinking of answers, then reacting. We can never be quite sure if what they are saying aligns with what they are actually feeling. With eye tracking and biometrics, we can collect raw, pre-cognitive data that tells the true story of the users' experiences.*
>
> **Dan Berlin, Mad*Pow, USA**

EEG data alone provide few conclusions on the general user experience; however, they can be quite revealing when the data is related to UX issues. Emotional effects of various websites can be compared using EEG, but individual differences, such as emotionally involved users versus rather pragmatic users, must be taken into account.

How Does EEG Measure Emotion?
Consumer EEG products measure a user's mental state through EEG electrical bands, and software suites provide automatic calculation of these bands. Varying combinations of different waves are correlated with different emotions. Software that is calibrated properly can accurately indicate the emotional state that a person is experiencing. As mentioned earlier, accurately indicating emotional state on a moment-to-moment basis is

important because a person may not be aware of the implicit emotional states they have experienced. There are four primary bands used in EEG research:

1. Delta waves (1–4 Hz): deep sleep, unconscious processing, trance-like state
2. Theta waves (4–8 Hz): daydreaming, creativity, intuition, memory recall, emotions, sensations
3. Alpha waves (8–14 Hz): cortical inactivity, mental idleness, relaxing
4. Beta waves (10–30 Hz): cognitive processes, decision making, problem solving, information processing, concentration

Lennart E. Nacke (2010) conducted a UX study using EEG electrical bands to compare the affective game play interaction modes between the Wii and PlayStation 2 remotes while gamers played the action horror game Resident Evil 4. The EEG results were then compared to a game experience questionnaire filled out by the participants after game play. The findings indicated a significant positive correlation between alpha power and negative affect ratings for both controller types. Alpha power also had a significant positive correlation with tension ratings for both controllers, while delta power had a positive correlation with tension ratings using the PlayStation 2 remote. Nacke (2010) proposed that the alpha power/negative affect correlation may stem from the idea that if players are not positively challenged it is possibly due to a low mental workload, which in turn is subjectively interpreted as a negative affective experience. The positive correlation between alpha power and tension may explain two opposite extremes of game play. First, when the game is not challenging it requires that the player exert greater alpha activity to maintain an adequate level of attention, while on the other hand, if the game is too challenging it again requires a greater mental effort in order to "keep up" with the game, with both extremes consequently leading to a subjective feeling of tension.

Findings like these suggest that employing EEG in UX evaluation can add great value by measuring moment-to-moment emotional reactions of users. Accurately measuring emotions and cognitive processes in real time can set you apart from other researchers and practitioners as you are finally able to understand what is going on in the user's mind.

MEASURING VALENCE

While physiological response measurements have the capability to provide us with invaluable information that is just not possible with traditional methods, a major disadvantage is that most of the measures do not measure valence (Figure 4.23). Some modern EEG software can display emotion states (as shown in Figure 4.19), and facial emotion recognition software claims to do just this, but other measures fail at identifying users' emotions. Thus, it is pertinent that other explicit measures, such as self-report questionnaires or think aloud, be used in conjunction with the physiological response measures.

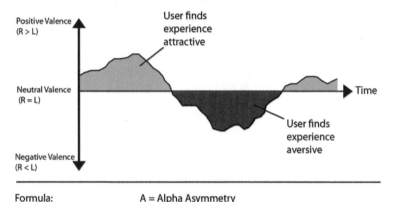

Alpha Asymmetry - A Measure of Valence

Positive Valence
(R > L)

User finds experience attractive

Neutral Valence
(R = L)

Time

User finds experience aversive

Negative Valence
(R < L)

Formula:

$$A = \left(\frac{(R - L)}{(R+L)}\right) \times 100$$

A = Alpha Asymmetry
R = Magnitude of alpha activity (measured in microvolts) in the F4 region of the *right* frontal lobe
L = Magnitude of alpha activity (measured in microvolts) in the F3 region of the *left* frontal lobe

FIGURE 4.23   Valence can be measured with EEG.

CONCLUSION

Many physiological response measurements are currently available for UX researchers to use, and they have the potential to fully explain the user's experience. While we struggle to find the best methods to allow us to understand more about users' unconscious desires, today it is possible. New biometric devices for measuring physiological responses, which are practical, reasonably priced, and suitable for practical research, have led to new opportunities in the UX field. We are now in a place where we can actually measure emotions and implicit reactions while users interact with products.

The great benefit of using physiological data is primarily that the measures of performance are purely objective and do not rely on the user's assessment. Rather than asking participants if tasks were difficult or if they were surprised when a stimulus appeared on the screen, we can now collect and examine physiological responses and in real time, without interrupting data collection.

In this chapter, we have provided an overview of physiological methods that are now applicable within UX research, and we shared concrete examples of physiological measures coupled with eye tracking that have led to a better understanding of the user experience. While the field is still relatively new, researchers should continue to include physiological measures in UX projects and share results in conference presentations and peer-reviewed articles so we can continue to learn from each other.

ACKNOWLEDGMENTS

Thank you to Sophie Belardi (users' delight), Georg Diener (users' delight), and Katja Kawan (users' delight) for assistance with EEG research and literature review, to Mehmet Arslan (users' delight) for assistance with graphics, and to Hadley Bergstrom (National Institutes of Health) for helpful feedback on an earlier version of this chapter.

REFERENCES

Andreassi, J., 2000. Pupillary response and behavior, psychophysiology: human behavior and physiological response. In: Andreassi, J. (Ed.), Lawrence Erlbaum Associates, Mahwah, NJ, p. 218.

Capra, M., 2002. Contemporaneous versus retrospective user-reported incidents in usability evaluation. In: Proceedings of the Human Factors and Ergonomics Society 46th Annual Meeting, pp. 1973–1977.

Demiral, S.B., Schlesewsky, M., Bornkessel-Schlesewsky, I., 2008. On the universality of language comprehension strategies: evidence from Turkish. Cognition 106, 484–500.

Ekman, P., Friesen, W.V., 1976. Measuring facial movement. Environ. Psychol. Nonverbal Behav. 1, 56–75.

Fong, J., 2012. The Meaning of Pupil Dilation. Retrieved from, http://www.the-scientist.com/?articles.view/articleNo/33563/title/The-Meaning-of-Pupil-Dilation/.

Hackney, H., 1974. Facial gestures and subject expression of feelings. J. Couns. Psychol. 21, 173–178.

Iqbal, S., Zheng, X., Bailey, B., 2004. Task-evoked pupillary response to mental workload in human-computer interaction. In: CHI '04, CHI '04 Extended Abstracts on Human Factors in Computing Systems. ACM Press, pp. 1477–1480.

Józsa, E., 2010. A potential application of pupillometry in web-usability research. Periodica Polytechnica Social and Management Sciences 18 (2), 113–119.

Kim, B., Dong, Y., Kim, S., Lee, K.-P., 2007. Development of integrated analysis system and tool of perception, recognition, and behavior for web usability test: with emphasis on eye-tracking, mouse-tracking, and retrospective think aloud, pp. 113–121. http://link.springer.com/chapter/10.1007/978-3-540-73287-7_15.

Kretschmar, F., Pleimling, D., Hosemann, J., Füssel, S., Bronkessel-Schlesewsky, I., Schlesewsky, M., 2013. Subjective impressions do not mirror online reading effort: concurrent EEG-eyetracking evidence from the reading of books and digital media. PLoS One 8 (2), e56178.

Lajante, M., Droulers, O., Dondaine, Th., Amarantini, D., 2012. Opening the "black box" of electrodermal activity in consumer neuroscience research. J. Neurosci. Psychol. Econ. 5 (4), 238–249.

Lang, P.J., Greenwald, M.K., Bradley, M.M., Hamm, A.O., 1993. Looking at pictures: affective, visceral, and behavioral reactions. Psychophysiology 30, 261–273.

Liversedge, S.P., Blythe, H.I., 2007. Lexical and sublexical influences on eye movements during reading. Lang. Linguist. Compass 1, 17–31.

Loijens, L., Krips, O., 2013. White Paper Noldus Information Technology, Based on Version 5 of FaceReader.

Nacke, L.E., 2010. Wiimote vs. Controller: Electroencephalographic Measurement of Affective Gameplay Interaction. In: Proceedings of Future Play 2010, Vancouver, BC, pp. 159–166. http://dx.doi.org/10.1145/1920778.1920801.

Olmsted-Hawala, E.L., Romano Bergstrom, J.C., 2012. Think-aloud protocols. Does age make a difference? In: Proceedings from the Society for Technical Communication Summit, May 2012, Chicago, IL.

Palomäki, J., Kosunen, I., Kuikkaniemi, K., Yamabe, T., Ravaja, N., 2013. Anticipatory electrodermal activity and decision making in a computer poker-game. J. Neurosci. Psychol. Econ. 6 (1), 55–70.

Powell, W.R., Schirillo, J.A., 2011. Hemispheric laterality measured in Rembrandt's portraits using pupil diameter and aesthetic verbal judgements. Cognit. Emot. 25 (5), 868–885.

Romano Bergstrom, J.C., Olmsted-Hawala, E.L., 2012. Effects of age and Think-Aloud Protocol on eye-Tracking Data and Usability Measures, Paper presentation at EyeTrackUX, Las Vegas, NV, June 2012.

Russell, J.A., 1994. Is there universal recognition of emotion from facial expression? A review of the cross-cultural studies. Psychol. Bull. 115 (1), 102–141.

Russell, J.A., 1995. Facial expressions of emotion: what lies beyond minimal universality? Psychol. Bull. 118 (3), 379–391.

Terzis, V., Moridis, C.N., Economides, A.A., 2010. Measuring instant emotions during a self-assessment test: the use of FaceReader. In: Spink, A.J., Grieco, F., Krips, O.E., Loijens, L.W.S., Noldus, L.P.J.J., Zimmerman, P.H. (Eds.), Proceedings of Measuring Behavior 2010, Eindhoven, The Netherlands, August 24–27.

Tullis, T., Albert, B. (Eds.), 2008. Behavioral and Physiological Metrics, Measuring the User Experience: Collecting, Analyzing, and Presenting Usability Metrics. Elsevier, Amsterdam, pp. 167–188.

Van Den Haak, M., De Jong, M., Schellens, P., 2003. Retrospective vs. concurrent think-aloud protocols: Testing the usability of an online library catalogue. Behav. Inform. Techn. 22 (5), 339–351.

Wiswede, D., Russeler, J., Munte, T.F., 2007. Serial position effects in free memory recall: an ERP-study. Biol. Psychol. 75, 185–193.

EYE TRACKING FOR
SPECIFIC APPLICATIONS

5

FORMS AND SURVEYS

Caroline Jarrett[1] and Jennifer Romano Bergstrom[2]
[1]*Effortmark, Leighton Buzzard, UK*
[2]*Fors Marsh Group, Arlington, VA, USA*

INTRODUCTION

Most parts of a web experience are optional. Forms usually are not.

You want to use a web service? Register for it—using a form. You want to buy something on the Internet? Select it, then go through the checkout—using a form. Want to insure a car, book a flight, apply for a loan? You will find a form standing as a barrier between you and your goal.

Some surveys are similar. Your response may be required by law, and lack of response may be punished by a fine or worse.

But in some ways, even "mandatory" forms and surveys are optional. When faced with a challenging form, the user may delay, abandon, or incur the cost of asking someone else, such as an accountant or family member, to tackle the form. All of these options increase the burden for the individual and pose potential problems for data quality. As a result, low response rates are now threatening the viability of the ordinary everyday survey, historically a powerful tool for social, academic, and market research. And costs increase—for the user and for the organization that wants the user's data.

In this chapter, we explore what eye tracking can tell us about the user experience of forms and surveys. We then discuss when eye tracking is appropriate and when it can be misleading.

Our conclusions are:

- For simple forms and straightforward surveys, eye tracking can guide your design decisions.
- For more complex examples, consider your eye-tracking data only in light of data from your other usability findings and cognitive interviews.

FORMS AND SURVEYS HAVE A LOT IN COMMON

There are different types of forms, varying in the amount and type of information they ask for. For example, in some, users need merely to enter their username and password. However, in others, they need to enter quite a bit more. The amount of information and the cognitive resources required to complete forms can greatly impact eye-tracking data.

In this chapter, we focus on the form or survey itself (a sequence of questions and places for users to answer) rather than on the entire process of the users' transactions or the data collection.

In this narrow sense, what is the difference between a form and a survey? Not very much. Both ask questions and provide ways for users to answer those questions. Broadly, we call something a "survey" if the responses are optional and will be used in aggregate, and a "form" if the responses are compulsory and will be used individually. But there can be overlaps. For example, sometimes a survey begins with a form (Figure 5.1).

And sometimes a survey asks questions that will be used individually, or are compulsory (Figure 5.2).

We can talk about the two together in this chapter because whether it is a form or a survey, users interact with it in similar ways.

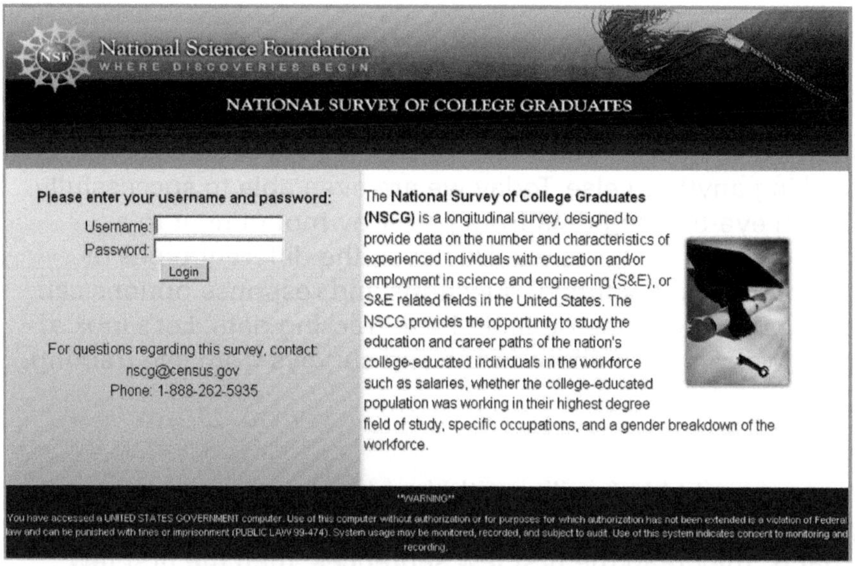

National Science Foundation
WHERE DISCOVERIES BEGIN

NATIONAL SURVEY OF COLLEGE GRADUATES

Please enter your username and password:

Username:

Password:

Login

For questions regarding this survey, contact:
nscg@census.gov
Phone: 1-888-262-5935

The **National Survey of College Graduates (NSCG)** is a longitudinal survey, designed to provide data on the number and characteristics of experienced individuals with education and/or employment in science and engineering (S&E), or S&E related fields in the United States. The NSCG provides the opportunity to study the education and career paths of the nation's college-educated individuals in the workforce such as salaries, whether the college-educated population was working in their highest degree field of study, specific occupations, and a gender breakdown of the workforce.

WARNING

You have accessed a UNITED STATES GOVERNMENT computer. Use of this computer without authorization or for purposes for which authorization has not been extended is a violation of Federal law and can be punished with fines or imprisonment (PUBLIC LAW 99-474). System usage may be monitored, recorded, and subject to audit. Use of this system indicates consent to monitoring and recording.

FIGURE 5.1 A form that requires users to provide a username and password to log in to the survey.

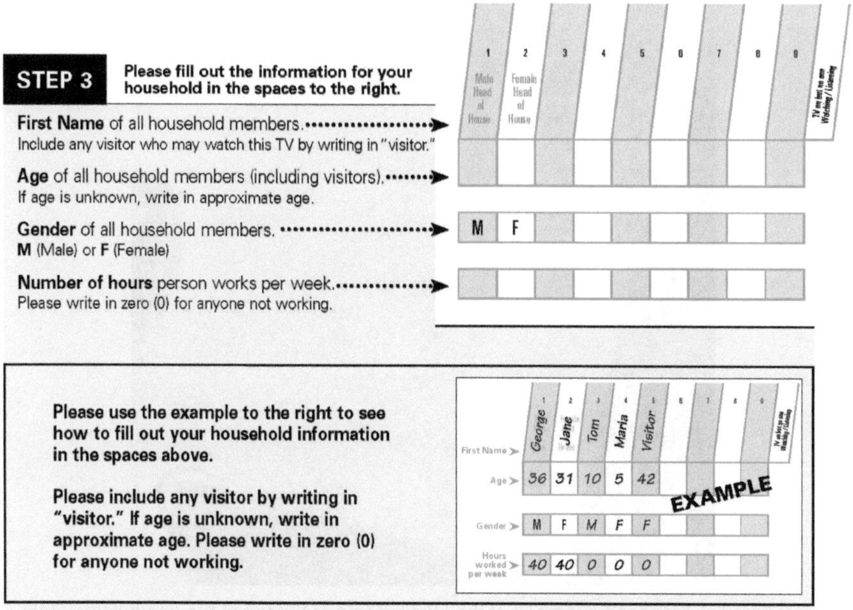

STEP 3 **Please fill out the information for your household in the spaces to the right.**

First Name of all household members.
Include any visitor who may watch this TV by writing in "visitor."

Age of all household members (including visitors).
If age is unknown, write in approximate age.

Gender of all household members.
M (Male) or **F** (Female)

Number of hours person works per week.
Please write in zero (0) for anyone not working.

1 Male Head of House	2 Female Head of House	3	4	5	6	7	8	9
M	F							

Please use the example to the right to see how to fill out your household information in the spaces above.

Please include any visitor by writing in "visitor." If age is unknown, write in approximate age. Please write in zero (0) for anyone not working.

EXAMPLE

	1	2	3	4	5	6	7	8	9
First Name	George	Jane	Tom	Maria	Visitor				
Age	36	31	10	5	42				
Gender	M	F	M	F	F				
Hours worked per week	40	40	0	0	0				

FIGURE 5.2 A survey that requires users to enter household demographics.

SOME EXAMPLES OF WHAT WE CAN LEARN FROM EYE TRACKING FORMS AND SURVEYS

In many ways, eye tracking a form or survey is just like eye tracking anything else. Today we are even able to successfully obtain eye-tracking data from paper by mounting it to a clipboard, as in Figure 5.3. However, the different types of questions and layouts of questions and response options can play a big role in the quality of eye-tracking data. Let's look at what we can learn about forms and surveys from eye tracking.

People Read Pages with Questions on Them Differently from Other Pages

You are probably familiar with the idea that "people read web pages in an F-shaped pattern" (discussed further in Chapter 7). That is, they read the first few sentences, then the first few

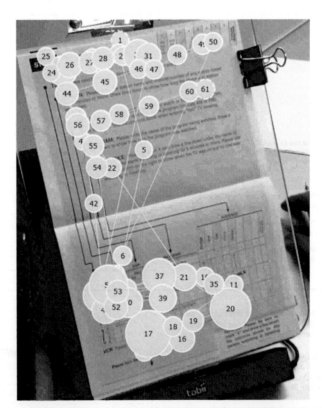

FIGURE 5.3 F-shaped eye track of the block of text at the top of the page; completely different pattern on the questions and answer spaces at the bottom of the page.

words of each line, and then a couple of sentences further down the page (perhaps in a new paragraph), and then the first few words of each line below that.

That F-shaped pattern may hold true for some content-heavy pages, but eye tracking reveals that people react entirely differently to pages that are full of questions and answer spaces. These differences are neatly revealed by the contrasting eye-tracking patterns in Figure 5.3.

When testing pages with questions on them, we consistently find that users avoid looking at the instructions. Instead, they focus on the questions.

In Figure 5.4, we see a typical example: gaze plots reveal that most people quickly looked for the "slots" to put their information in so they could move rapidly to their goal of finishing.

Do people ever read instructions on forms or surveys? Not very often—unless they have a problem with a question. Then they might. Or they might bail out. Figure 5.5 shows a typical pattern for two pages full of instructions; the participant quickly scanned then turned the page to get to the questions.

FIGURE 5.4 Participants in the usability study did not read the instructions on the right—they went immediately to the actionable slots on the left. (From Romano & Chen, 2011.)

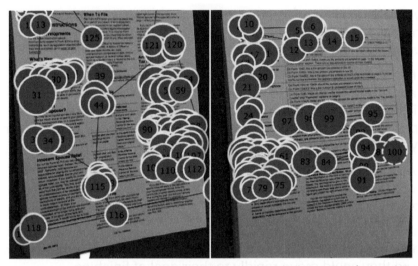

FIGURE 5.5 The participant did not read the instructions in their entirety (page 1, left; page 3, right); rather, he skimmed and then moved on to the form where he needed to enter information. Participants in this study flipped back to the instructions only when they needed help completing the form.

If your instructions are short, helpful, and placed only where needed, they might keep your users from giving up. If the questions themselves are too long, users may react to them as instructions and skip directly to the response options.

Eye tracking allowed us to identify some respondent behaviors that did not conform to the normative model of survey response. Whereas the model expects a respondent to read the question and then select a response option, we collected eye-tracking data that showed participants skipping questions and going directly to the response options. One thing we learned was that people take any shortcuts possible to finish a questionnaire, even in a laboratory setting. They have lives to live! If they can guess what the question was asking by looking at the response options, they will skip the question. Of course, their guess may not be right, and a design intervention may be needed to ensure that they have read the question. Thus, the results of eye tracking can inform survey design in many ways.

Betty Murphy, formerly Principal Researcher, Human Factors and Usability Group, U.S. Census Bureau (currently Senior Human Factors Researcher, Human Solutions, Inc.)

These eye-tracking results lead to three important guidelines about instructions for forms and surveys:

- Write your instructions in plain language.
- Cut instructions that users do not need.
- Place instructions where users need them.

Write Your Instructions in Plain Language

Many instructions are written by technical specialists who concentrate on the subject matter, not clear writing. It is up to the user experience professional to get the instructions into plain language.

For example, watch the jargon (Redish, 2012). The word "cookie" may be familiar to your users, but are they thinking about the same type of cookie (Figure 5.6)?

FIGURE 5.6   Users may not understand basic words, like cookies.

Cut Instructions That Users Do Not Need

Once users have clicked on an online form or survey, they do not want instructions on how to fill in the form. They have passed that point.

Limit yourself to the briefest of statements about what users can achieve by filling in the form. Provide a link back to additional information if you like.

Users do not want to be told that a form or survey will be "easy and quick," and they do not want claims about how long the form will take.

- If the form is genuinely easy, the users can just get on with it.
- If it is not, you have undermined the users' confidence straight away.
- Exception: if it is going to be an exceptionally lengthy task, perhaps several hours, then it might be kind to warn users about that. (And definitely, explain to them about the wonderful save-and-resume features you have implemented.)

Place Instructions Where Users Need Them

You may need some instructions on your forms and surveys. Some can actually be quite helpful, such as:

- A good title that indicates what the form is for
- A list of anything that users might have to gather to answer the questions
- Information on how to get help
- A thank-you message that says what will happen next.

The title and list of things to gather need to go at the beginning, the information about help in the middle, and the thank-you message at the end.

People Look for Buttons Near the Response Boxes

There is a long-running discussion in many organizations about whether the "OK" or "Next" button— properly, the primary action button—should go to the left or right of the "Cancel," "Back," or "Previous" buttons—properly, the secondary action buttons.

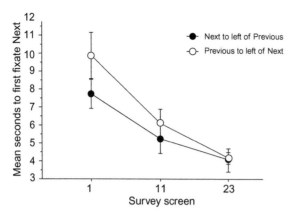

FIGURE 5.7   Users learned where to look for the primary navigation button by screen 23. (From Romano Bergstrom et al., under review.)

Eye tracking reveals that users learn where to look for the primary navigation button quite quickly, no matter where it is placed, as in Figure 5.7 (Romano Bergstrom et al., under review). By the time participants reached screen 23, the layout of the buttons no longer affected them.

But they do not like it when the Next button is to the left of the Previous button.

In a typical example where participants were asked to complete a survey with 'Next' to the left of 'Previous', many participants said that it was counterintuitive to have 'Previous' on the right. One participant said that she disliked the "buttons being flipped" although she liked the look and size of the buttons. Another participant said that having 'Next' on the left "really irritated" him, and another said that the order of the buttons was "opposite of what most people would design." In contrast, for the version with 'Previous' to the left of 'Next', no one explicitly claimed that the location of the buttons was problematic. One participant said that the buttons looked "pretty standard, like what you would typically see on Web sites." Another said the location was "logical."

Romano and Chen, 2011.

Eye tracking reveals that the important thing to users is not where the buttons are placed relative to each other, it is where the buttons are placed relative to the fields (Jarrett, 2012).

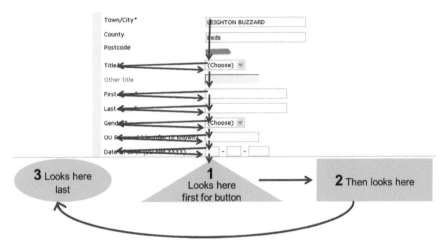

FIGURE 5.8   Schematic of a typical eye-tracking pattern for hunting for buttons. (Adapted from Jarrett, 2012.)

Users hunt for their primary action button when they believe they have finished the entries for that page of the form or survey, and they generally look for it first immediately under the entry they have just filled in, as in the schematic in Figure 5.8.

Place Navigation Buttons Near the Entry Boxes
To ensure that users can find your primary action button easily (and preferably before they get to page 23 of your form or survey), place it near the left-hand edge of the column of entry boxes. Then design your secondary action buttons so that they are clearly less visually obvious than the primary button, and placed sensibly, in particular, with Previous toward the left edge of the page.

People Fill in Forms More Quickly if the Labels Are Near the Fields
The schematic in Figure 5.8 also illustrates the typical reading pattern for a form page:

- Look for the next place to put an answer (a "field), then
- Look for the question that goes with it (the "label").

Just as with the placement of the primary action buttons, there is a long-running discussion over where the labels should go relative to the fields. Or at least this topic was discussed greatly

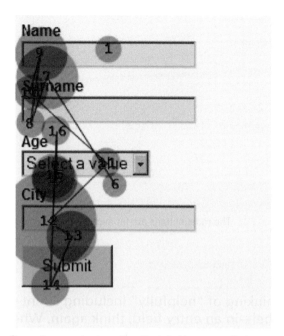

FIGURE 5.9 Saccades are shorter when the label is easy to find compared to the field. (From Penzo, 2006.)

until Matteo Penzo (2006) published an eye-tracking study that showed that users fill in forms more quickly if the labels are near the fields.

Penzo claimed that forms are filled in more quickly if the labels are above the boxes, as shown in Figure 5.9. A subsequent study (Das et al., 2008) found no difference in speed of completion, even in a simple form, but there appears to be an advantage for users if the labels are easy to associate with the fields.

For example, if the labels are too far away, as in Figure 5.10, then users' eyes have to work harder to bridge the gap, and they may associate the wrong label with the field.

Place the Label Near the Entry Field
Help users by putting the labels near the fields and making sure that each label is unambiguously associated with the correct field. Whether you decide to place the labels above or below the entry fields, make it easy on the user by being consistent.

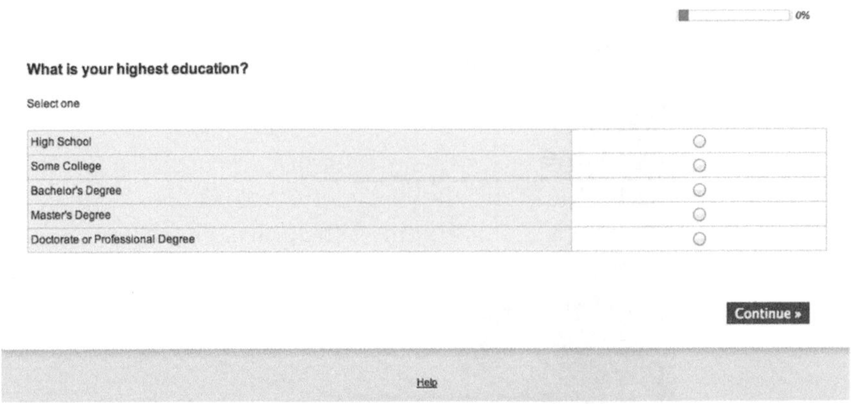

FIGURE 5.10 The radio buttons are far away from the response options.

Users Get Confused about Whether They Are Supposed to Write Over Existing Text

If you were thinking of "helpfully" including a hint—or even worse, the label—in an entry field, think again. When there is text in the entry field, users get confused about whether they are supposed to write or type over the existing text.

For example, in the form in Figure 5.11, participants consistently skipped over the first two entries and wrote in the names of household members starting in the third entry box, as shown. They did this even though there was an example at the bottom showing them how to use the form. They said things like: "If you want someone to write something in, you shouldn't have writing in the box," "I'm not sure if I'm supposed to write in over the lettering," and "Where am I supposed to write it? On top of this?"

We have many times observed the same behavior in web and electronic forms and surveys (Jarrett, 2010b).

Do Not Put Any Text Inside the Response Boxes

Do not put anything where users are meant to type or write. Leave the insides of boxes clear of labels, hints, and any other types of clutter so it is clear where they are supposed to write.

Users May Miss Error Messages That Are Too Far from the Error

The best error message is one that never happens, because your questions are so clear and easy to answer that users

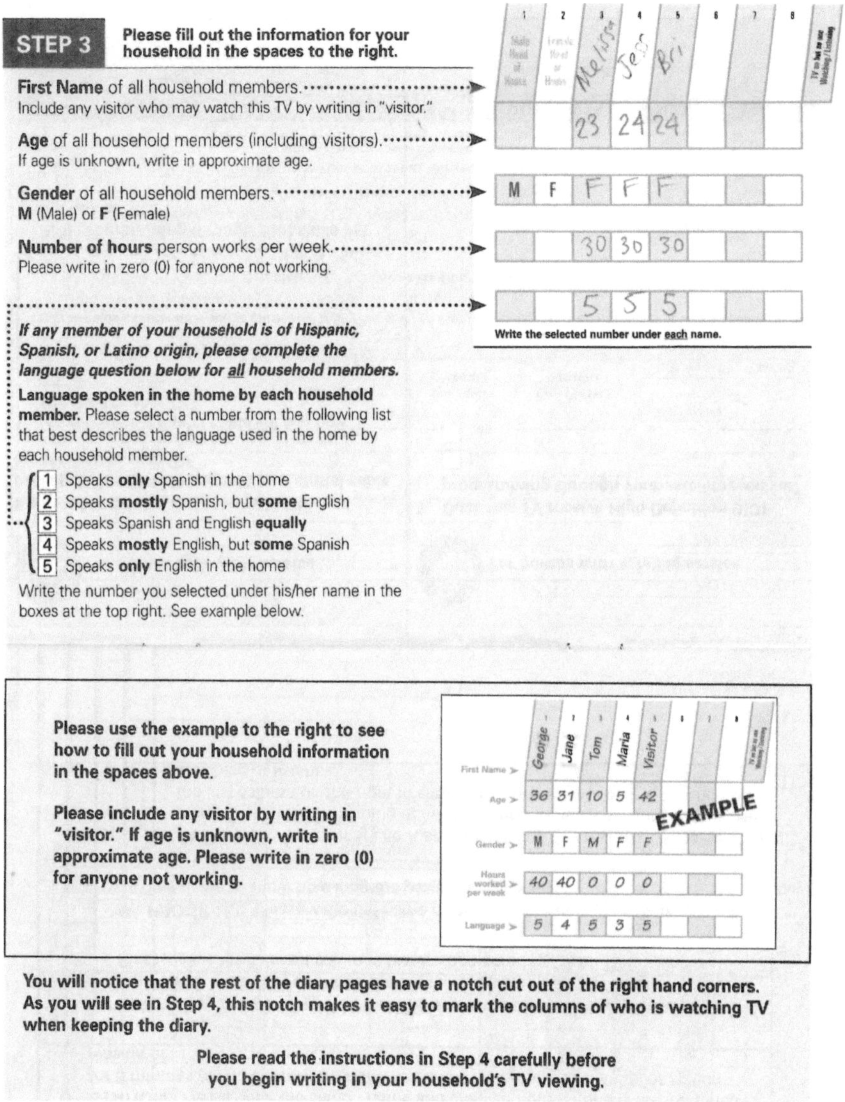

STEP 3 **Please fill out the information for your household in the spaces to the right.**

First Name of all household members.
Include any visitor who may watch this TV by writing in "visitor."

Age of all household members (including visitors).
If age is unknown, write in approximate age.

Gender of all household members.
M (Male) or **F** (Female)

Number of hours person works per week.
Please write in zero (0) for anyone not working.

If any member of your household is of Hispanic, Spanish, or Latino origin, please complete the language question below for all household members.

Language spoken in the home by each household member. Please select a number from the following list that best describes the language used in the home by each household member.

1 Speaks **only** Spanish in the home
2 Speaks **mostly** Spanish, but **some** English
3 Speaks Spanish and English **equally**
4 Speaks **mostly** English, but **some** Spanish
5 Speaks **only** English in the home

Write the number you selected under his/her name in the boxes at the top right. See example below.

	1	2	3	4	5	6	7	8
First Name	Male Head of House	Female Head of House	Melissa	Jess	Bri			
Age			23	24	24			
Gender	M	F	F	F	F			
Hours			30	30	30			
Language			5	5	5			

Write the selected number under each name.

Please use the example to the right to see how to fill out your household information in the spaces above.

Please include any visitor by writing in "visitor." If age is unknown, write in approximate age. Please write in zero (0) for anyone not working.

EXAMPLE

	1	2	3	4	5	6	7	8
First Name	George	Jane	Tom	Maria	Visitor			
Age	36	31	10	5	42			
Gender	M	F	M	F	F			
Hours worked per week	40	40	0	0	0			
Language	5	4	5	3	5			

You will notice that the rest of the diary pages have a notch cut out of the right hand corners. As you will see in Step 4, this notch makes it easy to mark the columns of who is watching TV when keeping the diary.

Please read the instructions in Step 4 carefully before you begin writing in your household's TV viewing.

FIGURE 5.11 The dark font in the entry boxes at the top misinforms users that they are not supposed to write in those boxes.

never make any mistakes. Realistically, some problems will occur: miskeying, misunderstanding, or failing to read part of a question.

When an error occurs, it is important to make sure that an appropriate message appears where users will see it, and that it is easy to find the problematic part of the form.

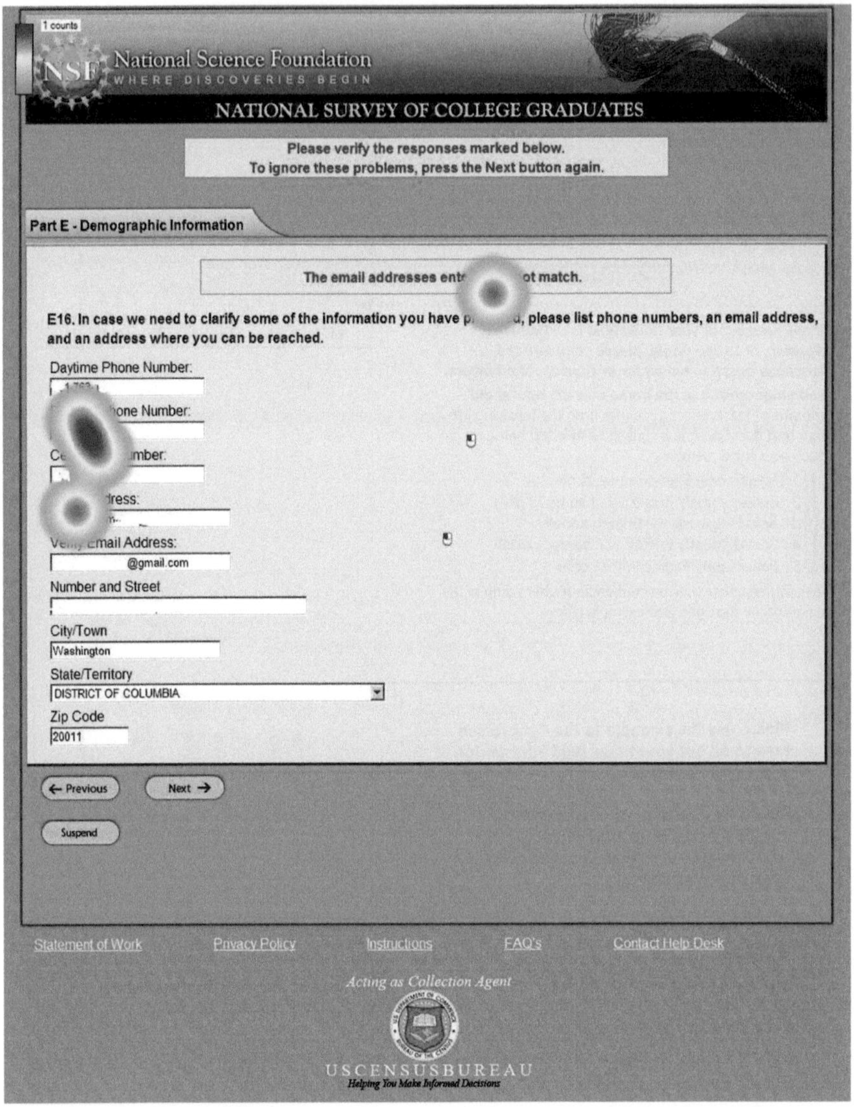

FIGURE 5.12 Users failed to spot one of the two overall error messages on this screen.

Romano and Chen (2011) tested a survey that had two "overall" error messages: one at the top of the page, and one at the top of the problematic question. The screenshot in Figure 5.12 illustrates the problem: users expect a single overview message, not one that is split into two places. In fact, they rarely or never saw the uppermost part of the message, which explained that the question could be skipped. Although correcting the problem is preferable, skipping the question would be better than

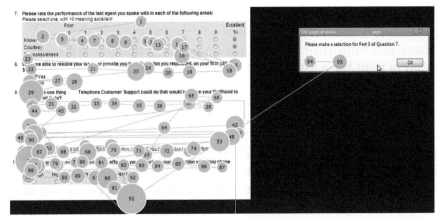

FIGURE 5.13   The error message on the right is too far from the field that it relates to.

dropping out of the survey altogether, and users who did not see the upper message might simply drop out.

We also often see users have difficulties when the error message is far away from the main part of the survey, as shown in Figure 5.13. This causes the respondent to turn his/her attention away from the main survey to read the error message then look back to the survey to figure out where the error is.

Put Error Messages Where Users Will See Them

Make it easy on your users. Place the error message near the error so the user does not have to figure out what and where it is. Be sure to phrase the messages in a positive, helpful manner that explains how to fix the errors.

Our recommendations are:

- Put a helpful message next to each field that is wrong.
- If there is any risk that the problematic fields might not be visible when the user views the top of the page, then include an overall message that explains what the problem(s) are (and make sure it deals with all of them).

For more information about what error messages should say, see: http://www.uxmatters.com/mt/archives/2010/08/avoid-being-embarrassed-by-your-error-messages.php.

Jarrett, 2010a

Double-Banked Lists of Response Options Appear Shorter

There is a long-running discussion among researchers about what is best for a long list of response options:

- A long scrolling list or
- Double-banked (i.e., split in half and displayed side by side)

A benefit of a long scrolling list is that the items visually appear to belong to one group; however, if the list is too long, users will have to scroll up and down to see the complete list, and they may forget items at the top of the list when they read items at the bottom of the list.

With double-banked lists, there is potentially no scrolling, users may see all options at once (if the list is not too long), and the list may appear shorter. But users may not realize that the right-hand half of the list relates to the question.

Romano and Chen (2011) tested two versions of a survey: one had a long scrolling list of response options (shown on the left in Figure 5.14), and one had a double-banked list (shown on right). Participants tended to look at the second half of the list quicker and more often when double banked. Most participants reported that they preferred double-banked lists.

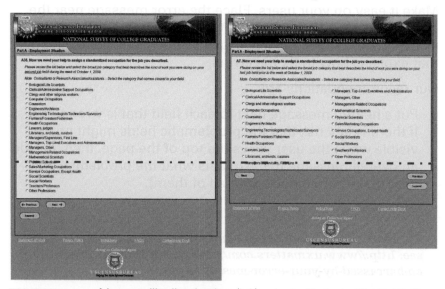

FIGURE 5.14   A long scrolling list of options (left) and a double-banked list (right). (From Romano & Chen 2011.)

Avoid Long Lists of Response Options

While eye-tracking data on this topic is still limited, double-banked lists can appear shorter, and shorter forms often seem more appealing to users. If you must present a long list of options, a double-banked display can help, provided the columns are not too far apart so that the two lists are clearly part of the same set of options.

But to be clear: we are talking about a double-banked set of response options within a single question. This is definitely not a recommendation to create forms that have two columns of questions, which is a clearly bad idea because users often fail to notice the right-hand column (e.g., Appleseed, 2011).

However, the challenge of the long list of options neatly illustrates the limitations of a purely visual approach to form and survey design. Better solutions to solve the problem include:

- Breaking long lists into smaller questions or a series of yes/no questions
- Running a pilot test, then reducing the list of options to the ones that people actually choose
- Running a pilot test, then reducing the list options to a small selection of the most popular ones, with a "show me more" option that allows users to choose from a longer list if necessary.

WHEN EYE TRACKING OF FORMS AND SURVEYS WORKS (AND WHEN IT DOES NOT)

Penzo's 2006 study was on forms that were simple, to the point of being trivial. As he points out, "users very quickly understood the meaning of the input fields." On such ultra-simple forms, the saccade time might indeed be an important proportion of the overall time to complete.

Instead consider the framework from Jarrett and Gaffney (2008; adapted from Tourangeau et al., 2000). There are four steps to answering a question:

1. Understanding the question
2. Finding the answer
3. Judging the answer
4. Placing the answer on the form or survey.

For most forms and surveys, the saccade time is only a small element of the time for Step 1, and the Penzo (2006) study ignores the times for Steps 3 to 4.

Eye tracking can clearly demonstrate problems with Step 1: Understanding the question. Eye-tracking data can show if users backtrack as they scan and rescan items in an attempt to understand the question. More difficult questions will often show up on a heat map as brighter spots because users will re-read the items, as in Figure 5.15.

Write Clear Questions That Users Can Answer

The implications of all this? Make sure that your questions are easily understood by the intended audience and understood in the same way that you intended them. Conduct cognitive testing to ensure that your audience understands your questions and that the information you collect is thus valid.

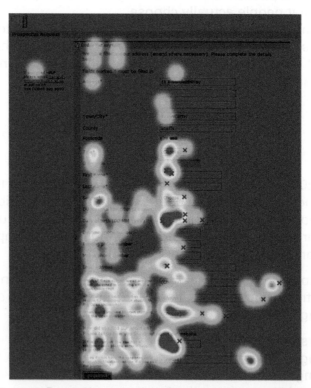

FIGURE 5.15 Eye tracking shows that users re-read the more difficult questions.

Cognitive interviews enable us to understand the respondents' thought process as they interpret survey items and determine the answers. In cognitive interviews, participants may think aloud as they come up with their answers to the questions. The interviewer probes about specific items (e.g., questions, response options, labels) and what they mean to the participant. We are able to determine if people understand the items as we have intended, and we are able to make modifications before a survey or form is final. For more on the cognitive interviewing technique, see Willis, 2005.

Gaze and Attention Are Different

In the examples above, we have focused mainly on the visual design of forms and surveys, and how those areas can influence Step 1: Understanding the question. Gaze patterns can give us some insights into what users look at, and how what they look at can influence their thinking ("cognitive processes").

Eye tracking gave us a way to document where participants were looking while doing tasks during usability testing. Heat maps and gaze patterns offered quite dramatic and undeniable evidence to show designers and survey clients how their layout of questions, response options, instructions, and other elements guided (or misled) the respondent's cognitive processes of navigating and completing an online questionnaire.

Betty Murphy, formerly Principal Researcher, Human Factors and Usability Group, U.S. Census Bureau (currently Senior Human Factors Researcher, Human Solutions, Inc.)

We use the term "gaze" to mean the direction the user's eyes are pointing in. Gaze is detectable by eye-tracking equipment as long as the gaze is directed somewhat toward the equipment.

In contrast, we use the term "attention" to mean: the focus of the user's cognitive processes. Ideally, when we are conducting eye tracking, we want the user's gaze and attention to both be directed toward the form, as in Figure 5.16.

We sometimes hear the phrase "blank gaze" used when a person's eyes are directed toward something but their attention is elsewhere, so they are not really taking in whatever their eyes are looking at.

FIGURE 5.16   Participant enters her name and date on a paper form while her eyes are tracked (eye tracker circled in red). Attention and gaze are both directed at the form.

The types of questions and responses affect eye-tracking data. Answering the question can mean at least four different types of answers (Jarrett & Gaffney, 2008):

- Slot-in, where the user knows the answer
- Gathered, where the user has to get information from somewhere
- Created, where the user has to think up the answer
- Third-party, where the user has to ask someone else

In general, when we are using eye tracking we assume that gaze and attention are in harmony. But for forms and surveys, that is not always true. We will illustrate what we mean in this section, by digging into Step 2: Finding the answer.

Let's say Jane wants to sign up for a warranty for a new television, and she has to complete an online form to do so. She has to find answers to a variety of questions, and each requires a different strategy, which in turn, affects eye tracking.

Slot-In Answers: Gaze and Attention Together Toward Questions

When dealing with slot-in answers—things like a user's own name and date of birth—users' gaze and attention tend to be in the same place: on the screen, as in Figure 5.17. These answers are in their heads, and they are looking for the right place to "slot them in" on the form or survey. It is cognitively simple to find these answers and does not take much attention.

Gathered Answers: Gaze and Attention Split

If users have to find information from somewhere other than the screen, such as from Jane's television receipt, or from a credit card, or from another screen, their gaze and attention will become split between the boxes on the screen and whatever gathered material they are using (Figure 5.18). They will have to switch back and forth between the two sources of information. For Jane, the sequence might be something like the process in Table 5.1.

That gaze switching away from the screen is a challenge for the eye tracker, which must try to acquire and re-acquire the gaze pattern after each switch.

Well, that's my email!

■ Attention
▨ Gaze

FIGURE 5.17   Users have slot-in answers in their heads and look for the right place to slot them in to the form or survey. Attention and gaze are both directed at the form.

Attention
Gaze

FIGURE 5.18 When users have to gather the required answer from an external source, not in their heads, attention and gaze are split.

Table 5.1 Mixed Gaze and Attention for a Gathered Answer

Action	Gaze	Attention
1. Jane reads a question on the screen that asks for a code from her receipt	On the screen	Toward the screen
2. She realizes that she needs to look at the receipt to get the code	Still on the screen	Toward her own thoughts: Where is that receipt?
3. She looks at the receipt	On the receipt	Mixed: thinking about the form, and finding the matching data on the receipt
4. She finds the code	On the receipt	Toward her own thoughts: storing the code in short-term memory
5. Jane looks back at the screen while holding the code in short-term memory	On the screen	Split: between retrieving the code from short-term memory, and finding the box to type into
6. If Jane forgets part of the code, Steps 2 through 5 will be repeated.	Mixed between screen and receipt	Mixed between screen, receipt, and her thoughts.

Created Answers: Gaze Toward Questions, Attention Elsewhere

Here are some examples of created answers:

- Thinking up a password that has complex rules,
- Writing the message for a gift card, or
- Providing a response to an open-ended question like "Why do you want this job?"

These typical created answers take a lot more attention. The user's gaze may still be directed at the screen, but the mind is elsewhere thinking about the answer (Figure 5.19).

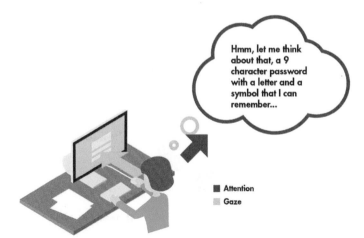

FIGURE 5.19   Users have to create an answer on the spot. Gaze is on the form, but attention is to their thoughts (inward).

For Jane, it might go something like this:

- Jane reads a question on the screen that asks her to create a unique password that contains nine characters, a letter, and a symbol (gaze and attention are on screen).
- Jane thinks hard about a password that meets these criteria and that she can remember (gaze is still on screen, but attention is to her thoughts).
- Jane creates a password and enters it in the box on the screen (gaze and attention are on screen).
- If the password does not meet the criteria, Jane will have to think of a new password, and Steps 1 through 3 will be repeated.

That attention switching away from the screen can give "false positives," where the eye tracker is reporting that some element on the screen is receiving the user's gaze, but the user is not actually making any cognitive use of that element.

Third-Party Answers: Gaze and Attention Elsewhere

A third-party answer is one where the users have to ask someone else, a third party, for the answer. To find that third-party answer, users are likely to switch both their gaze and their attention toward something else.

For example, when completing a warranty form, Jane might have to call her partner to look up the serial number

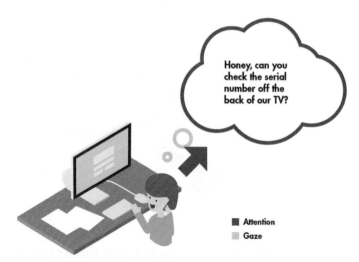

FIGURE 5.20   Users have to ask a third party for the answer—they do not know it themselves, but they know someone else who does: attention and gaze are both directed away from the form.

(Figure 5.20). She is fully removed from the original questions as she obtains the information she needs to complete the form. It might go something like this:

- Jane reads a question on the screen that asks her for the serial number (gaze and attention are on screen).
- Jane knows she does not have this information, so she picks up her phone and calls her partner who is at home and can check for the serial number (gaze is on something in the room, and attention is to her phone and partner on the phone).
- This phone call may last a while, and no eye-tracking data can be collected.
- Once Jane has the serial number, she enters it in the box on the screen (gaze and attention are on screen).
- If the phone call took too long, Jane may have gotten kicked out of the form and may have to log back in to proceed.

Third-party answers can present the ultimate challenge for an eye tracker: with gaze and attention both elsewhere, there is no gaze available for it to acquire.

For accurate eye tracking, you want users to have their attention and gaze going to the same place:

- If attention is elsewhere, you can get false readings: it appears the user is looking at something, but not actually seeing it (such as when Jane has to create a complex password).

- If gaze is elsewhere—or swapping back and forth, such as when Jane looks for the PIN number—you will get intermittent eye-tracking data. Each time the gaze comes back to the screen, the eye tracker has to re-acquire the gaze and make something of it.
- If both gaze and attention are elsewhere, you have got nothing to eye track!

These challenges are shown together in Figure 5.21.

The implications? Eye-tracking success depends on the proportions of the different answers in your form or survey. It may be the case that some data, for example for slot-in responses, is useful, while other data, such as for gathered responses, is not so useful. It is important to consider the type of questions you are asking and the strategy respondents must use to answer as you examine the eye-tracking data (Figure 5.22).

How do you find out what types of questions and answers you have? Inspecting the questions is a good start, but you will definitely get a more realistic assessment if you interview users, ideally as a cognitive interview.

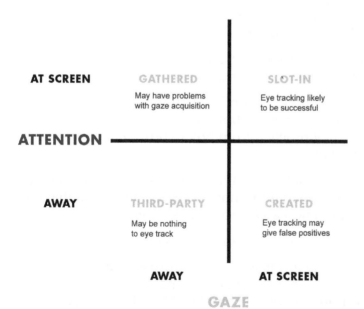

FIGURE 5.21 Eye tracking is most likely to be successful on forms and surveys that call for slot-in answers, where both gaze and attention are directed at the screen.

TYPES OF ANSWERS	TYPICAL RESULTS
Mostly slot-in	Accurate and useful
Mostly gathered	May get spotty results due to gaze switching
Mostly created	May find that users are looking at areas without seeing them
Mostly third-party	Poor

FIGURE 5.22 Different types of form/survey questions produce different types of eye-tracking results.

And do not forget that the classic observational usability test—watching a participant fill in your form or survey, as naturally as possible—is the single best way of finding out whether it works (Jarrett & Gaffney, 2008).

CONCLUSION

In this chapter, we have explained that eye-tracking data can help to learn about the visual design of pages with questions on them: forms and surveys.

We have found that eye tracking has been helpful in revealing how users really interact with simple forms, especially:

- How little they rely on instructions
- Where they look for buttons
- How they proceed from box to box when there are many questions.

But we have also found that eye tracking can be unreliable when users encounter more complex questions that take their gaze or attention away from the screen.

To repeat from earlier, our conclusions are:

- For simple forms and straightforward surveys, eye tracking can guide your design decisions.
- For more complex examples, consider your eye-tracking data only in light of data from your other usability findings and cognitive interviews.

ACKNOWLEDGMENTS

Thank you to Jon Dang (*USA Today*) for creating illustrations used in this chapter and to Ginny Redish (Redish and Associates) and Stephanie Rosenbaum (TechEd, Inc.) for helpful feedback on an earlier version of this chapter.

REFERENCES

Appleseed, J., 2011. Form Field Usability: Avoid Multi-Column Layouts–Articles–Baymard Institute. Retrieved on Sept 30, 2013, from, http://baymard.com/blog/avoid-multi-column-forms.

Das, S., McEwan, T., Douglas, D., 2008. Using eye-tracking to evaluate label alignment in online forms. In: Proceedings of the 5th Nordic conference on Human-computer interaction: building bridges. ACM Press, Lund, Sweden, pp. 451–454.

Jarrett, C., 2010a. Avoid being embarrassed by your error messages from, http://www.uxmatters.com/mt/archives/2010/08/avoid-being-embarrassed-by-your-error-messages.php.

Jarrett, C., 2010b. Don't Put Hints Inside Text Boxes in Web Forms from, http://www.uxmatters.com/mt/archives/2010/03/dont-put-hints-inside-text-boxes-in-web-forms.php.

Jarrett, C., 2012. Buttons on Forms and Surveys: a Look at Some Research. Presentation at the Information Design Association conference, Greenwich, UK, from, http://www.slideshare.net/cjforms/buttons-on-forms-and-surveys-a-look-at-some-research-2012.

Jarrett, C., Gaffney, G., 2008. Forms That Work: Designing Web Forms for Usability. Elsevier, Amsterdam.

Penzo, M., 2006. Label Placement in Forms from, http://www.uxmatters.com/mt/archives/2006/07/label-placement-in-forms.php (accessed 20.05.13.).

Redish, J., 2012. Letting Go of the Words. Elsevier, Amsterdam.

Romano, J.C., Chen, J.M., 2011. A Usability and Eye-Tracking Evaluation of Four Versions of the Online National Survey for College Graduates (NSCG): Iteration 2. Statistical Research Division (Study Series SSM2011-01). U.S. Census Bureau from, http://www.census.gov/srd/papers/pdf/ssm2011-01.pdf.

Romano Bergstrom, J.C., Lakhe, S., Erdman, C., (under review). Next belongs to the right of Previous in Web-based surveys: an experimental usability study.

Tourangeau, R., Rips, L.J., Rasinski, K.A., 2000. The Psychology of Survey Response. Cambridge University Press, New York.

Willis, G.B., 2005. Cognitive Interviewing: A Tool for Improving Questionnaire Design. Sage Publications, Thousand Oaks, CA.

6

INFORMATION ARCHITECTURE AND WEB NAVIGATION

Andrew Schall

Spark Experience, Bethesda, MD, USA

INTRODUCTION

An intuitive and easy-to-navigate website is the cornerstone to good user experience (UX). Nearly all digital products have some sort of menu system that must be navigated in order to complete a task. Usability issues often arise from navigation that has been poorly designed, usually because of the organization, placement, visual design, or terminology used. Eye tracking during UX testing can help to discover ways to diagnose and optimize information architecture (IA) and navigation elements.

Methods to Evaluate IA

IA is the science of organizing and labeling data and website links, and it forms the hierarchy of how information is organized and the paths available for the user to follow. There are several user research methods, such as card sorting and tree testing, which help to determine the effectiveness of an IA and the structure of a navigation system.

FIGURE 6.1 Card sort where participants place cards into piles that make sense to them, and then they label the piles.

Card sorting is a very useful activity for understanding how actual end users expect a menu system to be organized (shown in Figure 6.1) and the labels that should be used for each category of the IA. Card sorting can also be used to provide a comparison between how an existing IA is structured versus how a potential user would organize the IA. Card sorts are particularly useful for determining high-level categories and labels, but they do not lend themselves well to having users create deeper subcategories within an IA.

Tree testing is a method for validating the intuitiveness of an IA by having participants navigate through the information hierarchy (Figure 6.2). Participants are asked to perform a series of online information-seeking tasks whereby they navigate using the IA. Tree testing can be a very effective method for evaluating the depth and breadth of an IA, but it is limited to displaying a list of links without any page-level content or in-page links.

While card sorting and tree sorting methods are regularly used, they do not tell the entire story (e.g., how a user interprets the meaning of a link label, if they quickly understand the grouping structure of a series of buttons). Even the most intuitive navigation structure is useless if users never notice it. Eye tracking allows us to gain a real-time understanding of what

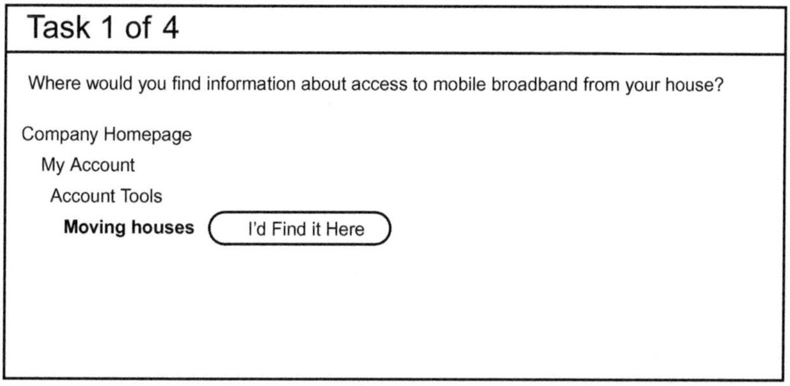

Task 1 of 4

Where would you find information about access to mobile broadband from your house?

Company Homepage
  My Account
    Account Tools
      Moving houses   (I'd Find it Here)

FIGURE 6.2   A tree study is a user research activity whereby a participant attempts to locate information based on a series of tasks by navigating through a navigation menu system.

users see as they navigate through a user interface. Whereas card sorting and tree testing evaluate an IA in isolation, eye tracking allows us to analyze the effectiveness of a navigation structure in the context of all of the elements on the page.

EYE TRACKING TO EVALUATE NAVIGATION IN CONTEXT

Menu systems can take on many forms and can function and look different from one system to the next. When presented with a new interface, users rely heavily on *mental models*. Mental models are explanations of how things work in the real world, and they are formed from past experiences. In order to effectively navigate, users use mental models that are based on past experiences with other navigation systems. The labeling and terminology used in a navigational interface can negatively impact usability if it does not match the user's mental model. Eye tracking can often identify issues associated with poor labeling when there are a relatively high number of fixations and high fixation duration of a link label. Regressive saccades are a common fixation movement that can indicate that a user did not see a link that they were expecting to find, or that they are evaluating and/or reevaluating the meaning of a given set of links, possibly due to a lack of cues (Sibert & Jacob, 2000). Goldberg and Kotval (1998) suggested that optimal scan patterns include long saccades, short scan paths, and few fixations in a small area of focus.

There are several common paradigms used in most digital interfaces to help the user navigate.

Primary Navigation

Primary navigation represents the core categories for the interface and the highest level of the IA. This navigation is almost always available from anywhere within the interface and is typically located in the same place from page to page (Figure 6.3).

At present, users are accustomed to seeing the primary navigation toward the top of the page and either in a horizontal or vertical format. It is critical for a user to quickly be able to identify the primary ways they can navigate and use the interface. When the primary navigation is not in a prominent location, users can miss the main way to navigate the interface. In these situations the navigation becomes overshadowed by competing visual elements and is often initially missed by users.

Using design conventions based on location alone does not always help users to find the primary navigation. For example, researchers discovered through eye tracking that participants did not notice the Continuing Education of the Bar (CEB)'s primary navigation due to its relatively small size and the high visual prominence of the left-located quick links (shown in Figure 6.4). In this example, the primary navigation is located horizontally across the top of the site. While the homepage quick links were a helpful feature for participants, the fact that most users did not notice the primary navigation caused usability issues later in their experience. Participants who did not initially notice the primary navigation were unable to locate the category for practice areas, a key category in the IA that was necessary to complete tasks on the site.

FIGURE 6.3 A horizontally positioned primary navigation at the top of the page.

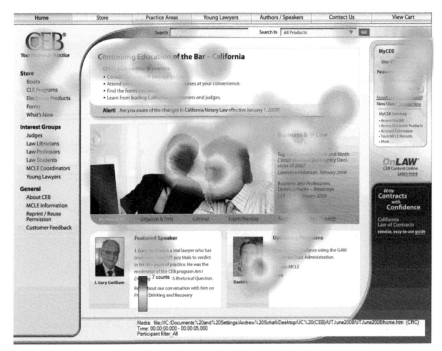

FIGURE 6.4   None of the participants noticed the primary navigation at the top of the page, due to its relatively small size and the high visual prominence of the left-located quick links. Most of the attention was on the central content area, quick links, and log-in box on the right.

WHY USERS SHOULD NOT SPEND MUCH TIME LOOKING AT NAVIGATION

It is the job of a UX designer to effortlessly guide a user through an interface to reach their goal. A good user experience is when a user does not have to spend a significant amount of time locating, evaluating, and using the navigation. Jakob Nielsen puts it this way:

> It may seem like people should look at global navigation more than a quarter of the time, but think of it as you would a lifejacket stored under your seat on an airplane. You may confirm its existence during the safety instruction presentation, but you are not going to put it on, inflate it, and wear it just in case you need to evacuate. Nor will you repeatedly look to make sure it's still there during your flight. But you know where it is if you need it. You ignore it when you don't. That's the way it is with Web site menus.

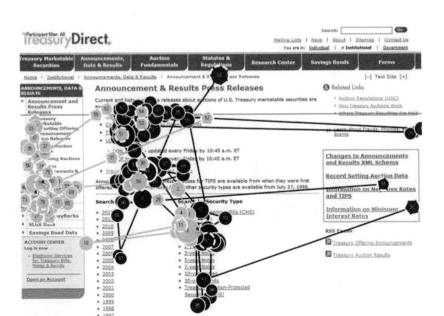

During an evaluation of the TreasuryDirect website, participants did not read the primary navigation at the beginning of their visit (Figure 6.5), and this significantly impacted their experience. Not only were the primary links a key way to navigate the site, but they also provided an overview of the types of information and features that the site offered. Participants were not able to gain a full understanding of the types of information available on the site and how to complete key tasks without noticing the primary categories.

There have been few studies about the optimal viewing position of primary navigation elements, and there does not seem to be a consensus on which format has the best user experience. Kingsburg and Andre found that navigation times were slightly faster when the primary menu was located on the left. Kalbach and Bosenick found no evidence that vertical left-located menus were significantly faster and concluded that top-aligned menus performed the best.

DeWitt sought to gain a better understanding of how the placement of primary navigation impacted a user's experience. They studied the eye-tracking behaviors of 147 participants across 15 navigational menus. They found that designing a vertical or horizontal menu does not seem to impact how quickly users can locate the desired item within the menus, although vertical menus run the risk of requiring page scrolling, which slows down navigation.

These studies indicate that there is still plenty of room in the user research field to continue to explore the optimal layout for navigational elements.

SUBNAVIGATION

Most IAs contain multiple levels within their hierarchy and can be divided into primary and sublevels of navigation. Subnavigation represents the lower levels of the information hierarchy and is often accessed by first selecting one of the primary categories. Figure 6.6 displays an example of subnavigation—once users click on Manage Your Mail, they see a secondary navigation on the left. Subnavigation is typically located in the same place from page to page.

FIGURE 6.6   An example of left-aligned vertically positioned subnavigation displaying secondary and tertiary links.

Users are accustomed to seeing the subnavigation in close proximity to the primary navigation either in a horizontal or vertical format. In the Kingsburg and Andre study, navigation performance was best when the secondary and tertiary menus were placed together. User experience problems arise when users cannot easily identify the subnavigation elements on a web page. For example, participants did not notice the subnavigation menu in Figure 6.7, which is located directly below the primary navigation. Depending on which page participants were on, some did not notice the secondary navigation at all, instead relying on the links embedded in the page. This often caused participants

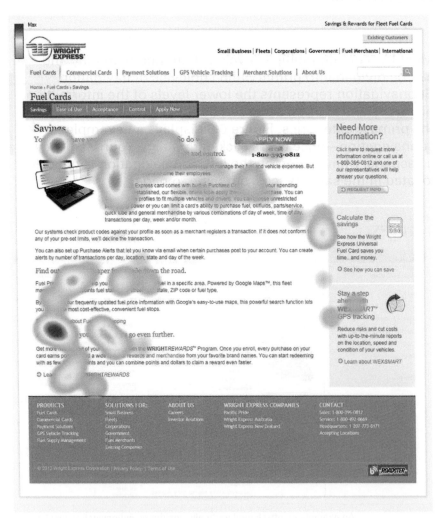

FIGURE 6.7   Participants did not notice the subnavigation menu, which is located directly below the primary navigation.

FIGURE 6.8   The redesigned GovSales website with secondary navigation displayed on the left side. Participants quickly focused on the secondary navigation after selecting a primary category, and they were able to quickly select a secondary navigation link.

to fail in their information-seeking tasks. Conversely, participants quickly focused on the secondary navigation in Figure 6.8 after selecting a primary category, and they were able to easily select a secondary navigation link.

The redesigned GovSales website incorporated a new IA structure into a horizontal primary navigation and a vertical, left-located secondary navigation. While this design is not revolutionary, it fits users' mental models. In this study, participants were very familiar with this layout and quickly focused on the secondary navigation after selecting a primary category. Participants were then able to quickly scan down the short list of choices to select a secondary navigation link. In this case, users were able to quickly glance at the subnavigation and understand how the links were structured. In the case of the TreasuryDirect website, participants had a difficult time understanding the subnavigation organization and were overwhelmed by the long lists of links within the tertiary navigation. There are also few visual cues to show where within the hierarchy the user is, and there is an unclear relationship between the contextual links located in the center area of the page and the left-located links.

BREADCRUMB NAVIGATION

A complex subnavigation structure that is not properly designed can confuse, mislead, and disorient users. Navigation elements take the user deeper into the IA and need to provide strong visual cues to highlight where the user is located at all times.

Breadcrumbs are a utility designed to let users know where they are within the site and a way to get back up to higher levels within the information architecture. Breadcrumb navigation tends to be less visually prominent than other surrounding elements and can easily be missed by users.

In a study of Moodle, an open-sourced online community platform, researchers found that participants frequently used the breadcrumbs. The breadcrumb navigation bar and "My courses" links were most frequently fixated (outlined in red, Figure 6.9) and used for navigating through the contents. Interviews identified that students preferred the breadcrumb navigation over the "My courses" links due to their fixed and central position as well as hierarchical references.

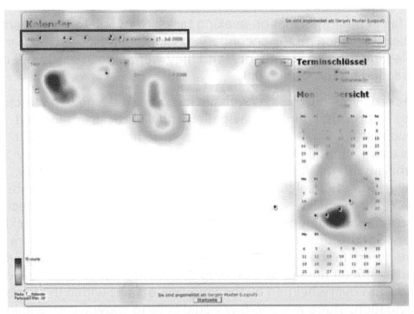

FIGURE 6.9   In Moodle, participants frequently referenced and used the breadcrumbs (outlined in red box) as a primary way to navigate back to previous pages.

CONTEXTUAL NAVIGATION

Contextual, or in-line navigation, represents links that are located within a page that are not part of the primary or subnavigation. The usability of in-line links is often greatly impacted by the content and layout of a given page (Figure 6.10).

In-line navigation can include text links located within a body of text, action buttons, or images.

Given that in-line links are often embedded within content, they need to have a strong *visual affordance* so that users can quickly identify them as links.

Visual affordance provides a cue to the user that a certain element is clickable. Users frequently miss in-line links when there is insufficient visual affordance. This is particularly problematic when links are embedded within paragraphs of

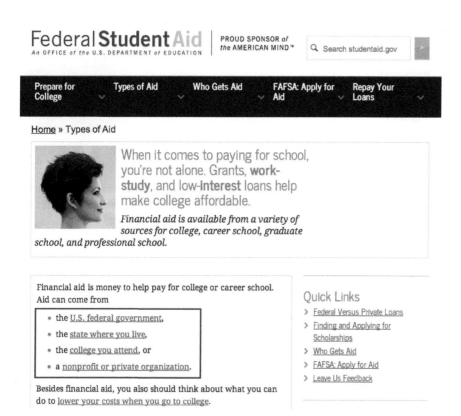

FIGURE 6.10   Links within the page (outlined in red box) provide opportunities for users to explore the website without using the top navigation.

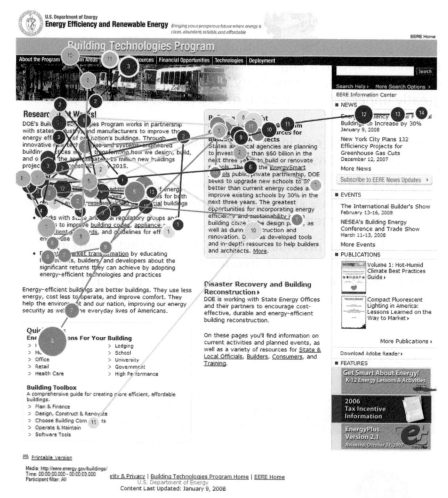

FIGURE 6.11 This page on energy.gov contains numerous contextual links embedded in paragraphs. The gaze plot diagram helps to highlight that participants randomly scanned the page without a clear way to locate specific links within the page content.

text where users typically scan the information very quickly and often skip over large areas.

While contextual links can be extremely useful, they can easily become lost within dense areas of text. The government web page shown in Figure 6.11 provides extensive content on energy efficiency and contained a great deal of information and links to more information. A lack of a clear visual hierarchy on this page contributed to an overall high number of fixations, and users had difficulty locating specific topic links within the page.

UTILITY NAVIGATION

Utility navigation represents necessary site functionality that is typically not associated with the core content of the website, such as contact information, shopping carts, language selection, sign-ins, etc. This navigation is often located in the header (Figure 6.12), footer, or sometimes both, and is always available from every page.

Eye tracking during usability tests often reveals that users pay little or no attention to utility navigation. However, there are certain circumstances where a user's mental model has a strong association to content being located in the utility navigation, such as when looking for contact information. Finding contact information is a common task for most websites and is often located in the utility links. Most users do not need to obtain this information on every page, but it should be highly accessible and easily located.

The SURL lab at Wichita State University compared the task of finding contact information across three websites: Toys to Grow On, Mastermind Toys, and Wonder Brains (Russell, 2005). The specific links that lead to the company contact information were located in different areas of the homepages for each respective site. Eye-tracking data was used to explore how users searched for these utility links on the different websites.

On the Toys to Grow On website, participants started their visual search for the appropriate link in the center of the page then examined other web components along the edges of the page, such as the top shopping cart links and left navigation bar (based on time to first fixation to each area of interest). The last place that most users looked was in the footer, which is where the contact information is actually located. The order of first fixations per area of interest (AOI) for Toystogrowon.com across all participants is shown in Figure 6.13.

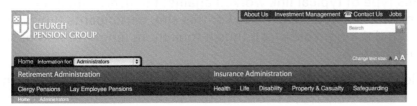

FIGURE 6.12   Example of utility navigation located in the top right blue bar on the Church Pension Group website.

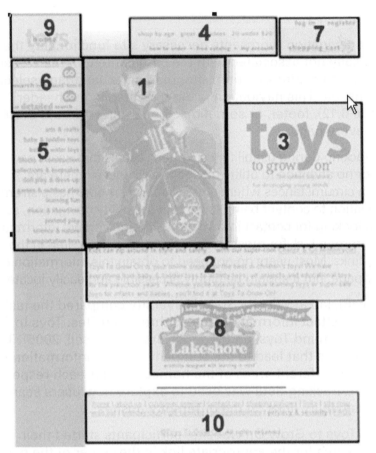

FIGURE 6.13   Order of first fixations per AOI for Toystogrowon.com across participants.

A similar bias for searching for the contact information link at the top of the page was shown by the first fixation data for MasterMindToys.com (Figure 6.14); however, the contact links for this site were located on the right side of the page. This demonstrates that expectations about the location of this type of typical link worked against the users when the link was located elsewhere. For this site, participants typically fixated the right side last; thus it took them longer to find basic information.

Heat maps revealed a highly distributed pattern of attention on the MasterMindToys.com (Figure 6.15) and ToystoGrowOn.com (Figure 6.16) websites. Both heat maps show that users directed their visual attention to several areas other than that where the correct link was located.

FIGURE 6.14   Order of first fixations per AOI for MasterMindToys.com for participants.

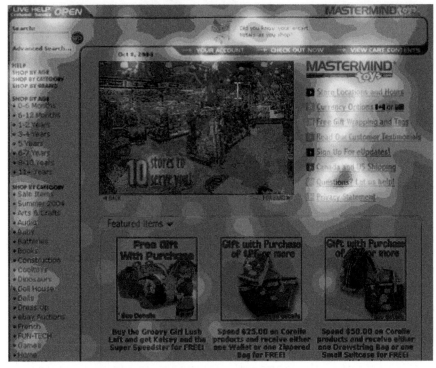

FIGURE 6.15   Homepage heat maps on MasterMindToys.com, demonstrating a high level of fixations in the utility navigation.

FIGURE 6.16 Homepage heat maps on Toystogrowon.com, demonstrating a high number of fixations in the footer and relatively fewer in the top navigation links.

Participants were better able to find contact information on The Wonder Brains website, because the information was located in areas where users expect them to be located—the top and bottom navigation. The heat map hotspots on WonderBrains. com were more concentrated (Figure 6.17) and were directed primarily at the correct utility links located at the top and bottom of the page.

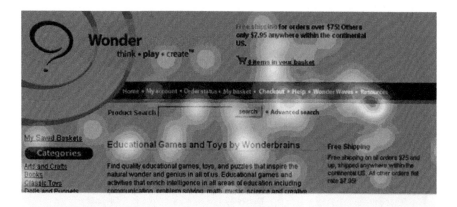

FIGURE 6.17   Homepage fixation hotspots on WonderBrains.com demonstrating that some participants looked for the contact information in the top right area of the page as well as the footer.

DYNAMIC MENUS

Dynamic menu systems, such as fly outs and dropdowns, have become commonly used navigation paradigms. These menus have the benefit of allowing users quick access to content without the need to fill up the valuable screen real estate with navigational elements. While these may be beneficial, dynamic menu systems also have their share of usability problems.

According to Cooke (2008), researchers have found that before people fixate a specific menu item, they first visually "sweep" the menu (Figure 6.18). Next, users view the first one or two items on the menu. Then users glance at items at the bottom of the menu and finally, at the middle of the menu.

Before users fixate a specific menu item, they first visually "sweep" the menu (left). Next, they view the first one or two items on the menu (center). Then they glance at items at the bottom of the menu and finally, at the middle of the menu (right).

To improve visual search efficiency, user interface designers can take advantage of this behavior. Important navigation items within the menu should be placed at the very top of the list, and items of least relative importance should be placed toward the middle.

Many news websites require users to hover over each of the primary navigation options to see the subnavigation options (as shown in Figure 6.19). Presenting both the primary and secondary navigation in a horizontal format can negatively impact users' ability to effectively scan the menu options. Users may hover over a category and then only scan the immediate subnavigation below, and they do not start at the very beginning of the subnavigation options (Figure 6.20). Instead, they quickly move their mouse over additional primary navigation categories while they continue browsing. This causes users to often miss subcategories that might be of interest to them.

FIGURE 6.19   The subnavigation options are not displayed until the user hovers over the primary navigation.

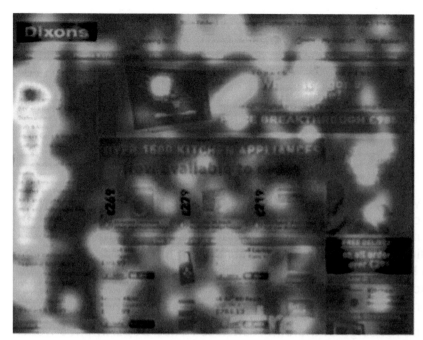

FIGURE 6.20   Usability issues can arise when menus do not function as users expect. This e-commerce website uses a left navigation menu layout. When a user clicks on a link within the navigation it then displays the subnavigations options immediately below. The eye tracker showed a high number of fixations for a relatively long duration as users tried to understand what was happening. (From Etre Ltd, 2013.)

Visual Hierarchy and Grouping

The visual design of navigational elements is equally as important in creating intuitive information architecture. Users often spend only a few seconds taking in all of the elements of the page. Within these few seconds, they establish a mental floor plan of the interface. During this short time, elements that are the most visually prominent will get the most attention and will help shape the user's perception of the interface.

Visual designers often rely on the *gestalt principles of design*, which are time-tested methods that shape the visual hierarchy that users will see. For example, the law of similarity reflects the idea that elements will be grouped perceptually if they are similar to each other. Applying gestalt principles to the design of navigation can help highlight the presence of navigational elements and provide a cue for users to know which elements are related to each other and which are not (Figure 6.21).

FIGURE 6.21   The PBS website uses color to visually distinguish the primary navigation from audience-based navigation. The audience-based options are all colored gray while the other navigation options are all represented in white. Objects similar to each other thus tend to be seen as a unit.

EVALUATING THE VISUAL HIERARCHY OF NAVIGATIONAL ELEMENTS

Eye tracking excels at helping UX designers understand how users perceive the visual hierarchy of the elements on a page. The navigational elements of an interface are in direct competition for the user's attention and can often take a backseat to other content. This can often result in users not noticing navigational elements and consequently not understanding how to get to the information they seek.

The redesign of the San Francisco Police Department's website (Figure 6.22) significantly altered users' eye gaze patterns. Much of the content and layout in the redesign changed with the exception of the right column navigation. However, the design changes led to large changes in user behavior in the right column, as evidenced by both the eye-tracking and click data. Sixty-four percent of participants clicked on the right navigation on the redesigned page, whereas only 14% of participants clicked on the right navigation on the old design. Participants looked at the new right navigation longer and more often, indicating that they read more in that

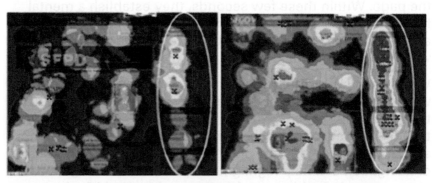

FIGURE 6.22   The old San Francisco Police Department website (left) and new redesigned website (right). Although the right navigation is exactly the same in both designs, in the redesigned page, it received more attention.

FIGURE 6.23   Eye tracking was done on two prototype designs during the redesign of GovSales.gov. In option A (left), participant's eye gazes were more distributed across the page, and in option B (right), eye gazes were more focused.

area, despite no change to the design or content of the right navigation. A change on one part of the page can impact other, unrelated elements on the page. The right navigation was used completely differently on the new redesigned website because the content to the left of it changed (Edwards, 2007).

We also use eye tracking to compare the performance of different interface design options. For example, in one recent study, the fixation patterns were analyzed for two prototype versions for the new website (Figure 6.23). The primary purpose of the homepage is to get visitors to explore product categories and find items that they wish to bid on. Homepage A (left) provided categories across the top as well as in a list of links in the lower left corner of the page. Homepage B (right) provided categories in a top-left dropdown menu and also in a list of links in the first column. In option A, participant's eye gazes were more distributed across the page, and attention was split when looking at the navigational areas. In option B, eye gazes were more focused, and participants noticed the list of categories much faster. Both designs performed reasonably well in exposing users to the content on the page; however, we found that the navigation areas in option B helped direct more users to where they needed to go next. A/B eye tracking test situations such as this are a useful way to understand the user's attention and can help designers to select the most optimal interface for their users.

Measuring Navigation Usability

Task performance is a key way to measure the efficiency and effectiveness of a navigation system. Users need to be able to quickly identify navigational elements, understand what they mean, and be able to keep track of where they are (Figure 6.24).

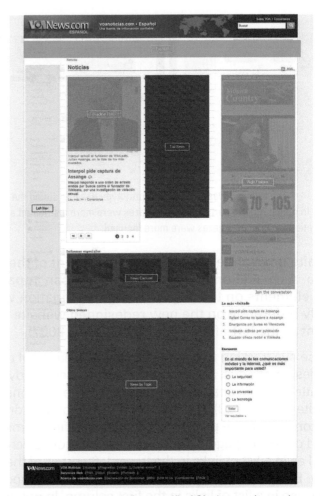

FIGURE 6.24 Researchers can define specific AOIs that can be used to understand the relative efficiency and effectiveness of each interface element.

Time to first fixation is a useful way to measure the amount of time it takes before a user notices navigational elements on the page (Figure 6.25). We can tell exactly how quickly users notice elements and the relationship between this measurement and where they notice other screen elements.

We can also analyze the specific elements within a given area, such as the number of links within a set of navigation items that the user looks at before deciding which one to click on. We can then measure the time it takes from noticing a navigational element to how long before the element is clicked. Task performance can be significantly slowed if users are forced to read through a long list of links before finding the one they want to click on (Figure 6.26).

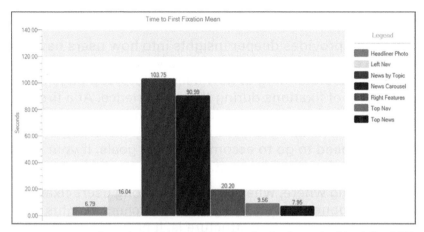

FIGURE 6.25   A graph showing the time to first fixation for each of the defined AOIs.

FIGURE 6.26   Participants scanned the long list of links looking for keywords that would help them get to the information they were seeking.

CONCLUSION

Eye tracking provides deeper insights into how users navigate a website beyond where they ultimately click. We can gain a high-level understanding of how users interpret a page based on the order of fixations during their experience. At a first glance, your visitors should be able to identify how to navigate where they are within the site's information hierarchy, and where they need to go to accomplish their goals. If your users do not see it, they cannot use it.

Understanding where, when, and for how long users fixate various components of a page gives researchers insights into how effective a navigation structure is. It provides designers the opportunity to fine-tune the placement and organization of menus so that users can quickly find what they are looking for. Eye tracking can provide indications that users do not understand labeling used in navigation menus.

As interaction designers invent new navigation paradigms and create more interactive forms of navigation, eye tracking will play a pivotal role in helping to understand the usability and effectiveness of these new designs.

REFERENCES

Cooke, L., 2008. How do users search web home pages? An eye-tracking study of multiple navigation menus. Technical Communication 55 (2), 176–194.

Edwards, G., 2007. Eyetracking a Navigation Bar—How Many Elements are Read? Well, it Depends. eyetools. [blog]. Available at: http://eyetools.com/articles/eyetracking-a-navigation-bar-how-many-elements-are-read-well-it-depends-dot (Accessed: 1 July 2013).

Etre Ltd, 2013. Five Days. Dixons.co.uk. [blog] May 8, 2006. Available at: http://www.etre.com/blog/2006/05/five_days_dixonscouk/ (Accessed: 1 July 2013).

Goldberg, J.H., Kotval, X.P., 1998. Eye movement-based evaluation of the computer interface. In: Kumar, S.K. (Ed.), Advances in Occupational Ergonomics and Safety. ISO Press, Amsterdam, pp. 529–532.

Russell, M., 2005. Hotspots and hyperlinks: using eye-tracking to supplement usability testing. Usability News 7 (2), 1–11.

Sibert, L.E., Jacob, R.J.K., 2000. Evaluation of eye gaze interaction. In: Proceedings of the SIGCHI Conference on Human Factors in Computing Systems (CHI 2000). ACM Press, New York, NY, pp. 282–288.

7

WEB CONTENT

Ian Everdell
Mediative, Toronto, ON, Canada

Content is king.

This is a common mantra in the user experience (UX) community. And rightly so: visitors to your website are there to consume content.

The majority of content is text. So let's take a look at how we find and consume digital text.

HUNTING AND GATHERING: INFORMATION FORAGING AND INFORMATION SCENT

On the web, humans are informavores: organisms that consume information. It only makes sense that we would develop strategies for looking for and consuming information that minimizes the effort required while maximizing the benefit obtained. Understanding those strategies helps us interpret eye-tracking data in light of how users naturally look for information.

Those strategies are shockingly similar to the way animals hunt for food. Just as animals forage for food, humans forage for information. And thus is born "information foraging" (Pirolli & Card, 1999).

The key concept of information foraging is that of *information scent*. As users browse the web, they evaluate how likely it is that a particular path will yield the information they are looking for. The scent has to get strong enough fast enough in order for them to pursue that path.

The flip side of this is that users also evaluate when to abandon a particular path and try a new one: Will it take more effort to continue down this path and potentially not get a whole lot of information in return than it will to change paths and look somewhere else?

Users will start deciding very quickly whether or not it is worth their time to read. Thus, it is important that your content— be it a website, brochure, form or survey (see Chapter 5), or advertisement—reinforces very quickly the idea that you have what your visitors are looking for. This is what will convince them to stay and read.

HOW MANY WORDS DO USERS SEE?

Reading is not a smooth process. Eye tracking shows that our eyes jump from word to word, sometimes skipping words, and sometimes going back to re-read words we have already looked at (Figure 7.1).

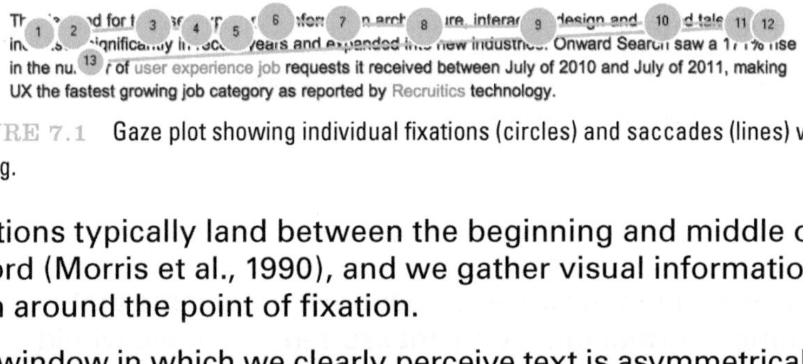

FIGURE 7.1 Gaze plot showing individual fixations (circles) and saccades (lines) while reading.

Fixations typically land between the beginning and middle of a word (Morris et al., 1990), and we gather visual information from around the point of fixation.

The window in which we clearly perceive text is asymmetrical around the point of fixation. Figure 7.2 shows a simulation of the perceptual window around the point of fixation: if users read left to right, the window extends 3 to 4 characters on the left side of

FIGURE 7.2 If you imagine that the red dot is the current point of gaze, this simulates roughly how much text is clearly visible in one fixation.

the fixation point and 14 to 15 characters on the right side of the fixation point, which means users can typically see 18 characters, at most, at a time (McConkie & Rayner, 1978; Rayner et al., 1980).

What Words Do Users Look At?

The chances of fixating a word depend on:

- The type of word—whether it provides information or simply connects other words (Carpenter & Just, 1983)
- The length of the word—2 to 3 letter words are skipped 75% of the time, but 8 letter words are almost always looked at (Rayner & McConkie, 1976)
- The difficulty and legibility of the text—more complex words are fixated longer and more frequently (for a review, see Richardson & Spivey, 2004).

Roughly 10–15% of fixations are made to words or characters that have already been looked at during a given reading session (see Figure 7.3 for an example of this "backtracking"), which is thought to be related to difficulties in processing the individual

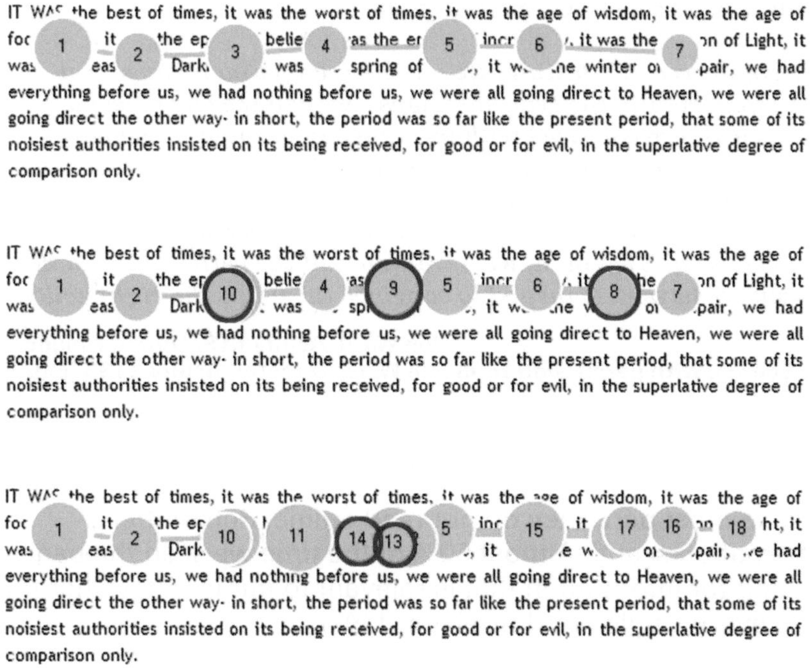

FIGURE 7.3   Gaze plots showing backtracking during reading. The first paragraph shows seven fixations along a line of text; the second and third paragraphs show backtracking (highlighted fixations) while reading that line. The reader was confused by the language "epoch of belief… epoch of incredulity" so went back and read those words again.

word or the meaning of the sentence (Kennedy & Murray, 1987; Murray & Kennedy, 1988).

See If Your Content Is Causing Confusion

If eye tracking shows lots of fixations close together or frequent backtracking, the content is probably tricky for the user to understand. Without eye tracking, we would have to rely purely on feedback from the user about the complexity or difficulty of the content. Since humans are notoriously poor at self-reporting behavior and also want to please researchers, it is likely that their feedback would underestimate this difficulty.

Things like click-through rates and Google analytics give us part of a story; we can also measure failure rates in tasks, but eye tracking allows us to see why and how users fail, what caught their attention and what didn't—at a conscious and sub-conscious level. We can see where they have to re-read text, what effect images or media have on their navigation and all while not slowing the cognitive process down by asking them to "think aloud" (a practice that shouldn't be employed with eye-tracking methodologies as it will pollute gaze data).

In e-commerce, UX testing, we see the reliance on images, and more importantly the type of images—we can see when people struggle or are confused with terminology or often—too many choices (sale items, specials, last minute deal, and so on—all listed on the same page (travel sites typically), we can identify when objects have been seen but not absorbed. So if users notice a call to action but don't act on it, we have won half the battle – they noticed it—but we haven't managed to convince them it is the right action.

Jon Ward, Acuity ETS, United Kingdom
Source: With permission from Jon Ward, Director, Acuity ETS Limited

HOW DO USERS READ ONLINE?

For the most part, they do not read online. Remember information scent? Almost 80% of the time we scan the page looking for information that is relevant to our intent, rather than read every single word (Nielsen, 1997).

In his research comparing average reading speed and the number of words on a web page to the amount of time that we actually spend on the page, Nielsen (1997) found that, for the most part, we spend enough time on a page to read at most

28% of the words. Taking into account the time needed to orient to the design and layout of the page and the time we spend engaging in other activities besides reading, it is likely that we actually only read about 20% of the words.

Eye-tracking research certainly backs up these findings. For example, it is extremely rare to see a heat map where the content of the page is covered by a uniformly red blob; Figure 7.4 shows examples of typical web "reading" heat maps. Keep in mind that this is an average. A user may decide immediately that the page is not relevant to their intent and hit the back button, or they may decide that the page is very relevant and read much more of the content. But if UX designers are mindful of the average and are aware of what 20% they are likely to read, we can be sure to structure and write content to capture users' attention and convince them to read more.

FIGURE 7.4   The heat maps show that reading is not uniform across the page. Viewers reading these pages scanned through the content looking for information that was relevant to their intent.

Reading versus Scanning

What makes up the 20% of content that users actually read? It is the content that will help them decide whether it is worth their time to read more:

- The page headline
- The first couple of sentences on the page
- Headings and subheadings that stand out from surrounding content
- The first few words of the paragraph immediately following an interesting heading or subheading

- The first few words of short paragraphs
- Image captions.

Conversely, visitors will almost never read:

- Long paragraphs
- Content below a headline, heading, or subheading that is not relevant to their intent.

Standard Scanning Patterns

While no two visitors will do exactly the same thing, and no two sites will elicit exactly the same behavior, the most common scanning pattern is roughly shaped like an "F" (Figure 7.5; as briefly mentioned in Chapter 2).

This scan is made of three parts:

1. A horizontal scan, typically across the top of the main content area.
2. The visitor moves down the page and scans horizontally again, although usually does not go as far across the page.
3. A vertical scan down the left side of the content area.

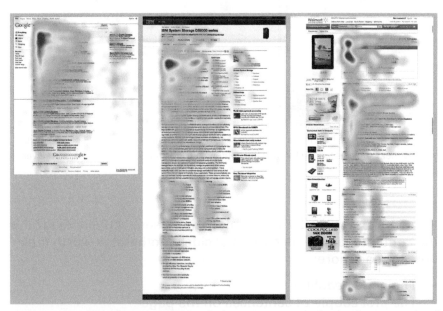

FIGURE 7.5 These heat maps show typical scan patterns—the first few lines are read, and then the visitor drops into a vertical scan. When they encounter information that is interesting or relevant to them, they read a few lines again. This behavior commonly results in a heat map that looks something like an F.

Variations on this pattern are certainly observed—more (e.g., E-shaped) or fewer (e.g., upside-down L-shaped) horizontal scans may be made; visitors may jump more irregularly around the page if they are seeking a very specific piece of information. Age (Romano Bergstrom, Olmsted-Hawala & Jans, 2013), literacy (Zarcadoolas et al., 2002), Internet experience (Loos & Mante-Meijer, 2012), and native language (Frenck-Mestre, 2005) can influence reading patterns, and the design and layout of the page can force the eyes to move in a specific way. But the implications remain the same:

- The content needs to capture the reader's attention at the place where they are likely to initially focus.
- The content needs to be "front-loaded" to keep the readers' attention as they move through the page.

Vertical Attention

If you think of a newspaper folded in half, you only see the top half; this content is said to be "above the fold."

For many years, web designers were encouraged to put everything important above the "fold"—the bottom of the first visible screen of a web page—because users really did not scroll. This led to many a cluttered web page.

With a newspaper, users know that there is content below the fold. But with a website, users do not necessarily know that unless there are visible clues that there is more content (for example, text or images that are partially visible).

Additionally, as digital interaction becomes more gesture based, it is now much easier to scroll (with scroll wheels, multitouch surfaces, touch screens, and "infinite scrolling"), and users will do so, assuming two key points:

1. The layout of the page encourages scanning.
2. The content that they initially look at makes them believe that it will be worth their time to continue down the page.

Note the second point.

The farther down the page a piece of content is, the less likely it will receive attention. In one study of scrolling across 541 pages from a variety of web sites, users spent 80% of their time looking at content above the fold; only 20% of time was spent looking at content below the fold (Nielsen, 2010).

There are obvious exceptions to this. For example, as discussed in Chapter 9, Facebook, Twitter, or LinkedIn—where one of the primary goals of the visitor is simply to "see what people I know are doing or talking about" (or possibly "waste some time!")–have taken advantage of the fact that visitors will scroll endlessly and introduced infinite scrolling. This works because the content is engaging and relevant to the visitor's intent.

There does tend to be a small uptick in attention for the piece of content that is near the bottom of the screen (just above the fold), and sometimes also for the piece of content right at the bottom of the page. UX designers can take advantage of this by putting the really important stuff at the top, and something interesting just above the fold to keep users engaged.

Horizontal Attention

The F pattern of scanning is a good indicator of how attention is allocated horizontally across the page, so designers will be better served putting important or attention-grabbing content on the left side of the page. A particularly compelling example of this is "banner blindness." Because we tend not to look at the right side of the page, ads that are placed there get significantly fewer views than ads placed elsewhere on the page (Owens et al., 2011).

The Chicken and The Egg

All of this research about how users read on the web brings up an interesting question: Do users read this way because of the way content is designed, or is content designed this way because it is how users read?

No doubt it is a combination of both of these. Web users have been accustomed to finding useful information in certain places (banner blindness, anyone?); UX designers know where to put that useful information so that it is most likely to be seen.

Mobile Content

As you read the rest of this chapter, you will likely wonder whether the research findings and best practices apply to content on mobile devices. Chapter 10 will provide more details, but the lessons in this chapter will help set you on the right path for mobile content as well.

WRITING FOR THE WAY WE READ

Now that we know how people scan and scroll and what they will actually read, we can understand how we need to structure our content to keep them engaged—the inverted pyramid (Figure 7.6; Redish, 2007).

Think about the inverted pyramid (see Figure 7.7) as being indicative of the number of people who will actually read that part of the content; many people will read the first little bit, but not very many will make it all the way to the very bottom. You need to provide what people came for right away: the majority of readers only want the conclusion.

The Lead

On the web, you have to lead with the essential message. If the visitor only reads the first sentence of your page, what do you

FIGURE 7.6   The typical approach to writing. This is probably familiar to you if you wrote anything in high school or post-secondary education.

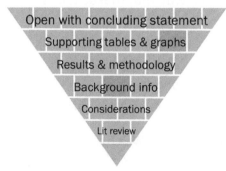

FIGURE 7.7   But if you want people to read your content online, you need to adopt the "inverted pyramid" style of writing.

want them to take away? Newspapers do this really well (The Poynter Institute, 2007). They start every article with one or two short sentences that draw readers in and make them want to read more. They describe the who, what, where, when, why, and how in the very first paragraph. It is important that the lead includes intent-related keywords (strong information scent) so that visitors will quickly know that the rest of the content is relevant to their needs.

The Body

The meat of the content should support the lead and present information in descending order of importance.

The Ending

This is the place for background information and "fluffier" content. Going back to the newspaper analogy, this is where users start seeing the less relevant information—the stuff that no one will really miss if an editor cuts it.

The only exception to this, as mentioned when vertical attention was discussed, is to include some sort of interesting tidbit or call to action to keep visitors on your site: something like a strong benefits statement, a compelling call to action, a highly relevant image, or a glowing testimonial.

DESIGNING EFFECTIVE WEB CONTENT

Aside from the inverted pyramid, writing content is beyond the scope of this book, and there are several other books that will tell you all you need to know. But well-written content is worthless if it is not designed in a way that makes it easy to read.

Top 3 content books: if you want to learn more about writing effective content, check out:

- Letting Go of the Words: Writing Web Content that Works *by Ginny Redish*
- Content Strategy for the Web *by Kristina Halvorson*
- Influence: The Psychology of Persuasion *by Robert Cialdini*

Visual Hierarchy

A good visual hierarchy (see Figure 7.8) tells your brain the order in which to look at objects on the page. This is accomplished by creating good contrast between a piece of content and its surroundings.

As mentioned earlier, our eyes are naturally drawn to headlines, headings, subheadings, bulleted lists, and short blocks of text. Why? Because they stand out from the other text around them, and have been designed to do so.

Visual hierarchy helps users understand the structure of content, and how to jump around within it to pick out the most important information or determine where to stop and read in more detail.

White Space

Let's actually call white space "negative space," because it does not have to be white. It is the background, the space between content, the part of the design that we often do not pay much attention to.

Imagine walking into a store looking for a specific product. The store sells a lot of different stuff, and in an effort to cram in as

FIGURE 7.8   The page on the left shows no visual hierarchy; it is impossible to see where important parts of the content are. In contrast, the page on the right uses color, size, and white space to break the content up and make it easy for users to see where they should look to pull out the highlights.

much different stuff as possible, they have created very narrow, cramped aisles. Chances are you are going to turn tail and get out of there, or at least be uncomfortable navigating your way through the store. Now, imagine you find the product you are looking for sandwiched between two other products, making it hard to get a good look at it and to get it off the shelf. There are two kinds of negative space, and this store has not done a good job of either of them:

- Macro negative space: The space between the shelves (the aisles)
- Micro negative space: The space between the products

Now imagine that this store is really a web page. Cramped "aisles" (blocks of content) and cramped "products" (letters or words) make it harder to find the product users are looking for. White/negative space gives the eyes a chance to rest, helps to structure the content, and influences visual hierarchy (Figure 7.9). When too much is crammed together, users get overwhelmed and ignore large parts of the content (Outing & Ruel, 2004).

Front Loading

Starting every content piece with attention-grabbing, information scent-rich words is called *front loading* (Figure 7.10). This is important because as seen with F pattern scanning, only the left side of much content is going to be scanned. We also know that a standard fixation will take in somewhere around 14 characters (jump back to Figure 7.2 for a refresher on the perceptual window around the point of fixation). This means that

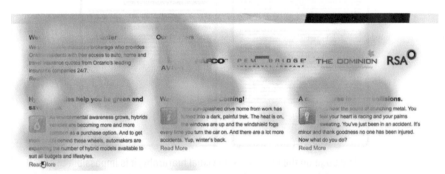

FIGURE 7.9 This heat map shows how the white space between the three columns of text helps users interpret them as three separate columns. Rather than reading each line across the entire width of the page, users look at the three individual headers and briefly glance at the content in each section.

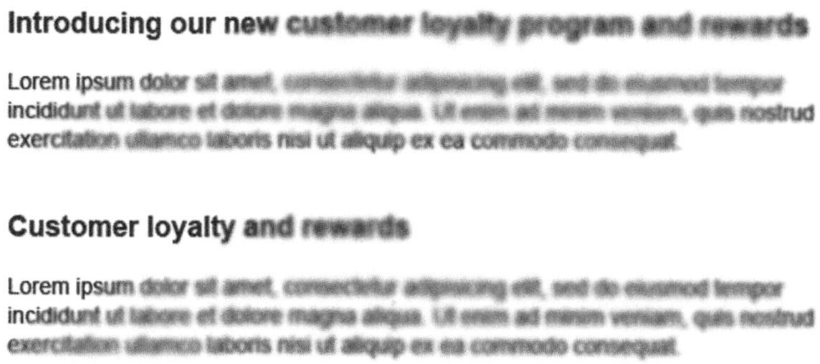

Introducing our new customer loyalty program and rewards

Lorem ipsum dolor sit amet, consectetur adipisicing elit, sed do eiusmod tempor incididunt ut labore et dolore magna aliqua. Ut enim ad minim veniam, quis nostrud exercitation ullamco laboris nisi ut aliquip ex ea commodo consequat.

Customer loyalty and rewards

Lorem ipsum dolor sit amet, consectetur adipisicing elit, sed do eiusmod tempor incididunt ut labore et dolore magna aliqua. Ut enim ad minim veniam, quis nostrud exercitation ullamco laboris nisi ut aliquip ex ea commodo consequat.

FIGURE 7.10   This simulation shows why front loading is important—if a viewer only makes one fixation at the start of each heading, he will not be able to determine what the first paragraph is about.

the first few words of every content element are very important for capturing attention and enticing the user to stop and read.

Headlines

Headlines are typically the first thing users look at when they land on a web page, and larger headlines attract more attention than smaller headlines (Outing & Ruel, 2004).

Because they are so frequently looked at, headlines are incredibly important in conveying the theme of the page. If they do not reinforce the user's intent, the user will likely leave the page.

Headings and Subheadings

Headings and subheadings serve as anchor points in content. Assuming an effective visual hierarchy, the users' eyes will naturally move from one heading to the next (as is shown in Figure 7.11) until it finds something that matches their intent. Every heading and subheading should capture the essence of the content below it. If it does not, the content should be broken up more.

Paragraph Text

Paragraph text is likely to make up the bulk of the content, so it is important to get it right. Since we now know that web viewers tend to ignore long paragraphs, we can infer that short paragraphs provide the best user experience. Paragraphs should be three to four sentences at most, but one to two sentences are ideal. Think again about newspapers: just about every paragraph is a single sentence.

Within those short paragraphs, sentences should be short. Content should be trimmed to half the length of traditional print

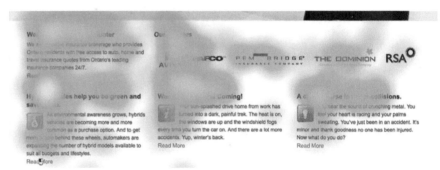

FIGURE 7.11   Most of the users' visual attention goes to the headings rather than the paragraph text.

material to somewhere around 15–25 words maximum per sentence is a good target (Olson, 1985). The research in this area also suggests that varying your sentence length can help maintain users' interest.

Eye tracking has demonstrated that familiar words take users less time to read and process (Clifton et al., 2007). Thus, UX designers and content developers should change complex words to simple, familiar words. For example, consider replacing "obtain" with "get," "assistance" with "help," and "purchase" with "buy." Your users will thank you for it.

Each paragraph should be a mini inverted pyramid: If the user only reads the first sentence, will they still get the gist of the whole paragraph? Just like there should only be one idea per section or subsection, there should also only be one idea per paragraph.

Finally, the first sentence should not be indented as the indent breaks up the visual flow along the left edge of the paragraph and makes it more difficult for users to orient to the beginning of the paragraph.

Justifying Text

Typical scan patterns show that users naturally scan down the left edge of text, so what happens when the left edge does not line up? It becomes more difficult to scan and find what we are looking for (Figure 7.12).

As much as possible, keep all text left justified to facilitate the natural scanning behavior. This includes headlines, headings, and paragraph text.

> The "Plain Language" movement is aimed at improving communication from the United States government to the public, but has lots of useful examples of writing in language that regular people can read. Check it out at http://www.plainlanguage.gov.

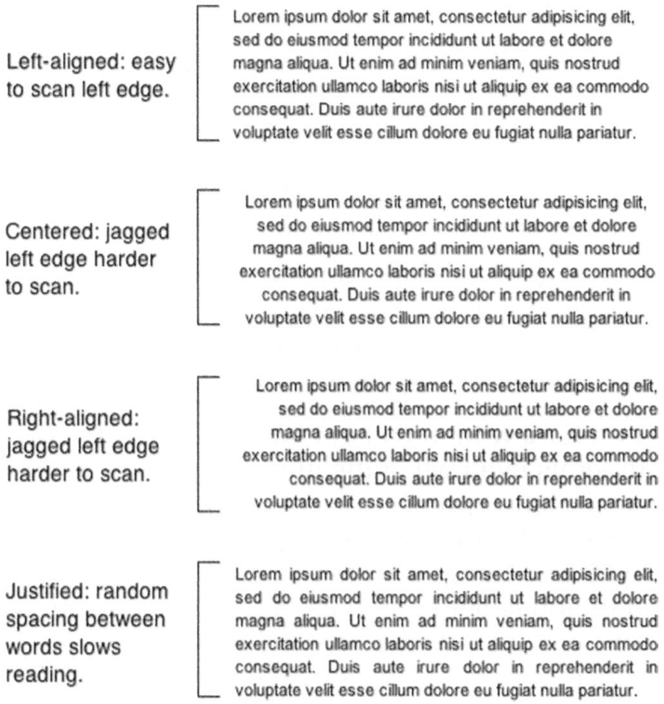

Left-aligned: easy to scan left edge.

Lorem ipsum dolor sit amet, consectetur adipisicing elit, sed do eiusmod tempor incididunt ut labore et dolore magna aliqua. Ut enim ad minim veniam, quis nostrud exercitation ullamco laboris nisi ut aliquip ex ea commodo consequat. Duis aute irure dolor in reprehenderit in voluptate velit esse cillum dolore eu fugiat nulla pariatur.

Centered: jagged left edge harder to scan.

Lorem ipsum dolor sit amet, consectetur adipisicing elit, sed do eiusmod tempor incididunt ut labore et dolore magna aliqua. Ut enim ad minim veniam, quis nostrud exercitation ullamco laboris nisi ut aliquip ex ea commodo consequat. Duis aute irure dolor in reprehenderit in voluptate velit esse cillum dolore eu fugiat nulla pariatur.

Right-aligned: jagged left edge harder to scan.

Lorem ipsum dolor sit amet, consectetur adipisicing elit, sed do eiusmod tempor incididunt ut labore et dolore magna aliqua. Ut enim ad minim veniam, quis nostrud exercitation ullamco laboris nisi ut aliquip ex ea commodo consequat. Duis aute irure dolor in reprehenderit in voluptate velit esse cillum dolore eu fugiat nulla pariatur.

Justified: random spacing between words slows reading.

Lorem ipsum dolor sit amet, consectetur adipisicing elit, sed do eiusmod tempor incididunt ut labore et dolore magna aliqua. Ut enim ad minim veniam, quis nostrud exercitation ullamco laboris nisi ut aliquip ex ea commodo consequat. Duis aute irure dolor in reprehenderit in voluptate velit esse cillum dolore eu fugiat nulla pariatur.

FIGURE 7.12   Left-aligned text is the easiest to scan because of the consistent left edge and the consistent spacing between words: the viewer's eyes always know where to find the next line or word.

Lists

Is there any type of content more suited to a quick scan down the left side than a list?

Lists should be short and to the point, so UX designers can easily convey the key message of each point in just a few words (remember to front load!). Conventional wisdom suggests that the last item in the list will be the one that the fewest people read, but eye tracking suggests that the last item actually gets a fair amount of the attention paid to the list (Graham, 2011). So consider building your lists like this:

- Most important item
- Second most important item
- Less important point (more likely to be skipped over)
- Less important point (more likely to be skipped over)
- Third most important item

Numerals

Numerals catch the eye, even when they are buried in a block of text (Figure 7.13 shows an example of a number catching attention on a Google search results page—a page where you want to catch as much attention as you can). Numbers represent data and facts, which web users are often looking for. They also stand out from text because of their different shape.

Traditional copywriting suggests that in many cases numbers should be written out, but based on the ability of numbers to capture the eye, Jakob Nielsen (2007) recommends the following guidelines for the web:

- Write numbers with digits, not letters (23, not twenty-three).
- Use numerals even when the number is the first work in a sentence or bullet point.
- Use numerals for big numbers up to one billion:
  - 2,000,000 is better than two million.
  - Two trillion is better than 2,000,000,000,000 because most people cannot interpret that many zeroes.
  - As a compromise, you can often use numerals for significant digits and write out the magnitude as a word. For example, write 24 billion (not twenty-four billion or 24,000,000,000).
- Spell out numbers that do not represent solid facts.

The final point is an important one. If you are just trying to convey an estimate or idea, write out the number: "thousands of people will love this book."

Image Captions

Perhaps surprisingly, image captions are one of the most frequently fixated pieces of content on a web page (Faria et al., 2004;

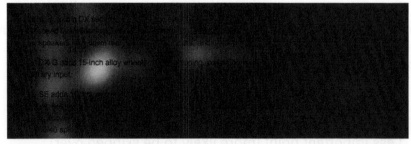

FIGURE 7.13   In this gaze opacity map, "15-inch" captured the attention of people reading about a car.

The Poynter Institute, 2007). They are often used to reinforce the key messages of imagery and content, because not only are they frequently looked at, they are frequently remembered.

> *In addition to image captions capturing attention, images themselves can also be used to both capture and direct attention. Humans are very attuned to faces and directional cues. Include an image of a face, and your users' eyes will be drawn to it. If the face in that image is looking somewhere, your users' eyes will naturally follow the face's eyes (Maughan, 2009). The same applies to directional cues like a body facing a call to action, someone pointing at something, and arrows (Patel, 2013).*

Fonts and Typography

The actual characters making up your content have a huge impact on legibility, readability, comprehension, and a user's willingness to actually read your content.

Choosing Fonts

Much has been written about serif versus sans serif fonts. Fortunately or unfortunately, depending on how you look at it, the overall conclusion of all of this research is that *it does not really matter*—there may be minor differences in reading speed or comprehension, but they are inconsistent and not significant (Poole, 2008).

The other characteristics give roughly equivalent legibility for two fonts as long as the actual letter size, not the point size, is the same (Poulton, 1972). So UX designers should choose the font(s) that best suits the aesthetics. The differences in legibility between mainstream fonts are so minimal that it does not really matter, as long as you make the font big enough.

Font Size

Unfortunately, there is no gold standard font size for web design. Most sites use somewhere between 10 and 16 points for body text, and arguments can be made for any of those sizes.

Smaller font sizes result in longer fixation durations and therefore slightly slower reading, but the difference in reading speed is often not significant (Beymer et al., 2008).

When choosing a font size, it is important to consider the characteristics of the users: for example, young or old, tech naive or tech savvy, alert or tired, or reading it on a mobile phone or a huge desktop monitor.

Line Height

Line height, or leading (from the old days of printing presses when lead strips were used to add space between lines of text), is one of the most influential factors in legibility (e.g., Dyson, 2004; Boulton, 2005).

Line height needs to vary with two things:

- Font size: The larger the font, the larger the line height should be.
- Line length: The longer the line, the larger the line height should be (see below).

Eye-tracking metrics show that a line height that is 130–150% larger than the font size typically leads to the most efficient reading.

Line Length

Research in the area of line length is somewhat inconclusive; however, the general consensus is that a line length somewhere between 50 and 100 characters will produce a good combination of reading speed and comprehension (Dyson, 2004). Additionally, other factors such as line width (the actual measurement from one end of the line to the other), margin size, and character density have minimal effect on speed or comprehension (Dyson, 2004). There is also interplay between line length/width and line height, as shown in Figure 7.14. As the line length increases, the line height needs to increase because the angle at which the eye travels down to the next line is important in helping the visitor identify where that next line starts.

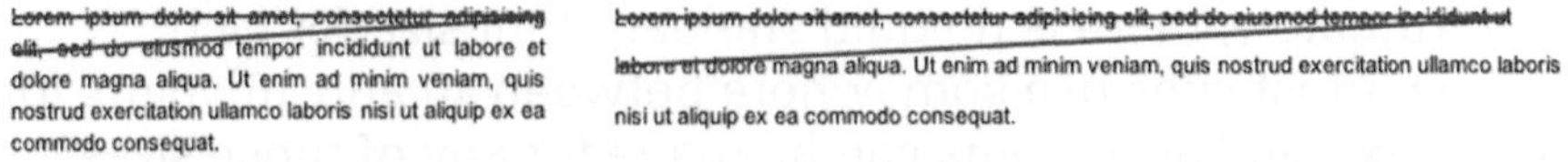

Lorem ipsum dolor sit amet, consectetur adipisicing elit, sed do eiusmod tempor incididunt ut labore et dolore magna aliqua. Ut enim ad minim veniam, quis nostrud exercitation ullamco laboris nisi ut aliquip ex ea commodo consequat.

Lorem ipsum dolor sit amet, consectetur adipisicing elit, sed do eiusmod tempor incididunt ut labore et dolore magna aliqua. Ut enim ad minim veniam, quis nostrud exercitation ullamco laboris nisi ut aliquip ex ea commodo consequat.

FIGURE 7.14   To make it easy for users' eyes to move from one line to the next, an appropriate angle between the end of one line and the start of the next (shown by the red lines) should be maintained. To do this, the line height needs to be increased as the line length increases.

Colors, Contrast, and Emphasis

In order to make certain pieces of information stand out on the page, colors, contrast, and emphasis can be used.

Colors and Contrast

There are millions of possible color combinations, and not that much research looking at how those combinations affect readability. The general consensus is that high contrast between foreground and background leads to better readability (Redish, 2007). The existing research suggests that dark text on a light background is more readable than the other way around; light text on a dark background is read more slowly, although retention of information is the same (Figure 7.15; Hill & Scharff, 1999; Hall & Hanna, 2003).

"Measuring Contrast:" The w3c has created an algorithm that assesses the difference in both hue and brightness, which accurately predicts readability in most cases. To play around with the formula, visit: http://www.w3.org/TR/ AERT#color-contrast.

It is important to note that even if you use different colors, they must still have different contrasts as well. Anyone who is colorblind to the colors you are using will not be able to tell the difference if the two colors have the same contrast.

Emphasis

UX designers can subtly influence users in their quest for information scent by emphasizing particular words or phrases. This is commonly referred to as *display type.*

The key to effective display type is to use it sparingly. If everything is bold, nothing will stand out. A good rule of thumb is

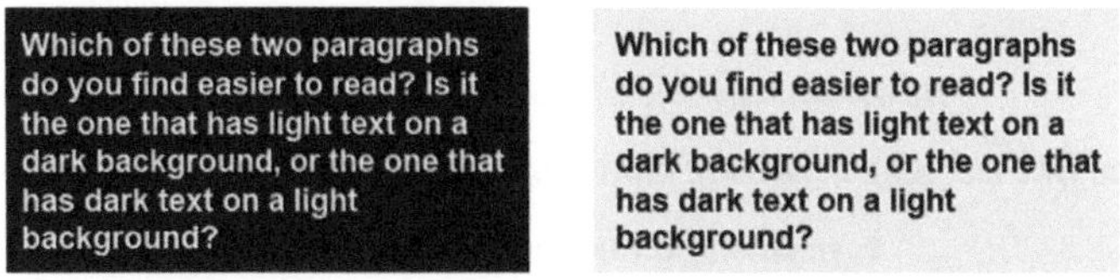

FIGURE 7.15   Dark text on a light background has been shown to be easier to read than light text on a dark background.

to add one type of emphasis at a time; for example, make the text bold first and if it still does not stand out, then change the color. A little variation in emphasis can go a long way (Chi et al., 2007).

Bold and Italics

Boldface text stands out because it contrasts in weight from the text surrounding it. Bold text is comparable in readability to plain text, provided it is used sparingly. Large blocks of bold text lose effectiveness because there is no longer a difference in contrast (Lynch & Horton, 2009).

Italicized text stands out because it is different in shape from the text surrounding it. However, italics should be avoided for large blocks of text because it is significantly more difficult to read than plain text, especially at screen resolutions (Lynch & Horton, 2009).

Redish (2007) anecdotally tells of research comparing headings in regular type, bold, and italics. Users typically assume that the bold heading is the most important, with mixed opinions on whether the italic heading is more or less important than the regular type.

Underlines

A throwback to the days of the typewriter, underlining is not a good method for emphasizing text. It interferes with letter shape, reducing readability (Lynch & Horton, 2009). Of course, underlining serves a special function on the web, as it typically denotes a hyperlink. This adds to the case against using underlining as a method to emphasize text.

Capitals

Capitalizing text is one of the most common and least effective ways of emphasizing text because capital letters are difficult to scan. Humans read primarily by recognizing the shapes of letters forming words, which is entirely eliminated by writing in all caps (see whether you can recognize the text in Figure 7.16).

We use the tops of letters to determine what they are

CAPITAL LETTERS ELIMINATE THAT SHAPE AND MAKE IT HARDER TO READ

Even Writing In Title Case Adds Complexity

FIGURE 7.16 We use the tops of letters to determine what they are. Capital letters eliminate that shape and make it harder to read. Even writing in title case adds complexity.

Even writing in "title case"—the capitalization of every word in a headline or heading, for example—disrupts the visitor's ability to read. Better to write in "sentence case," capitalize only the first word and proper nouns. A review of eye-tracking research looking at word recognition and reading speed reveals that all-capital text takes 5–10% more time to read (Larson, 2004).

CONCLUSION

Based on everything you have read (or skimmed, if we are being honest), you should now have the basics to make content easy on the eyes:

- Information scent helps to draw users' eyes toward content that is relevant to their intent.
- Visual hierarchy in design, inverted pyramid writing style, and front loading all help structure content so readers will see what is most important.
- Lists, numerals, and image captions help emphasize bits and pieces of your content to make important details stand out.
- Fonts, colors, and emphasis, when used wisely, enhance the legibility and readability of your content.
- Eye tracking can diagnose how you are guiding readers through your content, whether you have drawn attention to the right things, and whether your writing creates confusion or uncertainty. Test your content!

REFERENCES

Beymer, D., Russell, D., Orton, P., 2008. An eye tracking study of how font size and type influence online reading. BCS-HCI '08 Proceedings of the 22nd British HCI Group Annual Conference on People and Computers: Culture, Creativity, Interaction, vol. 2. pp. 15–18 (2008).

Boulton, M., 2005. Five Simple Steps to Better Typography | Journal | The Personal Disquiet of Mark Boulton. The Personal Disquiet of Mark Boulton. N.p., 13 April 2005. Web. 16 May 2013, http://markboulton.co.uk/journal/five-simple-steps-to-better-typography.

Carpenter, P.A., Just, M.A., 1983. What your eyes do while your mind is reading. In: Eye Movements in Reading: Perceptual and Language Processes. Academic Press, New York, pp. 275–307.

Chi, E.H., Gumbrecht, M., Hong, L., 2007. Visual foraging of highlighted text: an eye-tracking study. In: Human-Computer Interaction, Part III, HCII 2007, LNCS 4552. Spring-Verlag, Berlin, pp. 589–598.

Clifton, C. Jr, Staub, A., Rayner, K., 2007. Eye movements in reading words and sentences. In: Eye Movements: A Window on Mind and Brain. Elsevier, Amsterdam, pp. 341–372.

Dyson, M.C., 2004. How physical text layout affects reading from screen. Behav. Inform. Tech. 23 (6), 377–393.

Faria, I.H., Baptista, A., Luegi, P., Taborda, C., 2004. Interaction and Competition Between Types of Representation. An Example from eye-Tracking While Processing Written Words and Images. Laborátorio de Psicolinguástica. N.p., n.d. Web. 17 May 2013, labpsicoling.clul.ul.pt/investigadores/publicacoes/Faria_Baptista_Luegi_Taborda_2006.pdf.

Frenck-Mestre, C., 2005. Eye-movement recording as a tool for studying syntactic processing in a second language: a review of methodologies and experimental findings. Sec. Lang. Res. 21 (2), 175–198.

Graham, G., 2011. White Paper Article: Five Tips on Writing Better Bullets. That White Paper Guy. N.p., n.d. Web. 17 May 2013, http://www.thatwhitepaperguy.com/copywriting-article-five-tips-on-writing-better-bulleted-lists.html.

Hall, R.H., Hanna, P., 2003. The effect of web page text-background color combinations on retention and perceived readability, aesthetics, and behavioral intention. Proceedings of The Americas Conference on Information Systems. pp. 2149–2156.

Hill, A., Scharff, L., 1999. Readability of computer displays as a function of color, saturation, and texture backgrounds. Engineering Psychology and Cognitive Ergonomics, 4. pp. 123–130, Print.

Kennedy, A., Murray, W.S., 1987. Spatial coordinates and reading: comments on Monk. Q. J. Exp. Psychol. 39A, 649–656.

Larson, K., 2004. The Science of Word Recognition. Microsoft Corporation. N.p., 1 July 2004. Web. 26 Aug. 2013, http://www.microsoft.com/typography/ctfonts/wordrecognition.aspx.

Loos, E., Mante-Meijer, E., 2012. Getting Access to Website Health Information. Generational Use of New Media. Ashgate, Burlington, VT (pp. 185–202).

Lynch, P.J., Horton, S., 2009. Emphasis | Web Style Guide 3. Web Style Guide. N.p., 15 Jan. 2009. Web. 19 Jan. 2013, http://webstyleguide.com/wsg3/8-typography/5-typographic-emphasis.html.

Maughan, L., 2009. Cuing Customers to Look at Your Key Messages | Think Eye Tracking. THiNK Eye Tracking, Shopper, Media, Usability and Gaming research. N.p., 28 June 2009. Web. 1 Sept. 2013, http://thinkeyetracking.com/2009/06/cuing-customers-to-look-at-your-key-messages/.

McConkie, G.W., Rayner, K., 1978. Asymmetry of the perceptual span in reading. Bull. Psychonomic Soc. 8 (5), 365–368.

Morris, R.K., Rayner, K., Pollatsek, A., 1990. Eye movement guidance in reading: the role of parafoveal letter and space information. J. Exp. Psychol. Hum. Percept. Perform. 16 (2), 268–281.

Murray, W.S., Kennedy, A., 1988. Spatial coding in the processing of anaphor by good and poor readers: evidence from eye movement analyses. Q. J. Exp. Psychol. 40 (4A), 693–718.

Nielsen, J., 1997. How Users Read on the Web. Nielsen Norman Group: UX Training, Consulting, & Research. N.p., 1 Oct. 1997. Web. 17 May 2013, http://www.nngroup.com/articles/how-users-read-on-the-web/.

Nielsen, J., 2007. Show Numbers as Numerals When Writing for Online Readers. Nielsen Norman Group: User Experience Training, UX Consulting, and Usability Research Reports. N.p., 16 Apr. 2007. Web. 19 Jan. 2013, http://www.nngroup.com/articles/web-writing-show-numbers-as-numerals/.

Nielsen, J., 2010. Scrolling and Attention. Nielsen Norman Group. N.p., 22 Mar. 2010. Web. 19 Jan. 2013, http://www.nngroup.com/articles/scrolling-and-attention/.

Olson, G.A., 1985. Style and Readability in Business Writing: A Sentence-Combining Approach. Random House, New York.

Outing, S., Ruel, L., 2004. Eyetrack III. Eyetrack III. N.p., 2 Sept. 2004. Web. 16 May 2013, www.math.unipd.it/~massimo/corsi/tecweb2/Eyetrack-III.pdf.

Owens, J.W., Chaparro, B.S., Palmer, E.M., 2011. Text advertising blindness: the new banner blindness? JUS 6 (3), 172–197.

Patel, N., 2013. 7 Conversion Lessons Learned from Eye Tracking. Quick Sprout—I'm Kind of a Big Deal. N.p., 1 Aug. 2013. Web. 1 Sept. 2013, http://www.quicksprout.com/2013/08/01/7-conversion-optimization-lessons-learned-from-eye-tracking/.

Pirolli, P., Card, S., 1999. Information foraging. Psychol. Rev. vol. 106 (4), 643–675.

Poole, A., 2008. Which are More Legible: Serif or Sans Serif Typefaces? | Alex Poole. Alex Poole | User experience design and research. N.p., 17 Feb. 2008. Web. 19 Jan. 2013, http://alexpoole.info/blog/which-are-more-legible-serif-or-sans-serif-typefaces/.

Poulton, E.C., 1972. Size, style, and vertical spacing in the legibility of small typefaces. J. Appl. Psychol. 56 (2), 156–161.

Rayner, K., McConkie, G.W., 1976. What guides a reader's eye movements? Vision Res. 16 (8), 829–837.

Rayner, K., McConkie, G.W., Zola, D., 1980. Integrating information across eye movements. Cogn. Psychol. 12 (2), 206–226.

Redish, J., 2007. Letting Go of the Words: Writing Web Content That Works. Elsevier/Morgan Kaufmann Publishers, Amsterdam.

Richardson, D.C., Spivey, M.J., 2004. Eye tracking: research areas and applications. In: Encyclopedia of Biomaterials and Biomedical Engineering. Marcel Dekker, New York, pp. 573–582.

Romano Bergstrom, J.C., Olmstead-Hawala, E.L., Jans, M.E., 2013. Age-related differences in eye tracking and usability performance: website usability for older adults. Int. J. Hum. Comput. Interact. 29 (8), 541–548.

The Poynter Institute | EyeTrack07, 2007. The Poynter Institute. . N.p., n.d. Web. 17 May 2013, www.poynter.org/extra/Eyetrack/previous.html.

Zarcadoolas, C., Blanco, M., Boyer, J.F., Pleasant, A., 2002. Unweaving the web: an exploratory study of low-literate adults' navigation skills on the world wide web. J. Health Commun. 7 (4), 309–324.

8

E-COMMERCE WEBSITES

Wilkey Wong, Mike Bartels, and Nina Chrobot
Tobii Technology, Falls Church, VA, USA

INTRODUCTION

An e-commerce website has the goal of enabling the conduct of purchase transactions. Sounds straightforward enough, doesn't it? But in a context where essentially all the senses, save vision, are starved for stimulation and context, how exactly does a brand incite interest, passion, and commitment? Whether the device is a tablet, smartphone, or desktop computer, the primary and oftentimes sole modality for communicating information, value, and relevance is visual. And the mind and heart can only come to desire that which the eyes can see. Therein lies the essential motivation for including eye tracking in the study of e-commerce interface design and the user experience.

About 67% of e-commerce transactions are never completed (Cohen, 1999), and 60% of all users reach the check-out step and abandon before final completion (Loveday & Niehaus, 2007). In order to enhance e-transactions, the shopping process and the tool by which it is accomplished—the web page—must be designed to effectively help the user carry out a purchase. Unfortunately, only 36% of customers are satisfied with their transactions on the web (Chatham, 2002). The rest will try to find better service through alternate channels like call centers, catalogs, and brick-and-mortar stores.

One reason users may avoid shopping online is difficulty in finding the item of interest (Herschlag, 1998). There is wisdom, it seems, in the oft repeated aphorism, "unseen is unsold." And because of increasing competitiveness in a rapidly growing e-commerce market, e-commerce brands will have to pay greater attention to the online shopping experience as frustrated users simply go away or go to a competitor (Bhatti et al., 2000).

So, beyond satisfying functional considerations (such as providing a clear and efficient layout) and facilitating actions that are required of a non-commerce site (e.g., search, navigation), e-commerce sites must perform the additional function of convincing a visitor to engage, commit, and ultimately execute a financial transaction.

Eye tracking users' visual behavior from that very first glance on the landing page to the moment just before they click on the "buy" button can reveal both barriers and affordances in this process. Through eye tracking, user experience (UX) researchers are able to discover unintended patterns of viewing, quantify the attractive power of key interaction elements, identify the attentional or cognitive mechanisms behind missed opportunities, and differentiate the performance of design variants. In a domain that is so intensely visual, it makes eminent sense to include a methodology that can so naturally connect visual behavior and the outcomes that matter most to e-commerce businesses and brands: increased sales, satisfaction, and loyalty.

This additional goal of eliciting revenue from the user directly (as opposed to indirectly through ad impressions or click-throughs) particularizes the research focus on several accounts. First, the check-out or purchase process becomes a prominent item of study with the virtual "cart" becoming a common target of substantial interest. Second, the activities and tasks on a site may vary as a result of its commercial focus. That is, sites may be online front ends for product catalogs, outlets for commodity products and services, or gated sites with a "pay wall" separating free from premium content. e-commerce sites may further be categorized along the dimension of primary interactional relationship as business-to-business, business-to-consumer, consumer-to-consumer, peer-to-peer, or mobile commerce. This chapter focuses on two of the most commonly investigated site types: product catalogs and commodity product sites.

Types of E-commerce sites

The commercial focus, or type of e-commerce site, is a significant factor in guiding both its design and the evaluation of its usage. Let's take the case of the online product catalog.

Catalogs

The archetypal example of a catalog e-commerce site is Amazon.com (Figures 8.1 and 8.2). With likely millions of products across dozens of categories, the primary challenges for a site such as this, in addition to conversion, are to get shoppers to their desired product or to help them find a product they wish to purchase and then to facilitate that process. In addition, there are secondary goals such as increasing cart size through cross-selling or recommendations. With such a diverse product offering, locating a product becomes a significant source of cognitive demand, which can, unfortunately, lead to dissatisfaction and abandonment. Accordingly, navigation and search functions receive intense attention (Figure 8.3). Design and use of navigation in all its forms, from tabs to dropdowns with various expansion or bread-crumbing strategies (both vertical and lateral), are frequently studied both with and without eye tracking.

Search and results filtration strategies are another common target of study. Typical questions that are asked in navigation studies pertain to the logic and "intuitiveness" or naturalness of the categories with respect to moving from the broad to the specific or from category to rational subcategory. For example, in Figure 8.4 we have the top-level categorization for cameras at B&H PhotoVideo, a major retailer of photographic and video equipment. On this page, they present only the broadest

FIGURE 8.1   Amazon.com cross-selling opportunity features "Frequently Bought Together" and "Customers Who Bought This Item Also Bought."

FIGURE 8.2   Amazon.com landing page, unpersonalized.

categories of "digital" and "film" cameras. Clicking through either brings up a page format with detailed categorizations such as "point and shoot" or "35 mm" and "medium format" in the expanded left navigation pane and product listings in the center of the page. On Adorama's (a competitor to B&H) top-level camera page, not only are digital cameras shown, but there are also multiple film camera types such as dSLR, 35 mm rangefinder, and medium format displayed (Figure 8.5). Selecting any of these leads to another page that includes further options to click through to see the cameras and various accessory types. It is only after this additional step that the user is presented with a camera listing and left navigation filtration options that appear

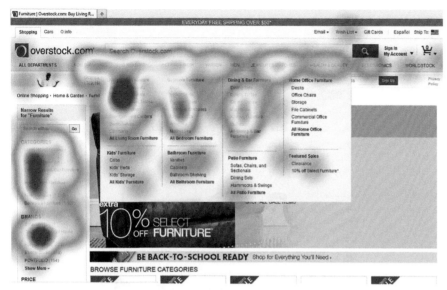

FIGURE 8.3 Count-based heat map of visual attention on Overstock.com showing concentration of gaze to left and dropdown navigation elements.

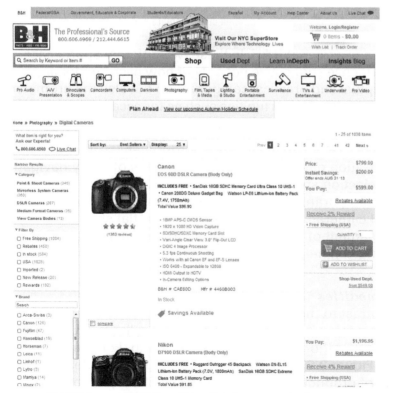

FIGURE 8.4 B&H PhotoVideo digital camera selection page.

FIGURE 8.5 Adorama digital camera and accessories page.

one stage earlier at B&H. In these two different approaches, we see evidence suggestive not only of how each vendor approaches conceptual and practical categorization but also the prominence of cross-selling opportunities such as for accessories.

So for browsing and search filtration, evaluating the efficiency of those filters, especially the appropriateness and number of the filtration parameters, are components of many navigation and selection studies. For example, how useful is the inclusion of a color parameter in top-level search for point and shoot digital cameras, and how hierarchical or flat should the arrangement of search and filtration parameters be? Eye tracking can help answer these questions.

Commodities

In contrast to multicategory catalog sites, commodities e-commerce sites generally offer a more limited range of product categories but with greater depth. For example, Petco. com (Figure 8.6) and Petsmart.com (Figure 8.7) deal with a vast array of products, but they are all specifically for pet care. While these sites employ many of the functions of a catalog site,

FIGURE 8.6   Petco landing page.

they also need to address the specific needs of new-to-market visitors (e.g., those considering becoming pet owners) and in-market shoppers. In-market shoppers, those who already have intent to purchase, will further be sensitive to site differentiators between vendors as well as product options and resources that are designed to move them along the purchase funnel to conversion. For example, the availability of testimonials (Romano Bergstrom, 2013), enhanced product information displays (such as 3-D virtual views), and targeted offers can be used to increase engagement and dwell time on the product page as well as provide a more complete context for product usage and its benefits. In studies undertaken by such e-commerce sites like Peapod.com and Safeway.com, shopping lists; the presentation of product information and imagery; recommendations, such as "you may also like" shown in Figure 8.8, or "other people who bought this"; and enrichment resources such as recipes are often investigated as to visibility, efficacy, and acceptability.

FIGURE 8.7   PetSmart landing page.

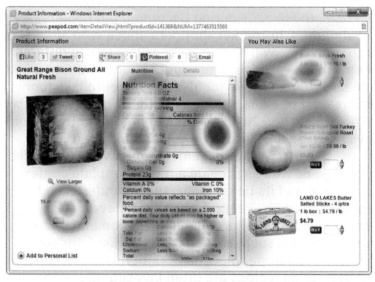

FIGURE 8.8   PeaPod product page including "You may also like" feature.

MEASURING INTERACTIONS

A fundamental question at the outset of any UX research project is how to measure performance baselines or discern performance differences among design candidates. In the case of e-commerce studies, UX researchers have metrics, or standards of measurement, that relate to usability, eye tracking, and commerce. Furthermore, these categories can be arranged in a number of ways, such as:

- Formative versus summative: Formative studies are conducted during the development process in order to understand user behavior, diagnose specific problems, and improve design. Summative studies, as the name indicates, summarize evaluations of the product through defined measures and make benchmark comparison possible. For example, on a grocery e-commerce site, a formative question might involve determining the acceptance of related-product recommendations. A summative study may determine the rates of use of various constructions and the effect of adjustments to the recommendation algorithm.
- Qualitative versus quantitative: Qualitative studies seek to understand the why and how of user behavior in a subjective way. Quantitative studies measure user behavior via statistical and mathematical methods, objectively answering questions of users' what, where, and when. A study may include both quantitative and qualitative investigations. In the case of a layout redesign, researchers could both categorize the overall user scan paths and then report fixation durations in the focal areas of interest as an indicator of engagement by design variant.
- Behavioral versus cognitive: Cognitive studies seek to understand users' cognitive processes during interaction with web pages (especially information processing). Behavioral studies aim to analyze user behavior on the web page and reactions to specific web elements or designs. For example, patterns of looking, clicking, and scrolling could be deconstructed to reveal the intelligibility and relevance of text blocks or informational displays.
- Descriptive versus diagnostic: Descriptive studies are used to describe specific phenomena of interest and describe user behavior, such as spatial or temporal patterns of viewing. Diagnostic studies try to identify good (strong) and bad (weak) points of any web pages, for example, by correlating viewing times with task completion rates or times.

*Usability testing with eye tracking gives us the insights we need
to keep improving our designs for KLM.com.*

**Marlies Roodenberg, User Experience Manager, KLM.com,
E-Commerce**

The selection of a metrics set for any given study is
determined by the specific goals of the study as well as the
stage in a product's development. It is also constrained by the
time and resources required to gather, analyze, and interpret
these measurements. For example, early stage studies with
wireframes may not benefit much from eye tracking, whereas
redesigns of established pages may have a significant history
of data captured via web analytics. The following section
will address selections of metrics from each of these three
categories that are commonly used in e-commerce UX studies
that provide particularly useful insights.

Commerce

There are numerous e-commerce website metrics that one
might choose to include in a study. Generally, they can be
grouped as pertaining to sales, marketing, or social activities.

Sales

In terms of sales metrics, some of the most commonly
considered include sales, profit or profit margin, conversion
rate, new versus returning visitors, and average sale (also
referred to as cart, especially in grocery or consumer
packaged goods settings). Nearly all of these can be
calculated and tracked on numerous timescales (e.g., hourly,
annually).

For some of these, it may be informative to track these data
by time of day to gain a comprehensive and dynamic picture
of the revenue aspects of a website's performance. Of all
the above metrics, the average sale per customer per visit is
often regarded as among the most important. One reason
this makes sense is that the average sale bears an obvious
relation to the cost of acquiring customers. Also, average
sale is directly linked to conversion through a site's shopping
cart. That is why it is extremely important to design checkout
processes that will not lead to abandonment. The overall cart

experience is a fundamental metric as well as a consummation of the entire on-site experience.

Marketing

Some of the most common metrics related to marketing effectiveness are related to visits. In addition to overall site traffic and unique and returning visitors, page views and time spent per visit are often included in marketing analyses.

Social Activities

A company's reputation is an important consideration and the most timely and dynamic indicator of reputation and sentiment is often found in the social sphere. Followers, subscribers, or fans on social channels such as Facebook, Twitter, Pinterest, and YouTube as well as HubSpot and YSlow grades and ranks are among the most obvious. Also of interest may be blog traffic, number and quality of reviews, retweets, and brand mentions.

User Experience

As discussed in Chapter 3, task success rate, time on task, and number of errors are basic UX measures that inform about the user experience. For e-commerce sites, the shopping cart and check out process provide clear targets and criteria for successful performance. Common tasks include finding the cart, adding an item to the cart, changing the quantity of items in the cart, and return to shopping, as shown in Figure 8.9. Eye tracking provides a natural complement to these performance measures precisely because it is capable of identifying the attentional factors that contribute to both success and failure, especially in a search or find task. For example, if a participant fails to meet a specific criterion for success (e.g., achieving a goal within a specified time frame) or fails altogether, an inspection of the gaze patterns during the task may reveal insufficient salience of key landmarks to calls to action. Alternatively, visual attention magnets such as images or superfluous information may be effectively drawing attention away from where it should be in order to complete a task. In addition, uncovering the allocation of total time spent attempting to carry out a task can provide a read on where people expect certain affordances to be located.

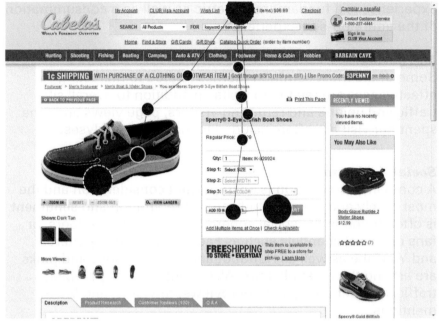

FIGURE 8.9   Gaze plot of Cabela's shoe product page, locating cart, and adding product to cart.

CONCEPTUAL MODELS FOR DESIGNING, ANALYZING, AND INTERPRETING EYE TRACKING

Assessing user performance on e-commerce websites is really no different from evaluations of any other type of site. The same kinds of questions are asked and the same metrics are gathered.

Eye-tracking metrics generally fall into several categories: durations, counts, and sequence or ordering. The value of selecting a useful metric can figure into the utility of the analysis. While a metric such as visit count may be tallied over an entire task exercise, the specificity of interpretation may be aided by examining, for example, only the number of visits made during a particular phase of the interaction on the e-commerce site, after a certain item is looked at, or in relation to actions such as immediately preceding clicks.

A conceptual model, as used in this chapter, is a structured way of thinking about a phenomenon or a process that makes it possible to achieve productive ends. In eye-tracking research on e-commerce sites, the ultimate goal is to answer questions that have both technical and business value.

Selecting a conceptual model starts with a process of uncovering the ultimate objective of the research and then ensuring that all subsequent steps from design of experiments, methodological considerations, analytical strategy, and through to the interpretive perspective are harmonious with the achievement of that goal. A well-constructed research question is generally the place to start and, at least in the early years of eye tracking, has been a step that has not received the rigor or scrutiny that it merits. Clients have said: "I'd like to know where people look. We've been asked to produce heat maps. We would like to include some eye tracking." These statements were once not at all uncommon to encounter as motivations for conducting eye tracking. However, these and similar requests fail for several reasons. First, they are not specific with respect to the behavioral insight sought. What is it about looking that we want to characterize? What is most attentionally salient? What gets looked at or missed? Second, the requests do not relate to measurable or describable behaviors. What is the order of looking? How long do people spend looking at these elements? And third, it is unclear how these statements relate to business priorities, objectives, or indicators. Without an understanding of the relationship of performance metrics to relevant business indicators (for example, the commerce metrics mentioned above), it is exceptionally challenging to broach the issue of return on investment.

Often the requestors are not prepared to formulate questions that meet these suitability requirements. Rather, the UX team needs to provide guidance and should start with the project brief and then probe and push back until the essential insight is uncovered. For example, we do not seek to learn if users look at a redesigned element; rather, we want to know if there is more meaningful looking (i.e., engagement), if the order of looking changes, and if any measurable behavior translates to an effect on completion or task efficiency and satisfaction. Ultimately, we want to know the effect on conversion.

Once a suitable research question is formulated, one that is specific, measurable, and relates to business goals or indicators, then one approach to framing the work would be to determine the type of process under study. That is, will you be investigating a search process where there is a defined target to be acquired, or are you interested in aspects of cognitive processing such as engagement, confusion, or effort. Alternatively, might this be a study that seeks to assess the visual and attentional salience of a design? This framework has been described by researchers (Olsen & Wong, 2012) as one that is particularly useful when the scope of research is relatively tight in focus and principally process based.

In this framework, subsets of eye-tracking metrics can be identified as being suitable and informative of these three classes of processes. For example, visual search efficiency with respect to acquisition of a given target can be constructively described by time to first fixation on target, fixations to other areas prior to first fixation on target, time from first fixation to click, and number of visits to other areas prior to click. Processing is informed by average fixation duration (and to a degree, number of fixations) and total visit duration (the sum of the saccade and fixation durations) to an area of interest bracketed by a single entry and exit.

Complimentary processing measures include pupil dilation and physiological responses such as electrodermal activity (commonly galvanic skin response) and electroencephalography, as discussed in Chapter 4. These can be used to assess engagement with e-commerce sites as well as points of frustration. Finally, attention and noticing can be measured through percentage of participants fixating on a region, though not necessarily a predetermined target such as a call to action, number of fixations prior to first fixation, and time to first fixation on an area of interest (AOI). Combining measures can increase the confidence of inferences made about cognitive effort, engagement, and affective arousal.

In the study of e-commerce sites, this model focuses the research effort on those aspects of task and design that are most important in, say, purchasing a product. For example, one might investigate the visibility of forms of "add to cart" button. Once a visually salient design is established, is any informative text unambiguous and easily understood? And finally, do all of these factors taken together relate to increased satisfaction and likelihood to purchase or a larger cart?

A recent case study involving research conducted by Valsplat for KLM airlines well illustrates the application of eye tracking to uncover the visual behavior underlying design efficiency and its relation to processing and decision making. Eye tracking was used to show that the existing design was burdensome with respect to finding the appropriate flight at the best price. Figure 8.10 presents a gaze plot that reveals a typical situation with numerous back and forth saccades across the width of the page. Feeding this information back resulted in a redesign that placed the price and schedule information next to each other, as shown in Figure 8.11, resulting in easier comparison shopping, reduced effort, and, ultimately, a 30% increase in online ticket purchase conversion.

FIGURE 8.10 Gaze plot of KLM.com flight search page prior to redesign showing many fixations and cross-page saccades resulting in difficulty making flight comparisons.

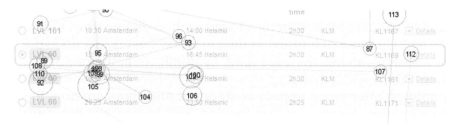

FIGURE 8.11 Gaze plot of KLM.com flight search page after redesign showing shorter saccades on the key price and schedule information place in proximal columns making flight comparisons easier and more efficient.

An alternative approach to establishing a study framework considers the entire journey undertaken with respect to an activity or mission. Here the researcher seeks to understand at least three differentiated stages in the interaction with e-commerce websites.

1. Attention and awareness is manifested (e.g., notice a suitable product as a candidate for consideration)
2. Initial cognitive processing or interest is developed (e.g., establish relevance and desirability)
3. Activation takes place (e.g., make a positive purchase decision by adding it to the shopping cart)

Arguments have been raised that this approach, which is structurally similar to the AIDA (i.e., attention, interest, desire, action) and related models (Vakratsas & Ambler, 1999) is more useful as a communications planning model rather than as a consumer process model (Pieters & Wedel, 2008). To be sure, research suggests that attentional, perceptual, and cognitive process are much more closely intertwined temporally than the stepwise nature of the model posits; however, it has demonstrated some utility as a practical framework for eye-tracking studies.

One reason this is so is that commercial research generally is more concerned with main effects rather than more fine-grained interactions. Partially, this is due to methodological constraints such as sample size, statistical requirements, and the complex nature of meaningful real-world behaviors. This is in contrast to the kinds of paradigms employed in fundamental cognitive and perceptual research aimed at elucidating truths or theory building. Additionally, this stage-based model is useful for analytical reasons because eye-tracking metrics can be readily grouped into attention, processing/interest, and action clusters for a structured approach to diagnosis of the three major loci of interest in design work. That is, we measure if a design catches the eyes (and, by implication, the mind), holds the eyes, and makes something happen. In this model, common attentional impact or standout measures are time to first fixation, location of first fixation, and percentage noticing. Interest measures include number and length of fixations, total gaze time, and scanning patterns on the stimulus. Eye-tracking metrics useful to consider with activation processes include number and location of fixations or visits prior click and time total looking time prior to the click.

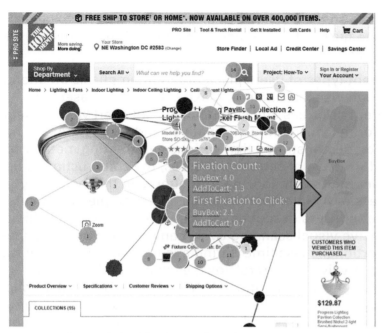

FIGURE 8.12   Gaze analysis of Buy Box and inset Add to Cart for ceiling lamp on HomeDepot.com.

In Figure 8.12, we see an analysis of the gaze characteristics involved in adding a product to the cart for an add to cart button inset in a larger buy box with additional shipping and delivery options. In this case, it was reported that there was only a slight difference in the number of fixations to the larger buy box versus the add-to-cart button. Additionally, once in the buy box, it only took about 1.5 seconds to fixate and click the target. This suggests that the additional delivery options were not a meaningful complication to the check out process, a finding that was further triangulated through post interviews.

USER TYPES AND MODELS

A useful approach to sense-making when investigating user behavior on e-commerce websites is to generate user types. To be clear, while this may appear superficially similar to the creation of personas, it is a far less intensive approach to understanding classes of behavior that is grounded primarily in gaze behavior. Furthermore, user types are useful as interpretive rather than predictive models. For example, from in-store market research studies, behavioral profiles may include: Explorer, Bargain hunter, Trip planner, One-shot v. Double-checker, and Revisitor.

Different types of users place different emphasis on attention (through visual scanning), make evaluations based on different priorities and sensitivities, and exert varying degrees of effort in considering alternatives and features. As we have already demonstrated that various eye-tracking metrics can be informative of certain processes, the construction of user profiles starts with looking for patterns in the metrics by process or by interactional stage. For example, a particular cluster of users described as "trip planners" might exhibit extensive visual scanning over many regions but then spend proportionally less time during evaluation and consideration. Alternatively, "explorers" look, evaluate, and consider extensively in preparation for action. Although construction of user types is not an indispensible step, it often has value when used in conjunction with user verbalization that reflects on the process.

DESIGN OF EYE-TRACKING STUDIES FOR E-COMMERCE

e-commerce user experience studies including an eye-tracking component have many of the same considerations as non-e-commerce studies. These include the number of tasks that can be reasonably executed during the session and order of presentation of stimuli (and any user–moderator interactions) to minimize bias or pre-exposure familiarization effects. Whether the study will be between-subjects or within-subjects is another fundamental consideration and one that will be driven by sample size and task similarity. In general, tasks to be eye tracked should be carried out prior to any activities during which dialog or questioning occurs. This is to ensure that visual scanning behavior is natural and not informed by prior interaction with the moderator (discussed further in Chapter 3). Of course, if the tasks involve substantially different activities on different pages, such as reading product descriptions to support making a purchase decision versus free looking at a page to assess attentional salience, then the risk may be minimal.

There are additional considerations specific to e-commerce studies. If the research involves purchasing goods, then one must decide whether to set up a generic shopper identity or account so that all users proceed from the same starting point with respect to preferences, recommendations, and other adaptive or personalizing features. This ensures a consistent starting point but risks some degree of ecological validity, as the common basis may be quite different from a user's actual circumstance. Of course, when testing non-users or first time users, the impact is relatively less severe. Alternatively, the study may require that a user log in with their actual account credentials. This approach allows the user to operate more naturally during shopping tasks particularly when employing saved shopping lists. Furthermore, it creates a scenario that is more realistic in that an actual transaction is considered and carried out. This also allows the researcher to gauge authentic reaction to functions made more relevant such as suggestions based on what has been purchased in the past, recent shopping history, or social inputs such as friends' actions or trending/popular items. If employing this approach, the UX researcher must be attentive to privacy and security issues such as cameras that might record log-in or payment key entries. Additionally, eye-tracking software automatically captures hardware-generated events such as loading of website URLs, mouse clicks, and keystrokes as a non-modifiable part of its normal operation. Thus, even though a site might replace letters typed into a password field with an obscuring symbol on screen, the identity of the keys that were actually pressed will be stored in the recording data file. Thus, researchers who engage in studies that require actual user log-ins should establish a protocol or policy regarding data access, storage, and retention similar to those in use at academic research institutions that engage human subjects.

Considerations Prior to Data Collection

The heading of this section could be applied to many research contexts, but it is especially true of eye tracking in e-commerce. Web pages are dynamic media with the capacity for highly variable user behavior compared to less interactive test stimuli (e.g., packages, advertisements). The fact that these are not just websites, but *e-commerce* websites adds further complexity, as it is difficult to realistically simulate the online purchase process with participants who may not be willing or able to make an actual purchase during a test situation. The challenge of evaluating visual behavior in this scenario can be daunting unless an analysis plan is generated before data collection begins.

It is also crucial to find the right participants that will represent real users. Only properly recruited participants (with similar needs, experience, and interest as actual users) can provide information on real search procedure and check-out process.

The first step in developing such an analysis plan is to understand the objectives of the research. Which specific pages are of interest? Which elements of the page are important to the purchase process? Are there specific products that are considered to be higher sales priorities? Which steps are associated with shopper abandonment? These and other questions must be carefully considered during study design in order to create tasks that are conducive to effective and efficient analysis. Otherwise, there is a danger of completing data collection only to discover that the goals of the research are not achievable within the study framework.

For example, imagine a study of an e-commerce site for air travel. Let's say that one of the goals of this research is to evaluate the extent to which online shoppers notice special low fares while searching for a flight. To address this objective, the researcher tests a sample of 20 participants as they purchase airfare on the site. However, after data collection, the researcher notices that some participants were never offered the special low fares because they were only applicable to certain destinations. These participants must be omitted from the analysis, as their experience of the pages of interest cannot be compared directly with those who encountered the special low fares during their airfare search.

The researcher's mistake was failure to account for the complexity of e-commerce interactions. There are many different paths that a shopper might take to complete a purchase, and the typical study does not include a large enough sample size to examine every permutation of user behavior. Thus, it is important to create well-defined tasks with well-defined start and end points to ensure that relevant pages are experienced in a comparable way by a large enough sample of participants to draw conclusions. In the previous example, the researcher might have been better served by identifying a specific travel location for the airfare search task. That simple detail turns a difficult analysis dilemma into a suitable approach to addressing a predefined study objective.

Approaches to Data Analysis of E-commerce Websites

There are countless ways to analyze and interpret numerical eye-tracking results. The most valuable approach to a given study is heavily dependent on the objectives of that research. There are, however, a few approaches that are typically taken for analysis of e-commerce sites. We will discuss those here:

- **Attention Distribution**: In other words, where do people look as they complete the purchase task? By analyzing the percentage of time allocated to each AOI on a given page, it is possible to determine which information is most important in the purchase decision and which information is not used. For example, what information is more heavily considered, the product detail or product description? Which row of results is viewed the most in the product search results? There are many different questions that can be addressed by considering the distribution of attention on a given page and a depiction like the one shown in Figure 8.13 is helpful in explaining attention distribution to clients.

FIGURE 8.13   Hypothetical percentage of visual attention allocated to different areas of an e-commerce homepage. This type of illustration is useful in determining how attention is allocated to different elements of the page over the entire interaction.

Product Description Page Elements	# of participants viewing element
Product Images	20 / 20 participants
Price	17 / 20 participants
Product Description	12 / 20 participants
Reviews	9/ 20 participants
Shipping Info	6 / 20 participants

FIGURE 8.14   A table demonstrating how many participants viewed various areas of interest.

■ **Element Viewing**: It is often useful to summarize how many participants viewed a given element (Figure 8.14), and how many people looked at a particular feature while completing the purchase. This is similar to attention distribution in that it is a measure of where people look, but it accounts for the fact that not all elements require the same level of visual engagement. For example, let's say only 1% of total attention was distributed to the product image. Does that mean that it was irrelevant to shoppers? Considering *element viewing* might reveal that although viewing time was relatively brief all participants looked at the image at least once. This is an important distinction.

■ **Perceptual Flow**: What is the typical order that page elements are seen? The dimension of time is an important consideration in eye-tracking analysis. It is not simply a question of *if* elements are visible; it is a question of *when* elements are visible. By analyzing the time to first viewing of page features it is possible to map the *perceptual flow* of the page (see Figure 8.15). Is the price of an expensive item seen

FIGURE 8.15   Hypothetical perceptual flow of a given web page—the most common order in which page elements are first viewed.

after the selling points? Is the *upsell* for a product seen in time to convince someone to take advantage before *adding to cart*? As any salesman will attest, it is important to control the sequence of the pitch, not just the content.

There are, of course, a great many other approaches that can be applied to eye-tracking research of e-commerce sites, including length of scan path, number of fixations, and duration of fixations just to name a few. These other metrics can be valuable, but are only applicable to specific research questions and certain types of web tasks. The three metrics described earlier can specifically be applied to most e-commerce testing scenarios.

Keep in mind that there is usually more to an eye-tracking study than eye-tracking data. Most analysis platforms allow recording and analysis of clicks, key presses, page visits, and task time. These data streams may be very important, depending on study objectives. In our air travel site example, the client will probably want to know about more than just visual behavior. They are likely to be interested in where users click, what they type into text fields, whether or not they could find acceptable flights, and what they thought of the site overall. Eye-tracking data cannot be used to directly address these questions, so other information must be considered. There are also physiological engagement (discussed in Chapter 4), workload, and appeal measures that may be included in the analysis. In today's UX industry, there are more ways than ever before to evaluate online shopping behavior.

Visualizing the Results of an E-commerce Study

The approaches described above are very useful in demonstrating trends in shopper visual behavior, although in many cases, *graphical displays* will make the case more persuasively than numbers. For example, it may be difficult for some clients to conceptualize the following research finding: *Users take an average of 17.5 seconds to notice the hotel offers on the lower part of an air travel homepage*. That is a very specific result, but what does it actually mean? To help put this information into context, one might include a gaze video example of a user demonstrating this behavior. Now the client has a numerical result *and* an accompanying visual example

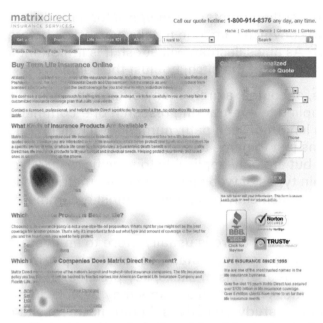

FIGURE 8.16 The heat map shows the fixations of all participants who completed a request form for a life insurance quote. The "About you and Health History" questions were viewed extensively, but the second column ("Your Quick Quote"/"Select a Term") was completed quickly as evidenced by the minimal visual attention. The upper branding and "Get Help" section were seldom viewed.

that illustrates *just how long 17.5 seconds* is. This combination of finding and illustration can be very effective in presenting the results of an e-commerce study.

Heat maps, gaze plots, and gaze video segments are the most commonly used visualizations in most fields of eye-tracking research. e-commerce is no exception. A heat map (Figure 8.16) is often used to illustrate findings related to *Attention Distribution*. As a snapshot of aggregated visual attention, the heat map is an extremely effective visualization. It is important, however, to keep in mind that this rendering of relative attention is limited. Some page elements require only a split second to process. They may be viewed frequently, but the heat map will not capture this because the overall visual attention was relatively brief.

Another limitation of the heat map is that it does not take into account the time course of the interaction. This is where a gaze plot can be most effective (Figures 8.17 and 8.18). Gaze plots are

FIGURE 8.17 The gaze plot shows that the user looked at the additional products offered on the right. This element is seen quickly when placed toward the top of the screen.

FIGURE 8.18 The gaze plots show that the user looked at the additional products offered on the bottom. This element is noticed much more slowly when placed at the bottom of the page.

often coupled with *Perceptual Flow* results. The metrics tell you the order in which elements are most often seen, and the gaze plot shows you what that looks like.

Many eye-tracking visualizations are static, but because e-commerce websites are dynamic in nature, a dynamic visualization is often required. Gaze replay video clips (either of a single participant or a group of participants) are often useful in demonstrating visual behavior as it relates to moving or changing onscreen content. For example, one might present a video clip of a user watching a promotional product video. Because the element of interest is a video, a static heat map or gaze plot may not be helpful in illustrating visual behavior. Gaze replay video is also valuable in demonstrating usability issues encountered during testing.

SO HOW DOES THIS HELP ME SELL SOCKS?

Throughout the process of study design, data collection, analysis, and reporting, the UX researcher must keep the study objectives firmly in mind. It is easy to get lost in statistical inference and finding the perfect gaze plot, to the extent that you forget the main purpose of the project—*to improve the means by which the website sells products*. So how do you make the leap from findings about the movement of a shopper's eye to conclusions about how to increase sales?

One path to actionability is through comparison. The best-case scenario for an e-commerce study is to test two versions of a site as a means of determining what works and what does not. Which version yields more attention to featured products? Which is associated with the quickest process from start through purchase? Which is associated with faster noticing of special offers? When an alternate version is not available, benchmarks from previous research or from a competitor's site can be used as a basis for drawing conclusions. In general, the presence of a comparative context is an excellent way of turning results into recommendations.

For example, in a recent comparative study, the visual attention and click behavior of shoppers was evaluated as they interacted with one of two versions of a product description page. In one design, the similar products were in a small box on the right (Figure 8.19, left), and in the other version, they were presented in an interactive carousel at the top of the page (Figure 8.19, right). By evaluating visual attention in an A–B comparison of these page versions, it was possible to reduce the main research objective to a pair of answerable questions.

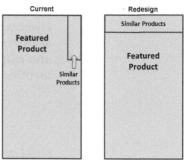

FIGURE 8.19   Two versions of the site were tested: the location of the "Featured Product" and "Similar Products" was different in each version.

We used eye-tracking data to assess if the Similar Products were more often seen on the redesigned page. Placing a page element in a higher and more centralized area of the page will not always result in increased visual attention. If the element is perceived to be irrelevant by the user, it might just as easily be ignored (as is often the case with banner advertisements in a similar page location). Here, we found that the Similar Products on the redesigned page did indeed capture and hold visual attention. The percentage fixated and total visit duration (shown in Figure 8.20) provided the evidence: users were significantly more likely to see this page element and spend significantly more time viewing it on the redesign compared with the current version. Another important difference was found in the sequence of visual attention. The Similar Products element was typically the first element seen on the redesigned page. On the current version it was seen significantly later (based on time to first fixation results).

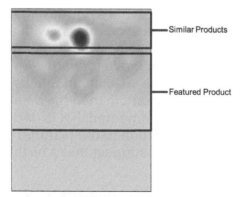

FIGURE 8.20   The heat map displays the first 10 seconds of visual attention of all participants interacting with the redesigned page. The Similar Products were heavily viewed as participants began interacting with this page.

Eye tracking is very useful in understanding information architecture. You immediately spot when a test person hesitates and can identify what needs to be adjusted, for instance, the terminology used in a menu.

Thor Fredrik Eie, User Experience Manager, Bouvet

Next we used eye-tracking data to assess if the placement of the Similar Products affects attention to the featured product. When a particular element is modified to increase visual salience, other page elements are likely to see decreases in visual salience. In this case, the product featured on the page was seen significantly later in the interaction on the redesign compared with the current version. Because participants focused heavily on the Similar Products as they first arrived at the page, it took them on average three times longer to make their way down to the main product (based on time to first fixation results). Participants were also less likely to see reviews, specifications, and the complete product description on the redesign (based on percentage fixated results). These results were red flags. One of the objectives of the research was to make sure that the featured product does not get lost in the shuffle as other products are presented more prominently.

So the new version pulled much more attention to Similar Products than the current version, but the product featured on the page was seen later, and some of the deeper product details often went completely unseen. While it may not be clear as to which page is best, the eye-tracking results provided site developers and retail decision makers with a detailed profile of shopper visual behavior. This information will help to determine whether or not to move forward with the redesigned page. If it is resolved that the visibility of Similar Products is the most important consideration, then the data suggest that the redesign should be implemented. If it is decided that the delay and reduction of attention to the featured product is unacceptable, then the data suggest that a further redesign is needed.

But what if there is no basis for comparison? What if the budget for the study allows only testing of one version of one site and benchmark data is unavailable? This is where eye tracking can be especially valuable. Let's say, for example, the client has identified a page in the purchase process that is associated with high shopper abandonment. Traditional usability research might demonstrate this fact, but eye tracking allows us to connect more directly with the shopper's experience. The UX researcher is able to report which specific elements are viewed immediately before abandonment, as well as which persuasive elements are ignored. Knowing that a page is associated with shopper abandonment is something of a black box; knowing that shoppers abandon after viewing the product star rating or when they fail to notice unique selling points is a much more informative and valuable finding.

Triangulation is key to creating actionable results. Just because you conduct an eye-tracking study does not mean that you cannot rely on other data streams. Follow-up questionnaires, interviews, mouse clicks, page visits, and any number of other results can be included alongside eye-tracking findings to generate useful conclusions. For example, to say that the *product filters on the left side of a product results page received 73% of attention* is not actionable alone. However, if you add to that finding the fact that shoppers only clicked the filters 12% of the time and described them as *not very helpful* on a post-test questionnaire, then you can say something more substantial, such as: S*hoppers are wasting a great deal of time looking at filters that they do not find useful.* From an isolated eye-tracking result, we now have a better understanding of the path toward improving the shopper experience.

CONCLUSION

Online transactions or e-commerce is becoming a greater aspect of the economic landscape, both in absolute terms and on a percentage basis. But unlike the dot-com bubble of a decade ago, this trend is not predicated on a new economic model per se, but rather on the same basic driving forces that have been around since antiquity. There are simply new avenues and approaches to buying and selling being introduced at a breathtaking pace. People still want things. Consumers want to buy things, and sellers want to satisfy this need. In e-commerce, all of these roles come together at the user interface of websites and mobile device applications. And, since the primary channel of communication at this interface is visual, it makes sense that a research method based on characterizing and interpreting visual behavior at the interface could be a powerful tool in understanding and optimizing the user experience. Eye tracking is a tool that is useful and unique in the insights it is capable of revealing about the processes of buying and selling online. And, ultimately, eye tracking is gaining greater acceptance and demonstrating greater practical value as practitioners become more adept at utilizing eye tracking technology and methods.

REFERENCES

Bhatti, N., Bouch, A., Kuchinsky, A., 2000. Integrating user-perceived quality into web server design. Computer Networks 33 (1/6), 1–16.

Chatham, B., 2002. Exposing customer experience flaws. Forrester Tech Strategy Report, December.

Cohen, J., 1999. The Grinch cometh. Neteffect, October.

Herschlag, M., 1998. Shopping the net. Time Magazine, July.

Loveday, L., Niehaus, S., 2007. Web Design for ROI: Turning Browsers into Buyers & Prospects into Leads. New Riders, Berkeley, CA.

Olsen, A., Wong, W., 2012. With eye tracking, you can't just wing it... workshop presented at the EyeTrackUX Conference, June 2012, Las Vegas, Nevada.

Pieters, R., Wedel, M. (Eds.), 2008. Visual Marketing: From Attention to Action. Lawrence Erlbaum Associates, New York, p. 52.

Romano Bergstrom, J., 2013, August 2. Testimonials can Increase the User Experience. Blog post, http://www.forsmarshgroup.com/index.php/blog/post/testimonials-can-increase-the-user-experience.

Vakratsas, D., Ambler, T., 1999. How advertising works: what do we really know? J. Market. 63, 26–43.

SOCIAL MEDIA

Lorenzo Burridge
Red C, Dublin, Ireland

INTRODUCTION

In February 2004, when Mark Zuckerberg first offered membership of Facebook to his fellow students at Harvard, YouTube was still a year away from launch; LinkedIn was a promising front room start-up with a few thousand members, and networking sites such as Friends Reunited, Bebo, and MySpace were already enjoying social media success with the concept of connecting networks of Internet users with common interests. However, the term "social media" had yet to become an everyday phrase.

In just a few intervening years, the importance of social media has skyrocketed. By 2012, Facebook achieved the milestone of 1 billion members worldwide, and social media sites were making a big impact socially, politically, and economically across the world. Unlike most other forms of websites, including informational and ecommerce sites, social media websites involve high levels of emotional engagement, and user behavior is markedly different. For businesses seeking to exploit social media to create more engaged relationships with their customers and markets, they must learn a new set of disciplines for dialog. In this chapter, we describe how eye tracking has been used to explore the fundamental structures underpinning user interaction with social media websites.

There are some unique challenges in creating effective web pages within the format constraints of a typical social network. Eye tracking reveals some powerful techniques for overcoming linear page structures.

Adrien Rowe, Red C Marketing, England

Why User Experience Testing of Social Media Is Important for Brands

An effective social media presence is increasingly viewed as an important part of a company's marketing mix, widely believed to influence perceptions about brands and propensity to purchase. Yet the instantaneous and transitory nature of conversations, the very personal nature of interactions, and the lack of control over content mean that traditional approaches to digital design may not be the most effective in social media.

Creating good feedback loops from research and testing is especially challenging. Traditional usability testing techniques can help with evaluating design concepts, but they are limited in providing insights on social media pages that contain high emotional engagement and frequently changing content. This is where eye tracking comes in.

Eye movements have been shown to be affected by both the visual design of the page and habitually preferred scan paths (a typical viewing path a user takes from the first point of fixation to the last; Josephson & Holmes, 2002). We can use eye tracking to identify how people view social media pages and discover what attracts and sustains their attention. We can also determine how they navigate the pages and what elements aid that navigation. This method has been shown to effectively identify high areas of interest and how they are approached (Habuchi et al., 2006). Eye tracking ultimately reveals the most efficient scan paths required for delivering maximum information and leading to a call to action.

Model of Visual Attention

The model in Figure 9.1 demonstrates how most users behave when they arrive at a web page. When users first see the web page, they begin by orienting themselves and looking for visual

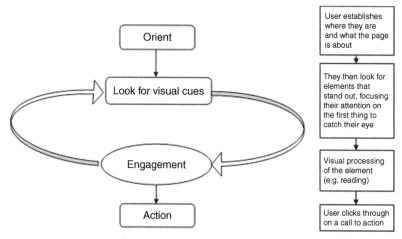

FIGURE 9.1   Model of visual attention for online communications.

cues to focus on. They are engaged in this element for as long as they deem necessary before either clicking a call to action, or repeating the visual cue search. The ultimate aim, of course, is getting that click-through.

Past eye-tracking research has investigated the use of images and text in a diverse range of media, showing each to receive varying levels of attention. Images are typically noticed first and take the least time to process. Text, on the other hand, requires more focus and attention and performs best at receiving attention when positioned in close proximity to other eye-catching elements (e.g., images, headlines, graphics; Rayner, 1998; Spool, 2006). The same principles are true in social media pages where it is essential to find the right positioning and balance for optimizing individual viewing behavior. For example, the food images on the Harvester Facebook page shown in Figure 9.2 are likely to get more visual attention than the text posts alone.

To date, there has been little eye-tracking research conducted on social media sites to understanding the user experience. One study from EyeTrackShop (2012) utilized eye tracking to investigate all major social media websites. While insightful, the sample was quite small ($N=30$) and the study required a more detailed, empirical approach in order to fully confirm the findings (to be discussed throughout this chapter).

Building on past eye-tracking and usability research, the current group of studies set out to test some of the top social

FIGURE 9.2   The Harvester Facebook page demonstrates how food images can be used to attract attention to text.

networking websites using eye-tracking methodology. It is one of the most exhaustive series of eye-tracking studies conducted in social networking to date, and the findings are discussed in detail throughout this chapter along with prior eye-tracking research in social media. We focus largely on Facebook, Google+, YouTube, and LinkedIn, social networking sites that rank highly in their member numbers and daily activity. These sites also share similar design layouts, but with notable differences, making them ideal for a direct comparison. It is clear that other social networks have since modeled design features on Facebook's features due to their subsequent adjustments in composition. For these reasons, the main focus in this chapter will be on Facebook, although the findings are still applicable to other websites.

FACEBOOK

Facebook is one of the most popular, continually expanding social networking services in the world, currently occupying over a billion active users (Figure 9.3). A typical user clocks around 30 minutes a day visiting the site, logging in an average of six times throughout that day to check out what is going on in their virtual network (statisticbrain.com, 2012).

With that much time devoted to such a task, it is essential that the site performs seamlessly in its design and functionality and with regular updates if the number of users is expected to continue growing. As discussed in Chapter 3, questionnaires and interviews are often used to discover user preferences. For Facebook, qualitative questionnaires

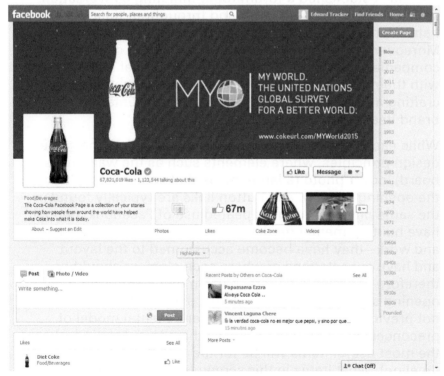

FIGURE 9.3 Coca-Cola's Facebook page delivers frequent updates and engaging images to increase traffic.

can help user experience (UX) researchers to understand more about users' page preferences, expectations, recall, and perceptions. In general, users typically favor pages that are well designed and pleasing to look at (Rodgers & Thorson, 2000). Moreover, a well-designed page is much more engaging and easy to navigate. Eye tracking can help UX researchers and designers identify ways to make pages engaging, pleasing, and easy to navigate, above and beyond traditional qualitative methods.

In recent years, Facebook has allowed companies to participate in the online phenomenon, offering them the opportunity to indirectly market their brands to other users. This trend took off very quickly, spawning a wave of interactive brand pages that formed a fresh conduit between brand and consumer. The availability of a plethora of content, including news feeds, polls, games, videos, and promotions meant individuals were now becoming an active consumer or "brand fan" by simply clicking the "Like" button for the page. This has established a forum for stimulating conversation among fans discussing the brand throughout their own network thus producing an invaluable tool for viral marketing. Moreover, by introducing this new marketing channel, companies were able to form a more personal relationship with their customers, reducing corporate anonymity and crafting a more emotionally engaged representation of the brand itself (Figure 9.4).

While each Facebook page is different, all follow the same design principles, where elements such as the wall (message board), cover photo (a large image that spans the width of the opening screen), and button links are typically found in the same place. Through repeated use of Facebook, people have built up mental models of how each page should look and work—they have become accustomed to the layout and have expectations of where each element should be, therefore adopting a general pattern of viewing from the opening screen. So when visiting a social network or website not previously encountered, the user's mental model of preconceived expectations allows them to determine where the most useful items will be for the task (e.g., apps or timeline). Most items in this screen tend to be scanned over quickly or viewed in the periphery, allowing users to decide

FIGURE 9.4   Miss Sixty's Facebook page includes a wide range of fashion-related content
that is noticed well and discussed among the fans.

what the page is about in mere seconds and whether to stay
on the page or move on.

In January 2012, Facebook underwent a complete design
overhaul with the introduction of the "timeline." This later
became a mandatory feature for all pages, which meant users
had to readjust their viewing patterns from the old layout and
develop a whole new model for viewing them. In the old design,
companies were able to create a storefront with clickable links
that resembled a "mini web page."

In the old version, fans could browse products and get
information directly from the brand page rather than going
to the website. Companies could also lock content, only
revealing it once a user clicked the "Like" button, as shown
in Figure 9.5—a clever tactic to increase followers. The main
downsides to this, however, were that this feature could actually

FIGURE 9.5 The old Facebook page for Red Bull includes an overlay that locks content until the user clicks the like button.

deter potential likes, as well as create an excuse for infrequent page updates from moderators (Figure 9.6).

The new timeline format, shown in Figure 9.7, has since brought a fresh look and feel to Facebook pages. Incorporating a large cover photo, image links, and a two-column timeline with wall posts, companies can now create more visually appealing and interactive pages than ever before. Furthermore, they have more control over the look and content displayed and can showcase their entire history over the timeline. Nonetheless, the new design has its setbacks. Pages are heavy in text content, and the two columns present posts in a linear format that create undirected viewing paths.

This new layout may be discouraging for users to read further down the page, and they could also miss out on crucial information. However, this could be overcome with the use of more imagery placed within text posts, and in diagonal placement—a point we will come back to later.

Research Findings

Eye-tracking data enables UX researchers to assess the main areas of interest within Facebook brand pages, highlighting fixation points and durations while illustrating individual gaze paths from the initial fixation to the last. When cross-comparing

FIGURE 9.6   Gaze plot illustrates how user attention becomes less directed after the cover photo section due to the lack of engaging imagery.

fixation counts with fixation durations, researchers can identify areas that generate interest and those that cause confusion.

The basic structure of each Facebook page is relatively similar in terms of where key elements, such as the cover photo, links, wall posts, and ads can be found. Therefore, individuals already have a clear and systematic approach to navigating Facebook pages before they have even seen the page. The cover photo is not only one of the largest elements on the page, it is also at the very top of the opening screen, so unsurprisingly, it tends to be the initial fixation point for users, as shown by the low numbers

FIGURE 9.7   Gaze plot on the Asos Facebook page clearly showing how diagonal placement of images helps to guide the user down the page to notice more content.

(early fixations) in Figure 9.8. This is consistent with results found in the EyeTrackShop study (2012), where the cover photo was also the main attraction (Figure 9.9).

From here, users orient themselves to the surrounding elements (e.g., company name, logo, and links) to discover further what the page is about. This normally occurs in three stages: encoding the visual stimulus, peripheral sampling, and preparation of where to look next (Viviani, 1990)—see model in Figure 9.10.

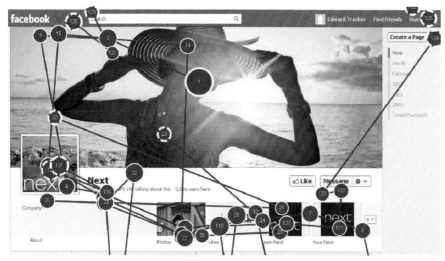

FIGURE 9.8 Gaze plot demonstrates how effective cover photos can attract attention and lead users from one element to the other.

FIGURE 9.9 Gaze plot showing that the cover photo guides user gaze to the rest of the page to other attractive elements.

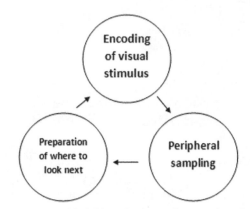

FIGURE 9.10   Model for orienting and processing of a page.

As is common with banner ads on web pages (discussed in Chapter 2), the ads on the right side of a Facebook page are either noticed last or simply ignored, as users already expect them to be there and have since become "blind" to them (see Figure 9.11). This finding is also consistent with previous studies that have identified frequent web users' awareness of ads and their familiar positions on a page. Picked up in their peripheral field of vision, they now instinctively know not to focus on them,

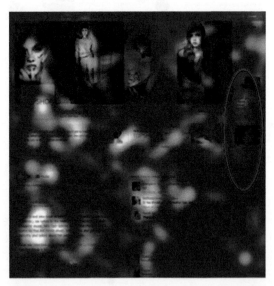

FIGURE 9.11   Gaze opacity map demonstrating how little attention is given to the ads compared to the rest of the page.

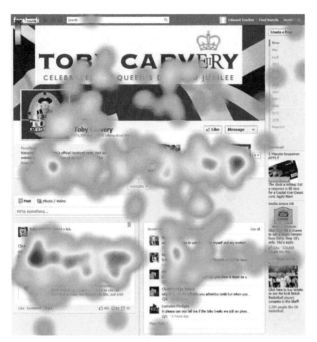

FIGURE 9.12   Heat map demonstrating how imagery can help lead users to other information and read any neighboring text.

as they are likely to be a distraction to their task at hand (Drèze & Hussherr, 1999). This is, however, more prevalent in profile pages than brand pages (EyeTrackShop, 2012), which suggests that when visiting a brand page, users are more likely to notice ads as they are more relevant to the page itself (Figure 9.12).

Each element within a stimulus (e.g., headline, body copy, image) receives differing levels of attention for encoding, and so each is attended to via an individual systematic approach (Royden et al., 1992). Put simply, whatever catches users' attention first, along with their own typical web viewing behavior, allows users to extract information more effectively for both task demands and further orientation of the page.

Moving down the page, the two-column structure of the wall presents elements in "sound bytes" (small blocks of either image/video/text information), separating everything into its own individual box. While previous tests indicate this as a preferred method of viewing information (Rowe & Burridge, 2012), the columns leave the viewing path more

FIGURE 9.13   Using elements effectively to guide attention to key areas.

open to diversion. In other words, the user is not being directly influenced to follow a particular pathway and thus may miss important information on the page (Figure 9.13).

As stated earlier, web viewing behavior is largely determined by previously viewed pages, causing users to develop a schema for each page they view and its defining characteristics (Herder, 2005; Habuchi et al., 2006). This enables users to quickly locate and identify useful information that is relevant to their objective while disregarding information that is not relevant. With this in mind, key information is recognized better when placed in the areas it is expected (e.g., logo or site links; Buscher et al., 2009).

Effective design structure is more evident in pages that employ the use of a diagonal framework. These pages have a good balance of images and text that are presented diagonally across columns, breaking up cognitive deterrents such as large blocks of text that require more work to process. This type of design is generally preferred by users as it is the most engaging and visually appealing. These pages are easier to process due to the neater sequential structure.

Not only do the images provide easy-to-process, light information, but they also serve to direct users to a piece of text that might otherwise have been missed or ignored (Wedel & Pieters, 2000). This type of structure also performs best for engaging users down the page, but also more importantly, these types of pages are much preferred to those that are unbalanced or particularly text heavy (Rowe & Burridge, 2012).

Making Elements Work for Their Place on the Page

Images nearly always get noticed regardless of content (Hughes et al., 2003). Not only are they some of the most salient elements on a page, but users are easily drawn to them via the peripheral field of vision. Eye-tracking studies have continuously shown that images consistently draw in users' gazes and lead them to read any neighboring text (Wedel & Pieters, 2000; Duchowski, 2003). This is demonstrated in Figure 9.14—the images attract users' attention to the text.

Facebook pages consist of mainly text posts, but when users incorporate a thumbnail image, the chances of reading the post significantly increases. Furthermore, images of people making direct eye contact (Figure 9.15) are noticed even faster, causing users to fixate them instinctively more than any other element.

In order to keep interest alive for a brand page, companies need to post frequently so that news appears in fans' live feed. But to encourage visits to the brand page, each post needs to be as good as the last, if not better, to generate interest and more potential fans. Promotions, competitions, and celebrity endorsements all perform well because they stimulate peer-to-peer conversation.

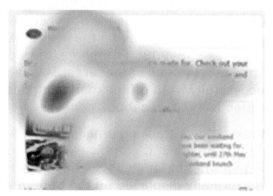

FIGURE 9.14   In the Harvester page, the use of thumbnail images increase levels of attention in text posts very effectively.

FIGURE 9.15   Eye contact imagery is one of the most effective attention grabbers.

Due to the column layout in the Facebook timeline, posts made each month are kept together, and those from previous months are hidden from view. This pathway interruption in the design pattern might not only cause interference in attention, but it may not even be seen among those who skim the opening screen. Creating engagement on a frequent basis with relevant posts is essential to keeping brand fans scrolling to view more posts and extend the dialog duration.

Content Hot Spots: Maximize Content Exposure Using Attractors, Directors, and Informers

Content should be eye catching, but in order to sustain attention, it also needs to be relevant. In general, no benefit is gained from "window dressing" (images that are only used for aesthetic appeal); they may end up diverting attention away from the areas one is trying to promote. When using images of people making eye contact, a user's gaze can be effectively directed to particular areas by having the eyes look toward another area (Figures 9.16–9.18). From here, the viewer follows the gaze and then takes notice of that area. This technique, transposed successfully from offline marketing design strategy, works just as effectively on Facebook pages.

In previous studies of eye-tracking emails (Rowe & Burridge, 2012), results found image and graphic elements to perform well in directing attention to hot spots while conveying snippets of information. Normally displayed on top of or in between elements, the same technique can be used within Facebook timeline posts. Due to the design constraints, however,

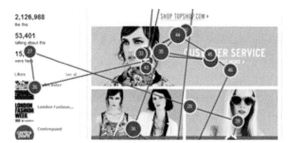

FIGURE 9.16   Individual gaze plots show how directional eye contact is followed to where it is looking.

FIGURE 9.17   The Burberry page uses a lot of irrelevant imagery and a little text. The end result is very little visual attention over the page.

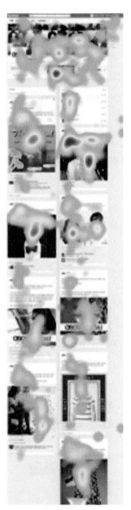

FIGURE 9.18   Asos uses diagonal frameworks, images, and graphics to direct user gaze to each post in turn.

strategic positioning is vital in driving attention to key areas. Diagonal frameworks are an effective way around this, and are commonly generated by frequent posting. This type of design is generally preferred by users as they are the most engaging and visually appealing (Fusaro, 1998; Andrews & Coppola, 1999). This design also makes it much easier to process due to the neater sequential structure.

The moving of elements such as number of likes, events, and apps to the top center of the page has improved their saliency on the page dramatically. As shown on the left of Figure 9.19, in

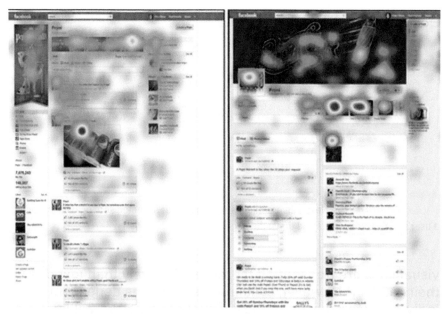

FIGURE 9.19   More attention is given to the additional links in new pages on the right as they use images and are easier to locate.

the old design, these elements were hardly noticed on the right-hand side, but now (right side of Figure 9.19) they receive just as much attention as the company logo. The whole area directly below the cover photo is now one that stands out and helps guide users to the information. This is a great example of how careful placement of elements can achieve excellent results.

Informational hot spots might include sales, promotions, new products, videos, recipes, etc., providing useful information to fans and thus attracting and sustaining their attention. These types of content are expected, preferred, and attended to the most across different pages (Figure 9.20).

Interactive elements (e.g., polls, games, videos) are also hot spots for visual attention and engagement as the user can take part in an activity rather than just look at a piece of information. Studies have frequently reported higher levels of interest in these areas as well as longer fixations, making them useful means to encourage page viewing and likes (EyeTrackShop, 2012; Rowe & Burridge, 2012).

Smart & Cappel (2003) proposed that the richness of information (e.g., graphic and multimedia stimuli) means that

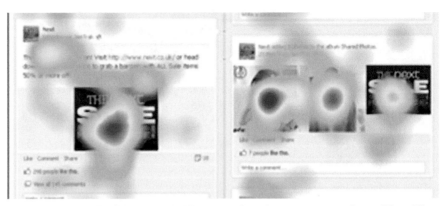

FIGURE 9.20   The Next sale graphic element is a clear attractor, serving well in guiding a user's gaze across posts and down the page.

visual cues are transmitted far more effectively than text due to their saliency. However, sustaining attention is dependent on individual learning styles, be it visual or verbal. Verbal learners are more attentive to text-based stimuli as opposed to visual learners who respond better to multimedia. So in order to appeal to both types of users, a careful balance of visual and verbal cues is required.

Attracting attention itself is easy. Using that attractor to direct attention takes a little more planning. Using eye contact imagery and graphic placement helps to achieve this, and if utilized throughout, the chances of leading to a click-through are dramatically increased. The idea is to attract, direct, and inform with the page elements until the user is taken to a call to action (Figure 9.21).

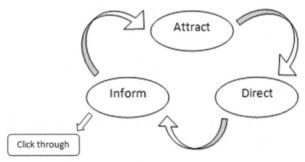

FIGURE 9.21   Model for using elements effectively to direct attention to the point of click-through.

Cover Crafting: Getting the Most Out of Cover Photos

In any online communication, the opening screen is extremely important when it comes to getting a user interested enough to stay on the page and keep reading. However, in Facebook, the rigid structural composition can be a limitation in designing original and effective opening screens. One of the most important elements "above the fold" of the page (see Chapter 2) is the cover photo—consistently the first element viewed—that is essentially a visual representation of the brand itself.

Facebook places a number of constraints on designers with the cover photo. For example, companies cannot advertise within the cover photo or display links or promotional information. Therefore, brands have to come up with more innovative ways of utilizing this feature and maximizing its potential to draw in fans. Bold, colorful images, as shown in Figure 9.22, work most effectively in attracting and sustaining attention. They also perform well in cleverly directing visual attention to the logo, and from there, to the brand name and site links.

Out with the Old In with the….Timeline?

The old Facebook design was quite simple in its layout, typically featuring a small profile image in the top left, text links below, and a main wall in the center for posts (Figure 9.23). This format allowed for companies to create a storefront that had clickable image and graphic links for exploring other pages. It had the look and feel of a mini web page or marketing email that could take users directly

FIGURE 9.22   Creating bold, colorful cover photos with directional images help to instantly attract attention and guide it down the page.

FIGURE 9.23   The Facebook page is confusing for users—mixing images of various sizes that are ambiguous in nature causes attention to derail.

to their websites. Scan paths overall were quite dispersed over the page. Attention was focused in many areas, and more time was spent on elements due to the smaller size of the page.

Much of this changed with the new timeline, meaning a new viewing approach was adopted by users. Rather than looking directly to the top left at the start (a behavior that is common in web viewing), focus is more centralized, due to the cover photo. Furthermore, the two columns split the normal gaze pattern and cause users to look to the first element that stands out to them (Figure 9.24).

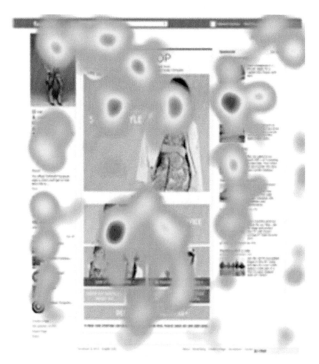

FIGURE 9.24 The old Topshop page is smaller but not too busy, making it clear to navigate; thus every element is attended to.

This not only breaks the traditional Facebook layout and viewing behavior but also the familiar structure that people instinctively attempt to impose from viewing other web pages. It is not so much about getting users to notice everything but to become aware of elements that are most salient. This is where the new design may be detrimental in generating sustained attention and interest to the point of a click-through (Figure 9.25).

Attention to the ads on the right side has also changed with the new design. In the old design, about a third of the page was taken up with ads comprising thumbnail images and accompanying text. In the new design, both the number of ads and the amount of space they occupy has been drastically reduced, thus significantly reducing the attention they receive. This in turn allows for more focus on the company page while reducing distractive elements, but it may have a detrimental effect on Facebook ad response rates.

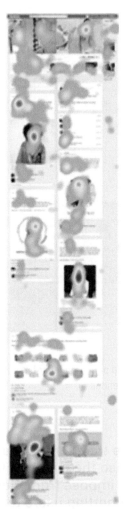

FIGURE 9.25 Elements are still noticed in the new design, but attention is less concentrated as the content is excessive and more dispersed.

Summary for Facebook

While there are elements that work in both the old and new Facebook brand page designs, to perform more efficiently, they must conform to user requirements and expectations (Moeller, 2001; Buscher et al., 2009). If users are going to land on a page they need a good reason to set up base and read it. You need to give the fans what they want!

Social networking sites are so fast-moving that traditional research methods just don't cut it. Eye tracking gives us the insight we need to design better social pages. There is so much "emotional investment" in a Facebook page that eye tracking is by far the most effective methodology to really understand how social elements influence perceptions.

Adrien Rowe, Red C Marketing, England

GOOGLE+

Google+ is another social networking service that arrived later on our screens (June 2011) with ambitions to offer a different experience than Facebook, and with greater integration with other Google products. Reaching over 500 million users by the end of 2012, the social network has not yet achieved anything like the frequency of use of Facebook. Initially the page design was not that different from Facebook, with similar elements placed in the same locations such as the profile picture and message wall. Subsequent development has resulted in a more unique interface, while still retaining some of the features that work so well on Facebook pages (see Figure 9.26).

The standard message wall is a single column as opposed to two and has the same posting format as Facebook, which allows for image and video posts with a comment box below. Google+ also has incorporated a cover photo to showcase brands and a profile picture positioned on the top right of the page. It even loads like the Facebook timeline, revealing past posts as the user scrolls. Additional links are all neatly displayed in one column on the far left of the page, which makes locating information easier for users. In general, Google+ pages appear to have been constructed with Facebook's design in mind, but it is much simpler to navigate, leaving little cause for distraction as a user reads through the page (Figure 9.27).

So what does eye tracking reveal about the design of Google+ pages? The layout is not too different from the original Facebook layout and therefore generates the same sporadic hot spots. The elements on the page are not cluttered and

FIGURE 9.26 Similar to Facebook, a cover photo and wall are used in Google+pages, but menus and links are different.

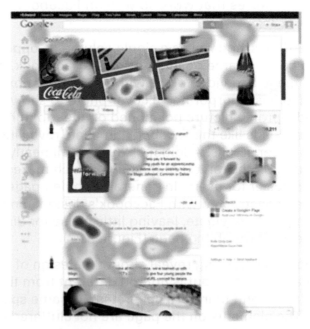

FIGURE 9.27 Attention is much more dispersed over the Google+ page, similar to the old design of Facebook pages.

are clearly defined in their own particular space on the white background, so each one is easy to find, and virtually all achieve good visibility.

The cover photo is the first thing that users notice, which is typically followed by the logo on the right. Thumbnails work like graphic devices and help to direct attention to the text posts. The single column wall makes visual scanning much simpler as users do not have to keep switching between two, which can be distracting.

Summary for Google+

Google + pages resemble the layout of the old Facebook pages, which makes navigation easy for users since they use their mental model that they have already built for this structure. Google + also makes good use of newer features such as the cover photo and sidebar links. It seems that while Facebook is leading in social networking, there are still elements that do not perform as well as Google+. It is possible then that Google has taken the best performing features from Facebook and negated the poorer performers, such as the dual-column timeline. They have taken a formula that works and added their own unique take on a page that maximizes usability navigation.

YOUTUBE

In 2005, YouTube was launched, allowing users to upload, view, and share videos all over the world. It was a huge hit and soon enough, there were millions of people sharing content on the site at the click of a button. As the site's popularity grew, like Facebook brand pages, it too started to allow brand advertising as well as a wide and diverse range of YouTube channels (Figure 9.28).

YouTube channels provided a way for users to display all of their video content in one place that other users subscribe to and comment on. It has become so successful that every day, millions of users continue to discover the weird and wonderful from all around the globe, bringing fame and fortune to the otherwise unnoticed (Figure 9.29).

More recently, YouTube has launched personal pages, where one user can have videos displayed with channel

FIGURE 9.28 YouTube pages include a main wall where content is presented and updated according to personal preferences.

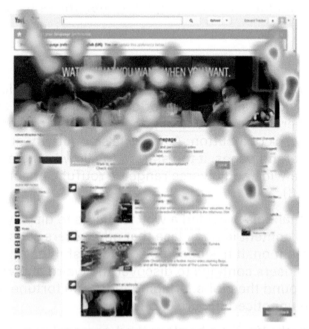

FIGURE 9.29 As most information can be found near the top of the page, there is more dispersion of attention as viewers are able to find everything in the opening screen.

subscriptions and share content among friends just as easily as other social networking services. A typical page will have video clips with descriptions, where a message wall would normally be. Additional links can be found on the left side, and recommendations are found on the right. The pages work similar to that of Facebook and Google+, but the content is purely video and comments, customizable through preference settings and recommendations based on a user's personal network and past viewings.

Eye-tracking results demonstrate that the YouTube pages perform very well in terms of attention and ease of navigation and use. The large ad at the top is noticed first and works much like a Facebook cover photo. The links on the left and right are easy to locate and make navigation a breeze.

Like the thumbnails on other pages, the screen captures help in attracting visual attention, which then leads users to read the description. The heat map clearly demonstrates quite a balanced level of attention among elements, which contributes considerably to its overall performance.

Summary for YouTube

This page performs especially well for the content involved. The top ad is the first thing users look at; however, since it is irrelevant to the content, it can be quite distracting and is often ignored. The content area makes good use of thumbnail images, which attract users' attention. Navigation links are easy to find, and the addition of recommendations on the right allows users to connect to a wide range of material. So for videos and YouTube channels, this format is ideal for sharing content over a wide network. Information is uncluttered and easy to navigate, making the page a great performer for visual content.

LINKEDIN

LinkedIn is the social network for working professionals. Hosting the platform for over 200 million users worldwide, it has become the go-to place for promoting one's own credentials while branching out into other professional circles. The site allows users to create a profile similar to an online resume for the eyes of potential employers and colleagues, while showcasing their work and career history among "links" or "connections" (Figure 9.30).

FIGURE 9.30 LinkedIn utilizes the wall space but also introduces a right-side feature that displays relevant information, ads, and other links.

In terms of the page layout, similar to Facebook and Google+, the central area contains a message wall where updates and related information are presented to the user when they sign in. This, like the other social network sites, can consist of images, videos, and text posts that can be commented on by other users (see Figure 9.31).

The right side of the page also includes items that may be of interest to the user, based on their profile and preferences. Sections include "People You May Know" which users can peruse, select, and add to their networks; related ads; jobs; groups; and companies as a way to market to specifically targeted demographics (Figure 9.32).

The largest element on the page is the recommended news feed, which consists of multiple images and headlines. This area is typically noticed first and also receives the most attention. The wall below feeds updates from links and groups and are usually the second element that users see. The links on the right also tend to receive a lot of attention.

Profile pages themselves are responded to in a similar manner but with a little more direction. Individuals notice the profile

FIGURE 9.31   Most attention is given to the main images, and the layout is separated into two defined sections, which helps users find what they want.

picture, name, and job title first, as they are positioned at the normal starting position when viewing web pages (EyeTrackShop, 2012). They are also the most salient elements at the top of the page.

The structure itself is easy to follow: listing all credentials on the left and other information, such as links and people you may know, on the right; thus, users attend to them accordingly. The simplicity in design makes for a very usable interface, and users rarely find themselves lost or distracted from their task.

Summary for LinkedIn

LinkedIn follows a similar layout to other social networking sites but with a few small additions that help to encourage more interest in the page. The main space is occupied by a collage of several image posts, each one with its own caption. Moreover, the right sidebar includes a variety of posts that are relatable to the user. It is these areas that receive the most attention due to the relevant content and their positioning on the page.

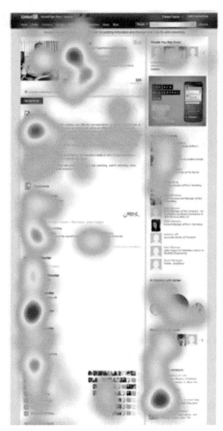

FIGURE 9.32 Personal pages differ significantly as attention starts with the profile image and leads down to user credentials before the right-hand information.

Relevance is key here. If the reader is disinterested or cannot relate, they tend to ignore the material and move on.

Personal pages follow a very direct structure presenting personal information in the larger left-hand column, stressing its importance. Related information such as links, groups, and ads are on the right side and are attended to second.

THE FUTURE FOR SOCIAL MEDIA

Social media networks are constantly evolving and dynamic digital communities, where emotionally engaged users are in the driver's seat for the first time in the development of the

Internet. And while technological advances play a part, all eye-tracking research to date suggests that consumer-led evolution will dictate the next wave of changes in the dynamics of the social marketplace. The present research points to three key trends that are important to sustain growth for the current leading social media networks:

1. *Increased use of rich content will be important to keep demanding consumers connected.* Users are attracted to engaging content, including images, videos, and interactive content (e.g., games, contests).
2. *Personalization and customization are crucial attention drivers in all the social networks.* Social media that continues to prosper will be those that offer increasingly enhanced personalization. Brands wishing to succeed in social media environments will embrace personalization or risk becoming "out of place."
3. *Social media content is not passively consumed—interactivity is an essential part of the attraction.* Most social media discussed in this chapter require dialog and interaction to maintain users' attention and encourage frequent visits. Interactivity is key to emotional engagement and will drive future development.

TEN THINGS EVERY COMMUNITY MANAGER SHOULD KNOW

1. Make Elements Work for Their Place on the Page

Every element should have a function, whether it is to serve as an attractor, director, or informer. If it is on the page it should be properly placed and contribute in some way to the overall objective.

2. Content Hot Spots—Maximize Content Exposure Using Attractors

Attractors can be bold headlines or images that instantly catch users' eyes in order to help them absorb other information. Attractors should be quick to process and should not distract from the ultimate goal.

3. Get the Most Out of Cover Photos

Cover photos should be exploited to serve the page and the user. Portray a positive representation of the brand and encourage consumers to read more about it.

4. Give the Fans What They Want

Capturing and sustaining attention on social media pages with rigid format constraints is a challenge. Keeping fans interested enough to make a return visit requires frequent updates of relevant and interesting posts.

5. Strategically Position Content

When designing a page or making a new post, think about the layout as a whole and place new content in strategic positions that engage the periphery. Eye tracking shows that in this way, more content is noticed and attended to while directing attention to desired actions, aiding overall to the user experience.

6. Use Constructs That Are Familiar to Users

Creating virtual signposts to aid navigation fosters positive engagement from users. Use familiar digital constructs to help users orient themselves on the page and assist in rapid absorption of information (e.g., left-side navigation menus or top menu bars).

7. Use Imagery to Highlight Key Information

On copy-rich pages that are common to social media, relevant images can be immensely effective in drawing and directing attention. Thumbnails within text posts make the text more salient and encourage users to read it to discover what the image is about. Each image should be purposeful and relevant to the content and interesting to the reader.

8. Consider Page Structure

Most social networking sites allow for posts on the main page in the message wall, which has particular constraints to the layout. Frequent posts with images as well as text help to break up the mundane heavy text and create visual pathways to lead users to more important areas such as calls to action.

9. Personalize Elements

Personalized elements perform very well at instantly attracting attention and generating positive engagement. Used effectively, personalization helps to increase repeat visits and possible click-throughs.

10. Use Ads "Right"

Users have become increasingly familiar with ad placements on the right side of the page on social networks. This can work well if they are relevant to the users but if not, they can easily be ignored. Successful ad placement demands relevancy and integration within the high interest areas to prevent users from ignoring them.

CONCLUSION

While images are key in portraying a company's impression on the public, they also play a huge part in directing user attention to information that might otherwise be missed due to numerous text-heavy posts. Increasing the use of images and graphics and placing them strategically about the page can enhance engagement. Moreover, this approach helps to break up the text-heavy posts and create a more positive position for the brand. If diagonal frameworks cannot be generated, the use of a one-column format provides a much clearer direction for the eye to follow and reduce uncertainty.

There has been little eye-tracking research carried out on social media, yet the findings suggest there is still much to learn. After all, while eye tracking has been around for many years, social media is relatively new and constantly evolving. Past research has shown how eye tracking can be used to learn how users visually interact with media and has since given the insight to make design adjustments. These principles can be carried over to social media platforms and tested to create the optimal performing page that keeps users interested and coming back for more.

In future research, it would be beneficial to compare Twitter, principally a text based social network, to Pinterest, which is image dominant. As images are processed much faster than text, it would be useful to discover how people are drawn to Twitter feeds. The content would also be relevant as users choose to follow whomever they like, but eye-catching elements are few. The advantage to Twitter feeds is that each post is limited in length, reducing the user's processing speed. Conversely, Pinterest is packed full of images, so users scan material quite quickly. Pinterest posts are also related to user preferences, so there should not be too many irrelevant posts to distract users.

REFERENCES

Andrews, T., Coppola, D., 1999. Idiosyncratic characteristics of saccadic eye movements when viewing different visual environments. Vision Res. 39, 2947–2953.

Buscher, G., Cutrell, E., Morris, M.R., 2009. What you see When you're Surfing? Using eye Tracking to Predict Salient Regions of web Pages, Boston, MA.

Drèze, X., Hussherr, F., 1999. Internet advertising: is anybody watching? J. Interact. Market. 17, 8–23.

Duchowski, A.T., 2003. Eye Tracking Methodology: Theory and Practice. Springer-Verlag, London.

EyeTrackShop, 2012. Here's What People Look at on Facebook Brand Pages. Retrieved May 18, 2013 from, http://mashable.com/2011/12/14/eyetracking-facebook-brand-pages/.

Fusaro, R., 1998. More sites use E-mail for marketing. Computerworld 32, 51–54.

Habuchi, Y., Takeuchi, H., Kitajima, M., 2006. The influence of web browsing experience on web-viewing behavior. In: Eye Tracking Research & Applications (ETRA) Symposium. ACM, New York, pp. 47.

Herder, E., 2005. Characterizations of user Web revisit behaviour. In: Buscher, G., Cutrell, E., Morris, M.R. (Eds.), What you see When you're Surfing? Using eye Tracking to Predict Salient Regions of Web Pages, Boston, MA.

Hughes, A., Wilkens, T., Wildemuth, B.M., Marchionini, G., 2003. Text or pictures? An eyetracking study of how people view digital video surrogates. In: Proceedings of CIVR.

Josephson, S., Holmes, M.E., 2002. Attention to repeated images on the world-wide web: another look at scanpath theory. Behav. Res. Meth. Instrum. Comput. 34, 539–548.

Moeller, E.W., 2001. The latest Web trend: usability? In: IEEE International Professional Communication Conference, Proceedings, pp. 151–158.

Rayner, K., 1998. Eye movements in reading and information processing: 20 years of research. Psychol. Bull. 124, 372–422.

Rodgers, S., Thorson, E., 2000. The interactive advertising model: how users perceive and process online ads. J. Interact. Advert. 1 (1), 42–63.

Rowe, A., Burridge, L., 2012. 10 inbox secrets: what eye-tracking reveals about designing more effective emails. The Institute of Direct and Digital Marketing.

Royden, C.S., Banks, M.S., Crowell, J.A., 1992. The perception of heading during eye movements. Nature, 583–585.

Smart, K.L., Cappel, J., 2003. Assessing the response to and success of email marketing promotions. Issues in Information Systems, 309–315.

Spool, J.M., 2006. Image Links vs. Text Links. Message archived at, User Interface Engineering. Retrieved on June 5, 2011 from, http://www.uie.com/brainsparks/2006/01/16/image-links-vs-text-links/.

statisticbrain.com, 2012. Social Networking Statistics. Browser Media, Socialnomics, MacWorld. Retrieved May 28, 2013 from, http://www. statisticbrain.com/social-networking-statistics/.

Viviani, P., 1990. Eye movements in visual search: cognitive, perceptual and motor control aspects. In: Kowler, E. (Ed.), Eye Movements and Their Role in Visual and Cognitive Processes. Elsevier Science Publishers, Amsterdam, pp. 353–393.

Wedel, M., Pieters, R., 2000. Attention capture and transfer in advertising: brand, pictorial, and text-size effects. J. Market. 68, 36–50.

statisticbrain.com, 2012. Social Networking Statistics. Brower Media. Socialnomics, MacWorld. Retrieved May 23, 2013 from, http://www.statisticbrain.com/social-networking-statistics.

Viviani, R., 1990. Eye movements in visual search: cognitive perspective and motor control aspects. In: Kowler, E. (Ed.), Eye Movements and Their Role in Visual and Cognitive Processes. Elsevier Science Publishers, Amsterdam, pp. 353-393.

Wedel, M., Pieters, R., 2000. Attention capture and transfer in advertising: brand, pictorial, and text-size effects. J. Market. 63, 36-50.

10

MOBILE

Jibo He[1], Christina Siu[1], Barbara Chaparro[1], and Jonathan Strohl[2]

[1]Wichita State University, Wichita, KS, USA

[2]Fors Marsh Group, Arlington, VA, USA

INTRODUCTION

The population of mobile users is growing at a rapid pace. In 2013, approximately 56% of U.S. adults (18 and older) were smartphone owners (Smith, 2013). That is a 10% increase from the 46% who owned a smartphone in 2012. More U.S. adults now own a smartphone than a standard cell phone. Annual smartphone sales have surpassed PC sales, and the gap only continues to widen (Canalys, 2012).

The use of tablet computers is growing even more rapidly than smartphones. In 2013, approximately 34% of U.S. adults reported owning a tablet computer, almost twice as many as the 18% of U.S. adults who owned a tablet in 2012 (Zickuhr, 2013). Steve Jobs predicted in 2010 that tablet computers would overtake computers for everyday usage. He compared this transition to when Americans turned in their trucks for cars as America became more urbanized. This prediction is becoming a reality. A worldwide sales forecast shows that tablets are expected to easily exceed notebook computers for 2013 (Himuro & Shim, 2013).

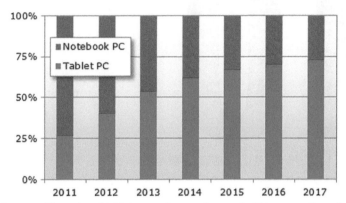

FIGURE 10.1   The sales of tablet computers are forecasted to surpass the sales of notebook computers in 2013. (From Himuro & Shim, 2013.)

As mobile devices continue to proliferate, the markets for mobile apps and mobile media will continue to grow. The experiences that these mobile products deliver to users will be a huge determinant for their market share (see Figure 10.1).

The mobile device boom has had a far reaching impact on many markets and industries. A strong user experience has been critical to the success of the organizations that only produce mobile products, whether they are mobile devices, apps, or media. However, the mobile user experience has also become integral to the success of companies in traditional industries. In the banking industry for example, 32% of U.S. adults transacted banking business on their mobile phones in 2012 (Fox, 2013). This demonstrates the number of customers who are influenced by their bank's mobile apps and websites. A strong mobile user experience gives a bank's customer a reason to stay with them and not switch to a competitor.

While a mobile user experience is clearly important for retailers that only operate online, the mobile user experience is also important for in-store retailers as well. A study of in-store shoppers during the 2012 holiday season reported that 28% of cell phone owners used their phone while in a store to look up reviews of a product to help decide if they should purchase (Smith, 2013). A store that provides their customers with a strong mobile app to augment their shopping experience is likely to be at an advantage over the store that does not (see Figure 10.2).

As companies continue to place more emphasis on the mobile user experience, effective methods to evaluate mobile product design become even more important. To design better mobile

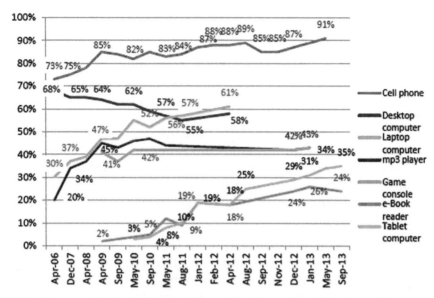

FIGURE 10.2   Adult gadget ownership over time: Percentage of American adults ages 18+ who own each device. Source: Pew Internet surveys 2006–2013.

user experiences, we need methods that can evaluate the unique features of mobile products. Usability testing (Chapter 3) is arguably the most effective method for the summative evaluation of designs. By using this technique, we can garner data about user performance, efficiency, and satisfaction with a mobile product. Until recently, eye tracking was limited to providing insights about designs on a traditional desktop computer display. However, with recent advancements in technology, eye tracking can now also be used during the usability testing of designs for mobile devices. Eye tracking provides a big advantage for organizations seeking to better understand and improve their mobile products.

In this chapter, we discuss the mounting pressure for organizations to improve their mobile products and how eye tracking can be used to drive exceptional experiences with mobile. We provide case studies in which eye tracking was used to test mobile device products and discuss the unique insights that eye tracking provided. We then examine what has made the eye tracking of mobile products possible and the recent technological improvements that have allowed for it. We conclude by predicting the future directions of eye tracking for mobile product testing.

WHAT CAN EYE TRACKING TELL US ABOUT MOBILE DESIGN?

Eye tracking is a valuable tool when examining the mobile user experience because it can tell us where attention is distributed when users interact with mobile devices. Eye-movement measurements provide user experience (UX) practitioners with practical information to help improve the usability of mobile products. Just as with websites and other user interfaces, eye tracking of mobile products helps us to understand confusing design elements, poor locations of important links and messages, and inefficient layouts. Eye-tracking findings help us make better design decisions.

Where users look, where they do not look, and how long they look at a location are important pieces of information for the development of mobile products. Eye movement measures, such as fixation duration, gaze duration, time to first fixation, number of fixations, re-fixations, scan paths, and even pupillometry (discussed in Chapter 4) can all be used to describe users' interactions with mobile devices. For example, eye-tracking fixation data may reveal that users do not look at an important image or text that we want them to see, which can indicate a design flaw. Often this means that the image or text is not salient enough or may be placed in an improper location. A high number of re-fixations in an area of interest on a mobile device may indicate confusion with how to advance to the next step in the task. And longer fixation durations can indicate that the information is not understood or, conversely, that it is interesting to the user. Like most types of data, eye-tracking data should not be used in isolation; it must be used in concert with other data to draw valid conclusions. Eye-tracking data often make our conclusions more accurate, but they can also reveal unique and valuable findings.

THE MOBILE USER EXPERIENCE

Mobile devices differ from desktop computers in many ways. They often have a much smaller display than desktop computers, and they are more likely to support touch gestures than desktop computers. The context in which they are used is also different. People often use mobile devices while on the go and desktop computers when stationary. Because of these differences, people use mobile devices in very different ways compared to a standard computer. Eye tracking helps to better understand how these differences affect users' experiences with mobile products.

Mobile Device Size Impacts the UX

The size of a smartphone typically ranges from 3.5 in. to 6 in., significantly smaller than a computer monitor. For example, the size of the iPhone 5 is 4.87 × 2.31 in., and the size of a Samsung Galaxy Note II is 5.95 × 3.17 in. Tablets are a bit larger in size than smartphones; for example, an iPad is 9.50 × 7.31 in., and an iPad mini is 7.87 × 5.3 in. The size of the mobile device changes how users interact with mobile apps and websites (see Figure 10.3).

Apple iPhone 4s
115.2 x 58.66 x 9.3 mm
4.54 x 2.31 x 0.37 in
140 gr / 4.94 oz

Nokia Lumia 800
116.5 x 61.2 x 12.1 mm
4.59 x 2.41 x 0.48 in
142 gr / 5.01 oz

Google Galaxy Nexus
135.5 x 67.94 x 8.94 mm
5.33 x 2.67 x 0.35 in
135 gr / 4.76 oz

3.5" screen
640 x 960 px
330 ppi

3.7 " screen
480 x 800 px
252 ppi

4.65 " screen
720 x 1280 px
316 ppi

FIGURE 10.3   Size comparisons of typical mobile devices.

A recent eye-tracking-based usability study of mobile devices conducted by Seix et al. (2012) explored whether display size affects users' eye movements. Participants interacted with websites on three different devices that varied in size including the Tobii T120 eye-tracker monitor (13.25 × 10.75 in.), Sony VAIO SJ (9.8 × 14.6 in.), and HTC Desire (4.69 × 2.36 in.). Eye-tracking data demonstrated that the smaller displays led to longer average fixation duration and fewer fixations compared to the larger display (see Figure 10.4). The smallest mobile display, cluttered with many elements, led to difficulties in reading the text on the mobile websites. Thus, the user experience of the same website proved to be quite different for each of the devices. The eye-tracking data confirm the importance of building websites that can be used similarly across multiple devices. Ideally, users should have a consistent experience when using a website on different devices.

Display and View

The size of a display also influences the appropriate font size and style for mobile applications and websites. A font

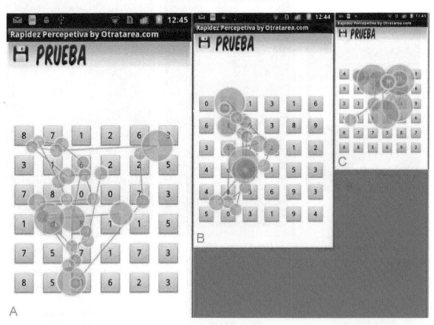

FIGURE 10.4   Gaze plot for a participant interacting with mobile devices of varied sizes: Tobii T120, Sony VAIO SJ, and HTC Desire display, left to right, respectively. (From Seix et al., 2012.)

size that is too small will be hard to read, and a font size that is too large will limit the amount of information that can be displayed, requiring frequent scrolling or touch to switch pages (Figure 10.5). Features such as zoom or a font size adjuster may help users with text-intensive pages. In general, when users hold a smartphone at an arm's distance, the text on the screen should be at least 12 point, which is about the same size as 16 pixels on most desktop computer screens. Eye tracking can explain a lot about users' interactions with fonts. Longer fixation durations as well as re-fixations indicate difficulties with reading text. In other words, users will need to look at difficult fonts longer and look back at the previous words more often if the information is difficult to read or understand.

Other important differences between the mobile UX and the desktop UX also need to be considered. On desktops, users have a lot to take in, but there is much less to interact with on mobile screens. One consequence is that the common

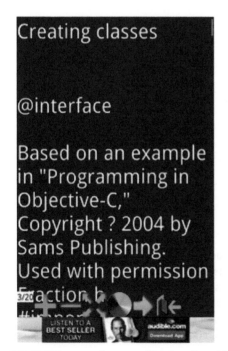

FIGURE 10.5   Improper font sizes in mobile designs: left, font size too large; right, font size too small.

F-shape eye-gaze pattern found when users interact with search results on desktop computers (described in Chapter 2) is often not replicated on mobile devices. This is likely due to the small size of the mobile screen compared to the size of the desktop computer monitor; the mobile display can only show several words per row. Rather, when viewing search results on mobile devices, users tend to focus on (1) the search bar, (2) the first AdWord advertisement, and (3) the first organic search results (Market Insights, 2011). Figure 10.6 presents data from an eye-tracking study that Google conducted. On average, participants spent almost twice as much time looking at the AdWords results compared to the organic search results. When participants searched on a desktop, the decline from the AdWords results to the organic search results was not as precipitous. These types of findings can guide UX practitioners when designing a search results page for their own mobile website.

FIGURE 10.6   Length of time participants looked at the different areas on a mobile search results page (left) and desktop search results page (right). On the mobile search results page, participants looked at the AdWords search results almost twice as long as the organic search results. On the desktop search results page, participants spent a similar amount of time looking at the AdWords search results and the first few organic search results. (From http://www.google.com/think/research-studies/eye-tracking-study-comparing-mobile-and-desktop.html.)

MOBILE DEVICE EYE TRACKING IN ACTION

We think the best way to demonstrate the utility of eye tracking mobile product usage is to present findings from actual usability tests of mobile products. In the following section we discuss the eye-tracking data from four usability tests of mobile products. The eye-tracking data are used in combination with the other types of data collected to determine usability issues and present design solutions. The first study we discuss is a usability test of a mobile app for an online investment product. Next, we discuss findings from the usability test of a pizza-ordering mobile app. The third usability test covered is that of a mobile app and website tool used to record television-watching behaviors. And the fourth study considers the eye tracking data collected from a usability test of several different e-readers. These studies demonstrate the kind of insights that eye tracking can deliver to drive exceptional mobile design.

Eye Tracking when Testing a Log-In Page on Mobile Apps

Users commonly need to log into websites and apps when using their mobile devices. Because this is often the first interaction that a user has with a mobile product, this experience anchors their perceptions for the rest of their experience with the site or app. An easy log-in process is important because it gives the user a positive first experience with a product; a difficult log-in process begins a negative experience, and this is often difficult to overcome. A site or app that has an easy log-in process with a smaller screen will likely lead to users logging in more often and, consequently, more usage. To log in, users typically input their email address and password and click a button to get started. A log-in page that is well designed will have the log-in button in close proximity to the email and password form. A poorly designed log-in page will force the user to spend a great deal of time searching for the correct button, and the user may miss it entirely if the button is labeled poorly or if it is located where it is not immediately seen.

Figure 10.7 displays a heat map for a study that assessed the log-in of a mobile app for an online investment product. On the log-in page, the only available button is labeled "Sign Up for Free" and is located directly below the email and password

FIGURE 10.7 A gaze path (right) and mean fixation count heat map (left) for a participant that typified other participants' eye-gaze interaction with the page. The poorly labeled button caused the participant to re-fixate multiple times on it (right).

fields. This design is not consistent with most log-in pages as most have the sign-in button labeled as "Sign in" in this location. As shown in the gaze path (Figure 10.7, right), this participant fixated heavily on the Sign Up for Free button while working on the task. However, after looking at the button, the participant looked at other elements on the page, presumably looking for the sign-in button. The participant eventually clicked on the Sign Up for Free button to complete the task. During the debriefing interview, the participant explained that he clicked on the button to test whether this would allow him/her to sign in. Having this eye-tracking data was powerful when making the case that users are unsure about how to sign into the app.

Eye Tracking the Core Features of a Mobile App

Most mobile UX studies do not present evidence that is as cut and dry as the case study of the log-in page in Figure 10.7. Mobile log-in pages are typically straightforward and do not allow for a lot of creative freedom in their design, because logging in is a simple and common task. We commonly have more complicated design questions about a particular design interaction. These more complicated design questions are typically about the core functionality of the site or app. Positive experiences with the core functionality of a mobile product are typically the most influential driver of an exceptional user experience.

In this mobile UX case study, we discuss two core features of a pizza-ordering application. This product was tested on a first-generation Apple iPad. The eye tracker was positioned above the iPad, and participants were asked to complete a number of tasks, including finding a Pizza Hut location, customizing toppings on a pizza, ordering a variety of items using a $100 budget, and deleting an item from the order. After each task, participants rated the perceived task difficulty on a 5-point Likert scale, (1=very easy to 5=very difficult) and completed a satisfaction questionnaire (Brooke, 1996) about their experience with the app.

Eye-tracking data revealed a critical design issue with the app's map directory. Participants were asked to order a pizza for carryout at a local store. To see the local store's pizza menu, participants needed to click on the green arrow button above the store's location pin. The app did not allow users to navigate to the local store's pizza menu by any other method. Participants were frustrated, and they reported that the steps required to successfully complete this task were not intuitive. Participants commented that they expected to be able to reach the menu by clicking on the local store address or the "Store Details" button as shown in Figure 10.8.

Eye-tracking data provided further details about the difficulties participants experienced navigating to the pizza menu (Figure 10.8). Participants typically looked at the store details and the map areas on the page. Across participants, the map area was fixated on the most with an average of 15.7 fixations. This demonstrated that participants looked at the map a lot, but another measure was even more telling. Participants re-fixated on the map area an average of 5.6 times. This indicated that participants looked at the map, looked at a different area on the page, and then came back to the map, and they did this often. This quantitative metric demonstrated the level of confusion with the design. A well-designed page would not cause participants to have to keep looking again and again at the correct button. Ideally, a user looks at the button to successfully complete the task, knows what to do, and clicks it. The eye-tracking data also provide a benchmark for a future

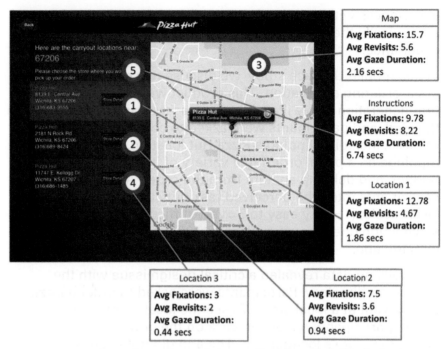

FIGURE 10.8 A page from a pizza-ordering app. Participants had difficulty figuring out what to click to begin the pizza-ordering process. The numbers that are circled in red represent the typical sequence of eye movements after these data were aggregated across participants. Participants typically looked at the first and second local store details on the left, then at the map area, and returned to the local store details again.

retest of a redesigned version of the app. If participants have fewer fixations on the page and fewer re-fixations on the correct button to complete the task, the designers can be more confident that they have improved the process.

Participants often looked at the instructions at the top of the page, presumably for guidance on how to move forward with the task. Unfortunately, the instructions on the page also did not test well. Participants' average gaze duration for the instruction area was 6.74 seconds, and they revisited the instruction area an average of 8.22 times. This indicates that the instructions were seen and referenced often and the low success rate demonstrates that they were not useful. These measures further emphasize the level of confusion with the task and provide an additional benchmark measure for a future retest.

The usability findings from this study demonstrated the need for a redesign of several key elements of the app. One option presented was to redesign the map directory section to allow users multiple ways to navigate to the local store's pizza menu. With this redesign, users would be able to get to the menu by clicking on the store's address or the "Store Details" button. Participants often looked at the Store Details buttons when working on this task, suggesting that this process can be made more efficient by having this button linked directly to the local store's menu.

The app's pizza-topping customization feature also did not test well. Participants were tasked with customizing the toppings on a pizza to be half mushroom and half green peppers. This feature of the app was designed to be an interactive pizza-building experience in which users could drag and drop different toppings to the left or right of the pizza. Before entering the feature, an instructional message popped up on the page to inform users on how to customize the toppings: "Remember, you can also drag your selection to the left or right of your pizza if you want" (shown in Figure 10.9). Three out of ten participants, however, did not look at the pop-up instruction and clicked the "OK" button immediately. The other seven participants looked at the instructional message for only 0.77 seconds, likely not enough time to fully read and understand the instruction.

Participants encountered difficulties when they attempted to customize the pizza's toppings (half mushrooms, half green peppers). Both the participants who fixated the pop-up message and those who did/did not realize they could customize the pizza by dragging the toppings to either the left or right of the

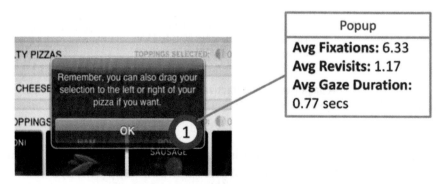

FIGURE 10.9   The pop-up message instructed users to drag and drop toppings to customize a pizza.

pizza. Participants' comments suggested that they thought the pizza graphic was simply a background of the page and not part of the topping customization feature. The eye-tracking data further detailed the problem. Participants looked often (average of 50.50 fixations) and spent a long period of time (average of 11.8 seconds for gaze duration) looking at the vegetable topping section at the bottom of the page (Figure 10.10). However, participants only briefly looked at the left and right side of the pizza where the toppings needed to be dragged. This further emphasized the ambiguity with the drag and drop method to choose pizza toppings. After a long period of time struggling to finish the task, participants typically started to explore other areas of the app. Some looked at the instructions and the "View Your Pizza" button for possible ways to customize the toppings.

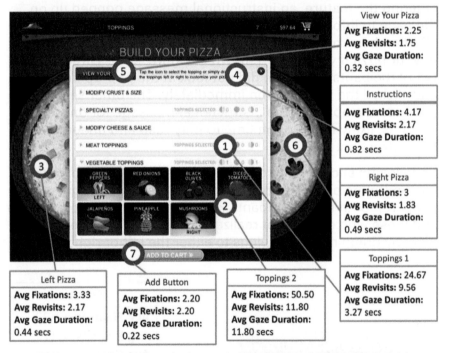

View Your Pizza
Avg Fixations: 2.25
Avg Revisits: 1.75
Avg Gaze Duration: 0.32 secs

Instructions
Avg Fixations: 4.17
Avg Revisits: 2.17
Avg Gaze Duration: 0.82 secs

Right Pizza
Avg Fixations: 3
Avg Revisits: 1.83
Avg Gaze Duration: 0.49 secs

Toppings 1
Avg Fixations: 24.67
Avg Revisits: 9.56
Avg Gaze Duration: 3.27 secs

Left Pizza
Avg Fixations: 3.33
Avg Revisits: 2.17
Avg Gaze Duration: 0.44 secs

Add Button
Avg Fixations: 2.20
Avg Revisits: 2.20
Avg Gaze Duration: 0.22 secs

Toppings 2
Avg Fixations: 50.50
Avg Revisits: 11.80
Avg Gaze Duration: 11.80 secs

FIGURE 10.10   A page from the interactive topping customization feature of the app. Participants struggled with customizing a pizza with half mushroom and half green pepper pizza.

The eye-tracking data from this pizza customization task suggest that (1) users expect to interact with a mobile app in ways consistent with other apps and (2) users often do not read instructions when attempting to complete a task. This reinforces the need for mobile apps and websites to be designed for a very intuitive first-time usage. In this case, users who are not able to find the pizza menu or customize their pizza topping are likely to discontinue using their app. While new and creative interactions such as this may at first seem enticing to design and build, complicated interactions often do not work with mobile users as they are typically multitasking, low on time, and distracted, which makes them less inclined to learn a new interaction. For this app, a simpler design is likely to work better.

Eye Tracking Mobile User Experiences across Multiple Devices

It has become increasingly rare to find a mobile application that is only available on one type of device. Typically, there are several versions of an application. The norm is to have a mobile website version, an iOS version, an Android version, and likely a Windows version. The difficulty with designing across these different platforms is that variability is often introduced. The applications may have the same primary features, but the application on one platform may produce a vastly better experience than on another.

In the next case study, an application was built to capture people's television viewing habits. Users log into the tool to record television shows that they are currently watching or have watched recently. The importance of a consistent experience across platforms is especially important for a data collection tool such as this. For example, if users typically make a particular error on the Android version of the app but not on the iOS version, the design issue will produce inconsistencies with the data collected. In other words, users could be watching the same television program but record the information differently on different devices, but it is impossible to know precisely how the design issue impacted the data.

To assess the user experience of this application, an eye-tracking-based usability study was conducted in which participants interacted with the application on an iPod Touch (fifth generation), HTC One (2013), and iPad (fourth generation). The web version of the application was also tested on the iPad. This study evaluated the application across these different platforms to determine any inconsistencies in the designs as well as common usability issues across them. Participants were randomly assigned three different devices to use. On the first device, participants were asked to register for an account and then complete the tutorial. On the second device, participants attempted to record two television programs they had watched in the last week. On the third device, participants were asked to record a third television program they had watched recently as well as edit previously entered information (e.g., the number of televisions in their home, the start time that a television program had begun).

For the account registration phase of the test, participants needed to enter information that was provided by the moderator into the "Household ID or email address" field and then click on the "Go" button on the device keyboard. The eye-tracking data demonstrated that most participants' eye movements progressed as expected: from the text describing the entry field to the entry field itself. While eye tracking confirmed that this step in the process was logical and straightforward, it also indicated a problem with the introductory text on the page. Most participants read the text directly above the text entry field; however, most did not read the information toward the top of the page (example gaze plot shown in Figure 10.11). The text at the top of this page contains

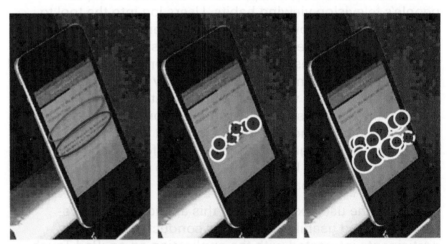

FIGURE 10.11   The text within the orange circled area (left) indicates the information to enter on this page. The red circled area is the field to enter the ID number. The center image shows a gaze plot from the first second that this participant was on this page: the participant looks directly at the section that describes the text entry field. The right gaze plot shows that the participant next looked at the field to enter the ID. The introductory text at the top of the page was not viewed by this participant.

important information about the purpose of the application, which was helpful to know before getting started. Not reading the introductory text may have indirectly caused issues with using the application later.

The process of registering for an account involved several steps. For the first step, participants were asked to enter information about the people who live in their household. Next, participants were tasked with entering information about the televisions in their home. Most of the fields on these pages were required, and if the participant did not enter information into the required fields, an error message appeared. The error message stated: "Fill all mandatory fields"; however, there was no indication about which fields were missing (shown in Figure 10.12). As discussed in Chapter 5, error messages should be meaningful and should help the user find the error quickly so they can fix it. In this case, participants had to search for the fields that were missed, which was a tedious and frustrating process. The eye-tracking data showed that, after receiving the error message, participants searched all over the page looking for the mandatory fields that were missed. An example gaze plot is shown in Figure 10.12.

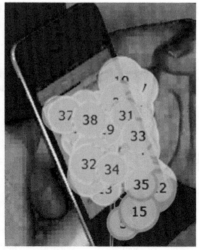

FIGURE 10.12   If the mandatory entry fields were not completed, participants received an error message that was not helpful. This gaze plot begins after the participant clicks "Ok." The participant looks all over the screen, searching for the missing mandatory fields. The error message did not indicate which fields were missing.

Eye tracking was also beneficial when comparing the iOS and Android applications. Although the primary functionality was the same across iOS and Android, there were slight differences in the designs. For example, when the iPad and iPod (iOS) were used to record the time that a television program stopped being watched, the previously entered start time was present on the page. This allowed participants to reference their start time when indicating their stop time. The quantitative eye-tracking data showed that participants looked at the time they had previously entered to help them with entering their stop time. When participants were entering their stop time, an average of 10% of the eye fixations on the page occurred on the area that contained the started watching time (see Figure 10.13). With the Android version of the app, however, participants could not see the start time when entering the stop time. This may seem like an inconsequential difference at first, but it created a significant efficiency problem as participants frequently clicked back to the previous page to look at the start time. Having the start time on the same page as the stop time helped to improve the efficiency of recording entries. The eye-tracking data suggest that users want to be able to reference their previously entered information when recording the time that they stopped watching a television program. Presenting information to users when they need it prevents them from having to rely on memory or having to take additional steps to remember what they entered.

FIGURE 10.13 The quantitative eye-tracking data showed that participants fixated on the area with the started watching time as they were recording their stopped watching time.

The eye-tracking data from this study provided additional findings in the assessment of the application. Without eye tracking, it would have been difficult to know if participants read the introductory message informing them about the purpose of the application. Some participants explained to the moderator that they did not read certain sections of a page, but not all did. Relying on verbalizations alone would have made it difficult to objectively assess how often particular text was read.

Without eye tracking, we would have known that participants often flipped back to the prior page on the Android smartphone when recording the time they stopped watching a television program. However, it would have been impossible to know if participants actually looked at the time they entered for starting to watch the program when recording the time they stopped watching the program on the iOS version of the app. Eye tracking confirmed that this design feature was helpful.

When conducting usability research on mobile devices, it is easy to make incorrect inferences based on the particularly vocal participants. But eye tracking helps to objectively assess usability issues.

Eye Tracking When Testing e-Readers

Mobile e-readers are an increasingly popular substitute for physical books. They are lightweight, portable, and, because they can hold many books on one device, they are extremely convenient. Despite the increase in their popularity, we still are not exactly sure how the experience of an e-reader differs across devices as well as how they compare to physical, paper books. To compare the reading experience and usability of e-readers, Siegenthaler et al. (2010, 2011) conducted an eye-tracking study of e-book readers and compared the experience to that of a paper book. Five e-readers were compared, including the iRex Iliad, Bookeen Cybook Gen, Sony PRS-505, BeBook, and Ectaco jetBook. Eye-tracking data showed that the mean fixation duration when reading the five e-readers was significantly shorter than when reading a paper book (see Figure 10.14). The iRex e-reader produced the shortest average fixation duration while the paper book produced the longest average fixation duration. The number of letters read per fixation was also significantly affected by the type of medium—participants could

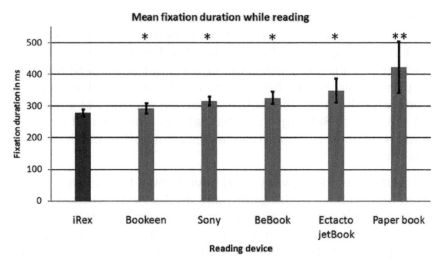

FIGURE 10.14   Participants, on average, spent a longer duration of time per fixation when reading a paper book than when reading on the e-readers. (From Siegenthaler et al., 2010.)

Reading device	Mean number of letters read per fixation (SD)
iRex	5.9 (1.5)
Bookeen	5.4 (1.2)
BeBook	5.8 (2.4)
Sony	5.7 (1.8)
Ectaco jetBook	6.5 (2.3)
Classic paper book	7.1 (3.0)

FIGURE 10.15   Participants were able to read more letters per fixation when reading a paper book than when reading on the e-readers. (From Siegenthaler et al., 2010.)

read the most letters per fixation using the paper book than all five e-readers (Figure 10.15). Eye-tracking data demonstrated that the reading efficiency of e-readers was lower than the paper book, but participants still preferred the e-readers.

New e-readers continue to hit the market with new advancements to the technology. One of these advancements is the low light display technology of the Kindle Paperwhite, which has been very successful in recent years. When designing an e-reader, eye tracking can provide UX practitioners with concrete benchmarks of performance throughout the iterative design process. Knowing the changes of these eye-tracking performance metrics is very powerful when determining whether a new design improves peoples' reading efficiency while using the device. In the case study discussed, participants preferred using an e-reader despite reading less efficiently on it. An e-reader that actually improves upon the reading efficiency of a paper book is likely to be very successful.

Text Entry Methods

Text input methods for mobile devices are quite different from desktop computers. Desktop computers often have a full-size keyboard. In contrast, mobile devices can provide input using a T9 keyboard, a QWERTY keyboard, or touch screen. Some mobile devices, such as Samsung Galaxy Note and Surface Pro, also provide a stylus. Traditional feature phones often use a T9 keyboard. Some feature phones and the Blackberry smartphone provide a full QWERTY keyboard. With the rapid development of smartphones, many mobile phones and tablets now provide touch input, with T9 keyboard or a soft QWERTY keyboard displayed on the touch screen of smartphones.

It is important for designers, product managers, and UX professionals to know that mobile inputs are less efficient than personal computer inputs with a mouse and a full-size keyboard. The keys on mobile devices are often smaller than the computer keyboard and do not provide physical feedback. The number of keys in a display is also smaller than on a computer keyboard. Users often have to switch to the symbol display to input a symbol or press a button multiple times to select the right key in the T9 keyboard. Therefore, it is helpful if the mobile application can provide auto-completion or word suggestions. Such features can significantly reduce the task duration and increase user satisfaction. For example, for the Google mobile search, the average search query is 15 letters long. But it takes 30 key presses and approximately 40 seconds to search in Google using a standard 9-key cell phone (Kamvar & Baluja, 2007, 2008).

FIGURE 10.16   Input methods for mobile devices (left, T9 keyboard; center, QWERTY keyboard; right, touch screen keyboard with stylus).

Cell phones with a QWERTY keyboard may be quicker for text input than a cell phone with a T9 keyboard (Figure 10.16). However, a cell phone is still less efficient than a computer keyboard for most users. Therefore, for websites, in which users have to produce many text inputs, query suggestion and word auto-completion is often implemented to facilitate text input.

The pointing accuracy of a finger is also less accurate than a pointing mouse. Therefore, designers of mobile products should make the buttons of a smartphone application larger and increase the space between functional buttons in order to reduce the chances of touching the wrong button. The recommended target sizes for touchscreen objects are 7 to 10 mm, which allow users to be able to reliably and accurately target them with their fingers. In its Metrics and Grids Guidelines, Google recommends that all touchable user interface components follow the 48 dp rhythm (Google, 2013). On average, 48 dp translates to a physical size of about 9 mm. Similarly, Apple has a 44-pixel rhythm (Figure 10.17). The iPhone has a 163 ppi screen resolution, 44 pixels is about 7 mm. Apple designs the size of elements for the iPhone to be precisely at 44 pixels. In portrait orientation of iPhone, 44 pixels is the height of the buttons in the Calculator app, and the height of the screen-topping navigation bar.

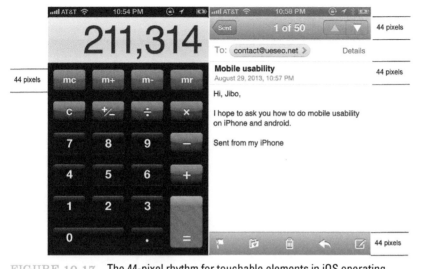

FIGURE 10.17 The 44-pixel rhythm for touchable elements in iOS operating system (From Clark, 2010.)

Touch Interaction

Mobile devices rely on touch for interaction. Although all screen pixels are built equally, their ease to reach and touch is not equal. According to Hoober (2013), smartphone users hold their phones in three major ways: 49% of users hold their phones with one hand, 36% users hold the phone in a cradled gesture, and 15% users hold phones using two hands. The easily touchable and reachable areas of the smartphone screen vary across users, devices, and holding gestures. Holding gesture is also a critical factor that mobile designers should consider. Mobile designers should put frequently used widgets in areas that are easily touchable regardless of holding gesture (Figure 10.18).

For an optimal user experience, designers can place essential buttons at easily touchable areas using a satellite menu design. Traditionally, menus and buttons are located at the bottom or the top of a smartphone. To select the menu or buttons, users often need to change their holding gestures. Frequent change of holding gestures can reduce the user experience and increase the chances of dropping the smartphone, especially when users travel.

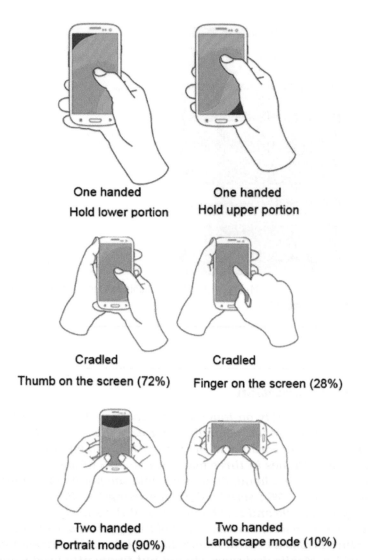

One handed
Hold lower portion

One handed
Hold upper portion

Cradled
Thumb on the screen (72%)

Cradled
Finger on the screen (28%)

Two handed
Portrait mode (90%)

Two handed
Landscape mode (10%)

FIGURE 10.18   Touchable areas for smartphones held in different gestures. Green area, easily touchable areas; orange area, somewhat difficult to touch area; and red area, most difficult to touch area. As shown, the easiest to touch area is often near the lower portion of the smartphone and near the fingers. The hard to touch area is often at the upper portion or at the corner of the smartphone.

The satellite menu design puts the menu icons around a quarter of a circle in which all buttons are easily touchable, alleviating the necessity to change holding gestures. The satellite menu design can also reduce the chances of clicking on the wrong icons, because the icons placed around a circle have a larger separation distance than icons placed horizontally in a row (Figure 10.19).

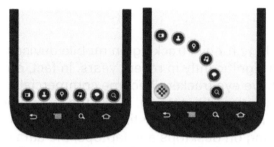

FIGURE 10.19   Comparison of traditional menu design (left) and satellite menu design (right).

Another optimal user experience example is the dial keypad for the Samsung Galaxy Note smartphone. In the first generation of the Note smartphone, the keypad covered the whole width of the display. Dialing with one hand is a common need, but it is hard for users to press all the keys with one hand on the large smartphone (3.17 in. wide). In the second generation, the keypad was reduced in its size, and an offset spacing was put at either the left or right. Users can choose to put the keypad to the left or right according to their handedness. The new design allows users to dial the phone more comfortably with a single hand (Figure 10.20).

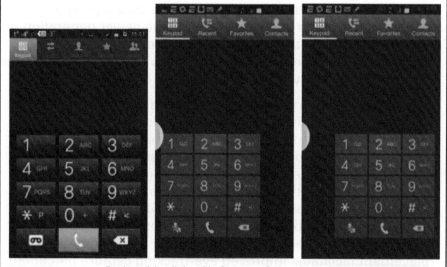

FIGURE 10.20   Design of the dial pad in Samsung Galaxy Note. Original design, left; new dial pad for left-handed users, center panel; new dial pad for right-handed users, right.

THE TECHNOLOGY BEHIND EYE TRACKING MOBILE DEVICE USAGE

The technology for eye tracking on mobile devices has progressed significantly in recent years. In fact, only in the last few years have eye trackers become commercially available for mobile device usability testing. While the technology for eye tracking on mobile devices is still in its infancy when compared to eye tracking on desktops and laptops, the data collected are now precise and reliable enough to provide meaningful insights.

Similar to eye tracking with gaming discussed in Chapter 11, the largest practical hurdle with eye tracking mobile devices is the time necessary for processing and segmenting the data to analyze. However, with the proliferation of mobile devices and the recent improvements in eye-tracking technology, there are great opportunities for eye tracking to help improve mobile devices.

Eye trackers for mobile devices can be categorized into three groups. The first category is the larger portable units that represent the previous generation of technology used for mobile device eye tracking. Examples of these types of eye trackers are the Tobii X60 and X120. These were two of the first eye trackers that allowed for eye tracking of an actual mobile device. Previous eye-tracking research was limited to simulating the mobile device interface on a computer monitor. While the eye-tracking accuracy for the X60 and X120 is robust enough for mobile devices at 0.5 degrees, the eye-tracking capture percentage is much lower than that on the newer generation of eye trackers. Because of their size, these eye trackers need to be positioned above the mobile device, which introduces issues with tracking fidelity (see Figure 10.21).

The second category of eye trackers used for mobile device testing are the candy-bar-sized devices like the Tobii X2 and SensoMotoric Instrument's RED-m. These eye trackers are lightweight, very portable, and yet have similar accuracy to the larger portable eye trackers (e.g., Tobii X60, X120). The sampling rates are typically lower, compared to the larger eye trackers yet acceptable for practical usability testing. Most importantly for mobile device testing, these eye trackers are slim enough to be placed underneath the mobile device. This placement facilitates improved eye-tracking capture percentage and overall tracking fidelity (see Figure 10.22).

FIGURE 10.21 The Tobii X120 eye tracker is placed above the mobile device.

FIGURE 10.22 The Tobii X2 is placed below the mobile device.

The third category is the head-mounted devices and includes the Tobii Glasses and the SMI Eye Tracking Glasses. These products are lightweight, fully portable, and allow for complete freedom of head motion. They are useful for shopping research (e.g., determining the optimal location for products on shelves), but they are more limited when it comes to usability testing in the lab. Because they are head mounted, the frame of reference of the participant is constantly changing. This makes aggregating across participants a very laborious task, as the mobile device will need to be centered and zoomed to the same levels for each frame for each participant. This limits these eye-tracking devices to only being practical in providing qualitative data such as single-participant gaze plots and heat maps (see Figure 10.23).

FIGURE 10.23   The SMI Eye Tracking Glasses are lightweight (<0.2 lb) and portable. They are more suitable for shopping research than usability testing of mobile devices.

A human factor consideration with eye tracking is the issue of properly positioning the eye tracker so that the infrared light lands on the eye. This issue becomes compounded with the use of a mobile device stand as the eye tracker needs to be positioned at a 20–45° angle for the path of infrared light to be projected onto the eye. Also, as participants use the bottom half of a larger mobile device, the eyelid typically drops and the pupil lowers as the eye moves farther down the page, as depicted in Figure 10.24. As the eyelid closes and the pupil lowers, the eye becomes a smaller target for the infrared light to project onto, and this leads to a lower eye-tracking capture percentage. The size of the larger portable eye trackers requires

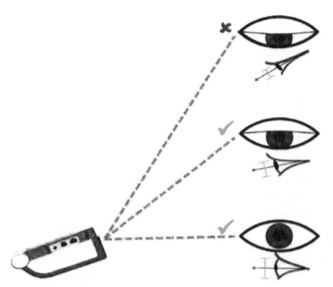

FIGURE 10.24   As people look down the eyelid drops, and it becomes more difficult for the eye tracker to locate the eye.

them to be placed above the mobile device, which increases the likelihood of the infrared light to be obstructed by the eyelid. Placing the eye tracker below the mobile device provides for a larger target and therefore decreases the likelihood of the infrared light to be obstructed by the eyelid.

Eye Movement-Based Interaction

The rapid growth of the computational power of mobile devices allows the possibility of using mobile devices as eye trackers. Eye-tracking technology is currently being developed to augment interactions with smartphones and text entries. Many modern smartphones have both a front-view camera and a face-time camera. The CPUs of smartphones are now fast enough to process complicated computer vision algorithms. New eye-tracking technologies are being developed to improve the user experience of interactions with mobile devices.

Face and eye-tracking technologies in smartphones can improve users' reading and video watching experience. When we read papers on a smartphone or watch a video on YouTube, the smartphone often locks the screen periodically. The auto-lock feature is intended to save the battery of the smartphone. Although the auto-lock is designed with good intentions, it does impair the user's reading and video watching experience. Users often have to touch the smartphone screen to prohibit it from locking or to unlock the phone manually from time to time. To provide a smooth reading and watching experience, the Samsung Galaxy smartphone provides a good design to solve the interference of auto-lock on reading. The Samsung Galaxy smartphone uses its front camera to capture the face of users. If the camera detects that the user is still reading, the auto-dim and auto-lock will be suspended, which allows users to continue reading without interruption. The SmartPause in the Samsung Galaxy smartphone uses face-tracking technology to improve the video viewing experience. If a user is distracted and looks away from the smartphone when watching a video on the device, the SmartPause automatically detects that the user's face is missing and can automatically pause the video. With the SmartPause feature, users do not need to take time to pause the video when they have distractions present.

Eye movement can be used for mobile-based text entry (Majaranta & Räihä, 2002; Drewes et al., 2007). The mobile phone uses the front camera to detect fixation locations. An item, such as a contact in the phone directory, can be selected either using dwell time or gaze gesture. For the dwell-time-based algorithm, a command is executed if users look at a specific area longer than a predefined time threshold. For the gaze-gesture-based algorithm, gaze directions are coded into strings, which are then converted into commands. Because users often use mobile phones outdoors and make frequent head movements while using it, a gaze-gesture-based algorithm to control the mobile phone performs better than the dwell-time-based algorithm (Drewes et al., 2007).

Setting Up a Mobile Eye-Tracking Study

There are two primary methods for collecting eye-tracking data that are comparable across participants. The first method is to transmit the mobile device's screen to a video capture card on a nearby computer. This method allows for a video recording that is clear and unobstructed by the participant's hands. Typically the mobile device is fixed on a stand, but this experimental setup also allows for the option of having participants hold the mobile device freely in their hands. As long as the eye tracker is placed in a fixed position beneath the mobile device, researchers can aggregate data across participants.

The second method for collecting eye-tracking data that are comparable across participants involves the use of a scene camera. This requires the use of a mobile device stand, which is a robust and practical solution to providing comparable and reliable eye-tracking data across participants. With this setup (shown in Figures 10.21 and 10.22), the mobile device is attached to a mounting plate and slides into the stand. The mounting plates can be removed and replaced with different plates, allowing multiple mobile devices to be tested in a single session. Because the mobile device and scene camera are in a fixed location, the data collected will have the same points of reference across participants. Once a test has begun, it is important to maintain the same scene camera position and angle for subsequent participants as a change in the scene camera will result in different points of reference in the recording. Without the use of a stand, researchers are required to manually adjust the location of the mobile device in the scene camera recording so that the device is in the same location across participants. The time required to make these adjustments makes this an impractical task.

While the use of a scene camera is a practical and acceptable solution for comparing eye-tracking data across participants, the setup has its limitations. Because the mobile device needs to be mounted to the stand, participants cannot hold the device freely in their hands. This may cause participants to deviate from their natural behavior. The use of a scene camera also means that a participant's hands may obstruct the view of the mobile device screen. Because of these limitations, a connection to a nearby computer is typically preferred if this is a feasible option.

Mobile devices with complete Windows Operations Systems, like the Windows Surface Pro, allow for the eye tracker to be directly connected to the mobile device. This is likely how all eye-tracking data will be collected on mobile devices in the future, with a direct connection to the mobile device itself, just as with testing on a computer. For this to happen, eye-tracker manufacturers will likely need to build software applications that run on different mobile devices' operating systems. Regardless of how the improvements actually occur, data collection is certainly becoming increasingly easier and producing higher quality results as the technology advances.

Analyzing Mobile Eye-Tracking Data

Analyzing mobile device eye-tracking data is a more tedious process than analyzing data collected directly by a computer with a full operating system. Unlike testing on a computer with a monitor, eye-tracking software cannot automatically segment the video recording per web page from the mobile device. This requires UX researchers to segment the individual test video recordings by page. These segments can then be grouped together across participants by the corresponding web page. A static image from the video recording is assigned to the segment grouping, which represents the web page. This is akin to assigning a URL to eye-tracking data that were collected using a computer and monitor. Using this static image, data visualizations and areas of interest for quantitative measures can be created with aggregated data.

The fact that we can analyze eye-tracking data from mobile devices is an astounding feat. Only until recently, researchers were limited to analyzing this type of data at the single participant level. This is often not very helpful, because we want to try to generalize our findings to a group of users rather than one particular user. When data are collected from mobile devices with full operating systems, like the Microsoft Surface Pro, analysis efficiency is the same as with a standard computer: fast and easy. As the flexibility of the software improves, we will also be able to perform efficient analyses on data collected from other types of mobile devices.

Smartphone as an Eye Tracker

With the advancement in technology, it is now possible to use smartphones and tablets as eye trackers (Miluzzo et al., 2010; Pino & Kavasidis, 2012; He et al., 2013; Iqbal et al., 2013). For example, the front camera of a smartphone can be used to capture images of users, and then the OpenCV computer vision framework can be used to detect face, eye, and eye blinks (He et al., 2013). The smartphone application can successfully detect eye blinks, head nodding, and head rotation and can be used to detect driver fatigue, driver distraction, and mobile usability in the near future.

Similarly, unmodified commodity webcams and iPads can track eye movements (Sewell & Komogortsev, 2010; Holland & Komogortsev, 2012). The camera of an iPad can be used to

*capture users' faces, and then computer vision algorithms can
be used to detect faces and eyes. A neural network algorithm
determines the gaze location. This iPad eye-tracking algorithm
can track the eyes at the rate of roughly one usable frame every
1.5 seconds. The eye-tracking accuracy is 4.42 degrees, or roughly
one-fifth of the iPad screen size (Holland & Komogortsev, 2012).
The smartphone- or tablet-based eye tracking is still in its early
development stages and cannot meet the requirement of real-world
eye tracking for usability research. However, as the hardware of
smartphone and tablets improves quickly, it is likely we will be
able to conduct eye tracking using mobile devices in the very near
future (Figure 10.25).*

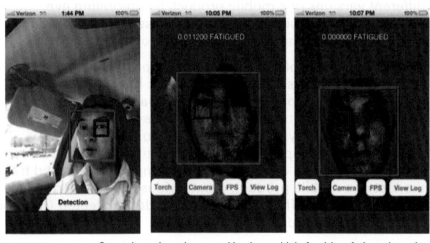

FIGURE 10.25   Smartphone-based eye tracking in a vehicle for driver fatigue detection.
As driving time increased, drowsy drivers produced more frequent head nodding and head
rotation, and the standard deviation of the percent of black pixels in the eye area also
increased. (From He et al., 2013.)

CONCLUSION

UX practitioners now have eye tracking as a powerful tool to identify
mobile design issues. Until recently, the technology was not robust
enough to produce reliable findings, but there are now several eye
trackers on the market that can be used with mobile devices. Just as
with testing a website on a computer, testing a product on a mobile
device informs about confusing button labels, improperly located
items, unread messaging, and improper font size.

We have discussed four case studies of eye tracking providing additional insights into the optimal design of mobile products. Each case study provides a unique example of the utility of eye tracking on mobile devices. Eye-tracking data from the first case study exemplified users' frustration with poor mobile log-in pages. In the usability test of the pizza-ordering app, eye-tracking data revealed several additional insights about usability issues with the core functionality of the app. The e-reader case study discussed how eye tracking can be used to produce benchmarks that can drive the improvement of an e-reader's user experience, and finally, the case study about the tool for recording television viewing behaviors demonstrated how eye tracking can be used to ensure consistency across different versions of a mobile product. Incorporating eye tracking into the design evaluation process provides a unique advantage when assessing all types of mobile products.

Eye-tracking technology is still being improved and customized for tests of mobile products; however, these improvements are occurring at a rapid pace. Now the technology for eye tracking on mobile devices allows a data collection and analysis process similar to the testing of products on desktops. While there are still typically additional steps involved with analyzing eye-tracking data collected from the test of a mobile product, great strides have been made so this process is as efficient as analyzing data collected from the test of desktop product.

The continual increase in mobile device ownership presents a great opportunity for developers of mobile digital products. The companies who produce exceptionally designed mobile products will continue to thrive. And eye tracking will continue to play an increasingly role for companies looking to gain that competitive edge.

REFERENCES

Brooke, J., 1996. SUS: a quick and dirty usability scale. In: Jordan, P., Thomas, B., Weerdmeester, B., McClelland, I.L. (Eds.), Usability Evaluation in Industry. Taylor & Francis, London, pp. 189–194. Retrieved from, http://usabilitynet.org/trump/documents/Suschapt.doc.

Canalys, 2012. Smart Phones Overtake Client PCs in 2011. Retrieved on September 12, 2013 from, http://www.canalys.com/newsroom/smart-phones-overtake-client-pcs-2011.

Clark, J., 2010. Tapworthy: Designing Great iPhone Apps. O'Reilly Media, Cambridge, MA.

Drewes, H., De Luca, A., Schmidt, A., 2007. Eye-gaze interaction for mobile phones. In: Proceedings of the 4th International Conference on Mobile Technology, Applications and Systems (Mobility 2007), pp. 364–371.

Fox, S., 2013. 51% of U.S. Adults Bank Online. Pew Research Center. Retrieved from, http://www.pewinternet.org.

Google, 2013. Metrics and Grids. Retrieved on October 28, 2013 from, http://developer.android.com/design/style/metrics-grids.html.

He, J., Fields, B., Peng, J., Cielocha, S., Coltea, J., Roberson, S., 2013. Fatigue detection using smartphones. In: International Conference on Psychology and Applications, Beijing, China.

Himuro, H., Shim, R., 2013. Quarterly Mobile PC Shipment and Forecast Report. NPD Display Search. Retrieved from, http://www.displaysearch.com/pdf/quarterly_mobile_pc_shipment_and_forecast_report.pdf.

Holland, C., Komogortsev, O.V., 2012. Eye tracking on unmodified common tablets: challenges and solutions. In: Proceedings of ACM Eye Tracking Research & Applications Symposium, Santa Barbara, CA, pp. 1–4.

Hoober, S., 2013. How Do Users Really Hold Mobile Devices? Retrieved on October 28, 2013 from, http://www.uxmatters.com/mt/archives/2013/02/how-do-users-really-hold-mobile-devices.php.

Iqbal, N., Lee, H., Lee, S.Y., 2013. Smart user interface for mobile consumer devices using model-based eye-gaze estimation. IEEE T. Consum. Electr. 59 (1), 161–166.

Kamvar, M., Baluja, S., 2007. Deciphering trends in mobile search. Computer 40 (8), 58–62.

Kamvar, M., Baluja, S., 2008. Query suggestions for mobile search: understanding usage patterns, CHI 2008, April 5–10, Florence, Italy.

Majaranta, P., Räihä, J., 2002. Twenty years of eye typing: systems and design issues. In: Proceedings of Eye Tracking Research and Application, ACM, pp. 15–22, New Orleans, LA.

Market Insights, 2011. Eye Tracking Study: Perception of Search and Display Advertising Mobile vs. Desktop. Retrieved on February 19, 2013 from, http://www.google.com/think/research-studies/eye-tracking-study-comparing-mobile-and-desktop.html.

Miluzzo, E., Wang, T., Campbell, A.T., 2010. EyePhone: activating mobile phones with your eyes. In: Proceedings of the Second ACM SIGCOMM Workshop on Networking.

Pino, C., Kavasidis, I., 2012. Improving mobile device interaction by eye tracking analysis. In: 2012 Federated Conference on Computer Science & Information Systems (FedCSIS). pp. 1199–1202.

Seix, C.C., Veloso, M.S., Soler, J.J.R., 2012. Towards the validation of a method for quantitative mobile usability testing based on desktop eyetracking. In: Interaction, October 2012, Elche, Alicante, Spain.

Sewell, W., Komogortsev, O.V., 2010. Real time eye gaze tracking with an unmodified commodity webcam employing a neural network. In: Proceedings of ACM Conference on Human Factors in Computing Systems (CHI), Atlanta, GA, 2010, pp. 1–6.

Siegenthaler, E., Wurtz, P., Groner, R., 2010. Improving the usability of e-book readers. JUS 6 (1), 25–38.

Siegenthaler, E., Wurtz, P., Groner, R., 2011. Comparing reading processes on e-ink displays and printed paper. Display 32 (5), 268–273.

Smith, A., 2013. Smartphone Ownership— 2013 Update. Pew Research Center. Retrieved from, http://www.pewinternet.org.

Zickuhr, K., 2013. Table Ownership 2013. Pew Research Center. Retrieved from, http://www.pewinternet.org.

11

GAMING

Veronica Zammitto[1] and Karl Steiner[2]
[1]*Electronic Arts Inc., Burnaby, BC, Canada*
[2]*TandemSeven Inc., Plymouth, MA, USA*

INTRODUCTION

Video games have become increasingly popular throughout the years. Multiple electronic devices can be used for gaming, ranging from computers to dedicated game consoles, handheld systems to smart phones, tablets to smart TVs. Games are present in home living rooms and in people's pockets.

The gaming population has also reshaped itself, becoming increasingly diverse. According to the Entertainment Software Association, gamers' average age is 30 years old, and the average gamer is as likely to be a female as a male. Moreover, playing games has been part of gamers' lives for 12 years on average (Entertainment Software Association, 2012). Such growth and diversity has also translated into the video game industry revenue, which reached $24.75 billion in the United States in 2012. Accordingly, the importance of understanding the user experience (UX) of video games has increased within the last years in the game industry, where more sophisticated evaluation techniques are needed. Eye tracking unveils the user experience at multiple levels, ranging from a utilitarian point of view on how people interact and navigate through menus to identifying visual aspects in the game that contribute to the experience of fun or frustration.

One of the distinctive characteristics of video games compared to other software products is that games do not only need to provide an environment that is efficient and easy to use but also an engaging and fun experience. Playing games is about having an enjoyable and entertaining experience. Therefore, traditional usability techniques discussed in Chapter 3 that are concerned with effectiveness, efficiency, and satisfaction are not sufficient to assess the user experience of video games. When evaluating games, we also need to consider other concepts, such as engagement, emotional profiles, attention, flow, challenge, and balance. These concepts bring forward the breadth and depth of the video game playing experience.

Within the last few years, the term Games User Research (GUR) has been used to identify the field of studies on video game players' experience. UX researchers and practitioners have proposed numerous new and modified techniques for addressing the unique needs of this audience, ranging from qualitative to quantitative and from subjective to objective. For example, GUR techniques include user interviews, journals, think-aloud protocol, heuristic evaluations, telemetry, and psychophysiology, among others (Isbister & Schaffer, 2008; Bernhaupt, 2010; Steiner, 2011; Zammitto, 2012). Recently, eye tracking has been increasingly employed by both practitioners and academics, and has provided new value to the understanding and enhancement of the video game user experience, as well as to game design.

Two Roles of Eye Tracking in Video Games

Eye tracking has been introduced into game development from two different perspectives: using gaze as an input technique, and using eye tracking as an evaluation method. This chapter focuses on the latter: diving deep into the use of eye tracking as a tool for assessing the UX of video games, and briefly touching on eye tracking as input for controlling games (see Chapter 10 for additional information about eye tracking as an input technique on mobile devices).

The idea of playing a game with your gaze has captivated many game developers and researchers. The renowned game company, Valve, developed a modification for their game Portal 2 that allowed the character's aim to be controlled by the player's gaze (Ambinder, 2011). Isokoski et al. (2009) reviewed several studies exploring eye-gaze control in different game genres and documented the strengths and challenges of implementation on each type. One main objective of eye tracking as a game input is accessibility. Approximately 11% of the U.S. population is affected by disabilities that prevent them from fully experiencing games (Yuan et al., 2011); this percentage increases to 20% when looking at the casual gamer audience (Barlet, 2008).

We use eye tracking in a variety of ways, but our primary goals tend to deal with investigations of player attention. We want to know where a player is attending while playing, and we can use eye tracking to generate an approximate map of their attentional focus over time. We use eye tracking to evaluate interfaces, examine novice-expert differences, investigate pathfinding and navigation issues in-game, determine attentional set, and a variety of other questions applicable to player experience and game design.

Mike Ambinder, Experimental Psychologist, Valve, USA

Eye tracking has enabled researchers to have and use new data about many different aspects of the visual dimension of the gaming user experience. In particular, eye tracking has assisted researchers and designers in better understanding when and for how long different elements of the display attract users' visual attention and what elements are overlooked. Given the complexity of video games and the many forms and types of information displayed in games, in this chapter we provide a classification of video game design elements that can benefit from eye-tracking evaluation.

At Ubisoft we've been experimenting with our eye trackers and looking at how we can develop a better understanding of what the player is seeing and looking at. With eye-tracking data, we can begin to develop a general understanding of how players are consuming the information that is presented to them. We've been exploring the consumption of text and visualizations, as well as evaluating the effects of visual cues in level design and menu structure. We've also been exploring how we can use the hardware in the long-term to develop effective metrics for important areas, such as learnability. It's our belief that eye trackers provide a clear opportunity to learn key generalizable lessons that can be applied across a broad spectrum of games and genres.

Ian Livingston, User Research Project Manager, Ubisoft, Montreal, Canada

I have used an eye tracker in a few different ways. The simplest, yet highly valuable, set-up has been to live stream play-test sessions with user's eye movements visualization. Beyond some anecdotal information, this approach allows me to introduce the tool to developers and entice them into using the tool in other usability sessions (UI, menu system, task based, etc.) using static or uniform experiences that can and should be evaluated with an eye-tracker.

Ben Lile, Senior User Researcher, Warner Brothers Games, USA

Overall, eye-tracking UX work on video games is fairly recent and the body of knowledge is still in development. Established eye-tracking concepts for productivity applications cannot be employed straightforward for video game evaluation. For example, long fixations on the same location in productivity software could be interpreted as related to confusion; however, in video games, long fixations could relate to engagement, or tracking the character controlled by the user. This happens often in certain types of video games like first-person shooter games where users fixate primarily on the center of the screen where the crosshair is displayed. Moreover, the diversity of video games (i.e., different types of games) and the multiple layers of information in games (i.e., game design elements, discussed in the next section) add to the shortage of generalizations for UX eye tracking in games. Efforts have been undertaken in sports video games (Zammitto, 2011) and first-person shooter games (Rodriguez & Steiner, 2010) that have shed light onto the different emerging gaze patterns. For example, sports video game users balance their gaze among the character they control, the assessment of the field situation (teammates and opponents positions), and visual cues about the time left in the period, plus secondary characters that add to the game's atmosphere (e.g., audience, players at the bench).

Overall, important guiding questions for eye tracking in video games include:

- Did players "see" a certain design element (or fail to see it)?
- When did players "see" such a design element?
- Are the patterns related to players' gaze and in-game behavior?

These questions are explained in more detail later in this chapter.

RELEVANT GAME DESIGN ELEMENTS FOR UX EYE TRACKING AND CHALLENGES

There are four distinct design element groups in video games where eye-tracking information is particularly useful in understanding and improving the user experience. Of course, all design elements in an application are intertwined and contribute to the final user experience, but understanding the distinctive characteristics of these design element groups can help to optimize the focus, planning, and execution of testing.

Nevertheless, employing eye tracking for gaming user experience evaluation has particular challenges, which are mainly related to the high interactive nature of video games. Although all users are exposed to the exact same conditions, video games are an interactive medium, and therefore what actually appears on screen (the stimuli) can vary greatly. For example, in a hockey video game, one player can win a match by scoring three points, whereas another person with the same user profile can lose without scoring and never see all the same visual cues as the first person. Every game session is unique, and each gamer's action shapes the UX evaluation session uniquely.

Accordingly, video game design elements present different degrees of interactivity; at a general level, it can be divided into low, medium, and high interactivity, depending on the amount of input required by the user.

The following areas shed light on how to address UX eye-tracking studies.

Menu

The first area that users interact with in a game is the menu. Players have to navigate through different options to start a game or to choose the desired settings.

Menus are highly important because first impressions of the game are forged at this stage, before the gameplay even starts. If a menu is too cumbersome, it can become a roadblock to the intended experience. Menus can take several forms and also appear throughout the game as well, for instance, when pausing or accessing different game modes.

In menus with list-like structures, the user's gaze has to cover the overall width of columns in order to gather all necessary information on how the game mode will work; for example, Figure 11.1 shows the menu of Madden NFL 13 in the Career mode settings. Such a gaze pattern promotes constant saccadic jumps, which over long periods can lead to tiredness. Conversely, when there is just one column or one row to inspect visually, users tend to employ a smooth pursue gaze pattern when exploring the possible selections; as shown in Figure 11.2, there is one key row to cover in Madden NLF 13 when choosing the team captain in the Ultimate Team mode.

Minimizing saccadic jumps is preferable; however, it is not always possible to completely avoid saccadic jumps when structuring information conveyed in menus. Tiredness would not be feasible to efficiently assess through regular UX methods such as think aloud, but analyzing users' gaze patterns can unveil the generated effort related to eye movements.

Menus in video games can range widely from a few options to rather complex menus in games with significant depth. Game menus often include a combination of static design elements (such as the relative position of menu items) and dynamic elements (such as the specific menu elements). While

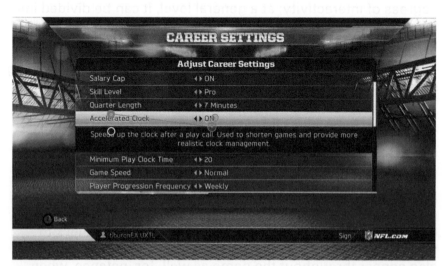

FIGURE 11.1   Madden NFL 13, Career mode settings menu. The user has to cover two wide columns in order to gather all necessary information on how the game mode will work.

FIGURE 11.2 Madden NFL 13, Ultimate Team mode. The user has to choose the team captain. The most important information is the score of the players (number 85 in the image).

traditional game instrumentation can capture when users open a menu and what options they select, eye tracking can provide additional information regarding scanability and which menu elements attract (or fail to attract) user attention.

The static elements in the menu do not present a challenge for understanding game user experience since they are laid out in fixed locations of the screen and in a predetermined flow. The challenging aspect of game menus is related to dynamic elements that can be modified by the users' choices and the contextual game situation. Thus, aggregation of data is relatively straightforward, but users' interactive timing and context can represent a challenge when analyzing eye-tracking data.

Cutscenes

It is common that video games include short cinematic videos. These video clips are generally scripted short movies, ranging from seconds to minutes, which are played during non-interactive moments. For example, a game begins and a cutscene shows the two main characters arriving to a location; the scene continues with a conversation between them.

Cutscenes are important for setting the atmosphere and for presenting key concepts of the game. For example, Figure 11.3 shows a screen shot from the NHL 13 opening cutscene that

FIGURE 11.3   During an intro match cutscene in NHL 13, the stadium is featured right before the hockey players get onto the ice rink. When showing the whole ice rink, the eye movement shows an expected behavior where the gaze sweeps toward the edges of the figure, in this case the boundary between the rink and the audience.

features the stadium. Eye tracking can confirm that the visual representations of the key concepts are intersected by a user's gaze.

Cutscenes present a lesser demand of interactivity; the only option is to skip them. They are mostly short movies that accompany the narrative of the game. Therefore all participants that watch cutscenes will see the same content in the same timely manner, which highly facilitates aggregating data.

Overlays

This concept encompasses all information that is visually represented as part of the user interface when playing. Another common term used in the game industry for these overlays is "heads-up display". This naming was borrowed from aviation: the transparent display in a cockpit that presents data to pilots that they can still see through. In shooting video games, like Battlefield 3, as shown in Figure 11.4, the usage of overlays is very frequent.

Overlays are an interesting challenge where eye tracking can be beneficial in improving the user experience. Overlays provide the user with critical information that can assist them in succeeding in the game; however, the placement and timing are key for their

FIGURE 11.4 Battlefield 3. The user can see the game world as well as information about how much ammunition is left, the direction to take to reach their objective, and teammates location—all of which are overlaid as part of the user interface.

success. Overlays should not be intrusive nor grab unwanted visual attention, yet they should still be visible when and if needed. Eye tracking can provide measures of if and when users look at overlays. Madden NFL 13, shown in Figure 11.5, presents an example of overlays, which only appear when the user requests it.

FIGURE 11.5 Overlays in Madden NFL 13 where the user's "play-call" information is displayed. The timing is triggered by the user, the different options for a play are drawn on the field, and the buttons to activate them appear over the football players that would execute them. In the screen shot, the user is assessing option "X" in blue on the left.

Overlays are the visual information that is part of the user interface while playing. Most overlays tend be permanently displayed or reappear on the same screen location. It can be relatively straightforward and valuable to capture eye-tracking measures such as which overlay elements capture user attention, and for how long. However, understanding "when" users look at an overlay is highly contextual and very important. To best understand these situations, it may be necessary to integrate (manually or preferably automatically) contextual information about events in the game with the eye-tracking data.

Gameplay

This concept encompasses the core mechanics of the game and its world. Gameplay is what people refer to as the "actual" game. It varies greatly based on the game genre, the game hardware, and the artistic crafting of the designers. Consequently, there is no unique way to infer user experience based on eye-tracking data. The importance of eye tracking in gameplay resides in revealing how the user visually engages with the game and if the game items are covered as intended by the design. In sports video games, like NHL 13 shown in Figure 11.6, users have the freedom to move the characters as they see fit, creating their own strategies.

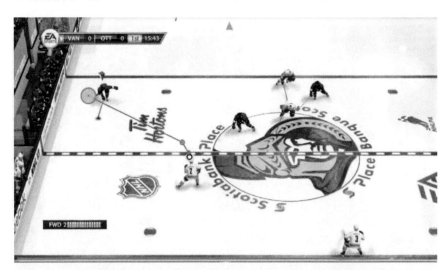

FIGURE 11.6   In NHL 13, gameplay is when the characters are on the ice and play hockey. The user controls the player on the far left, and the eye-tracking data show that the user is actively assessing the opposing players' position. Engagement and progression in this game is highly related to the assessment of the physical virtual world.

Gameplay is the core component of a game, where the inputs of the player completely shape the experience. Each game session is unique, and many aspects of the visual display presented to the user will be unique as well. Understanding what visual elements of the gameplay attract user attention under certain circumstances is of extremely high importance to the design team.

The highly dynamic nature of the gameplay is the most challenging type of eye tracking. The best approach to overcome this challenge is to employ multiple tags to the eye-tracking data. These tags serve to subclassify data based on what just happened and the overall situation in-game. An example of classifying a segment of the sessions based on what just happened could be that the character got shot and the overall situation is that the team is now winning. The multiplicity of variables during gameplay is the biggest challenge for user experience.

Table 11.1 summarizes the challenges of UX eye tracking for each game design element group.

Understanding that interactivity is the quintessential characteristic of games is critical. The ultimate goal of games is to entertain, which involves getting into a state of flow and immersion. The experience that we are trying to measure is in flux constantly and is driven by the user. Interactivity impacts the UX research design and analysis, and supporting this state while running an eye-tracking session is necessary for obtaining meaningful data.

Table 11.1 **Video Game Design Elements and Their Challenges for UX Eye Tracking**

Video Game Design Elements	Brief Description	Interactivity Level	Challenge of UX Eye Tracking
Menus	List of options for playing the game	Medium	Dynamic elements add to the complexity of analysis
Cutscenes	Short movies that support the narrative of the game	Low	Exact same stimulus for all users; easy data aggregation
Overlays	Visual information that is part of the user interface while playing	Medium	Stimulus is fixed in screen location, but its relevancy is highly contextual; AOI aggregation is relatively simple but further per user contextual analysis is needed
Gameplay	Playing the game	High	Each game session is unique; contextual and situational tagging is needed to find trends

The most time consuming use of eye tracking is to run a proper sample through a set of user sessions where many different areas of the game are evaluated. The downside of this is the sheer amount of time on the backend it takes to define and set scenes that the player is experiencing. A test looking at game elements that are static on screen are easier because all users see the same thing. When the action is moving and scenes are defined more by what the player is doing, it gets to be more difficult. Often I find that these are the hardest to do with the least amount of payoff when trying to positively affect an experience within a game due to the amount of time it takes to process the data. Unfortunately this is the type of test that is currently marketed to our field.

Ben Lile, Senior User Researcher, Warner Brothers Games, USA

Current eye-tracking technology is rather robust and allows a fair degree of movement while playing; nevertheless it has limits. Aggregation of data is invaluable for understanding the collected information and for analysis speed, which is vital in the game industry world. Current off-the-shelf eye-tracking software products do not offer an efficient approach for dealing with recordings from video games with multiple participants. Manual analysis of eye-tracking sessions, such as having a researcher review each recording and manually log when the user's gaze is directed at a certain design element on screen while tagging contextual information, can be burdensome. In-house solutions that integrate information from the game to the eye-tracking data can improve the analysis process; for instance, auto-generating areas of interest (AOIs) for overlays and auto-tagging the event that occurs can save a significant amount of effort.

When we play games, we move around without even thinking about it. As things become intense in such an interactive and engaging experience, we have a tendency to lean closer or shift in our seat. All these things can make it difficult to collect good eye-tracking data. It can also be difficult to determine what information is being processed peripherally, but that's where other tools can fill in the gaps.

Ian Livingston, User Research Project Manager, Ubisoft, Montreal, Canada

COMMON EYE-TRACKING RESEARCH QUESTIONS AND ANALYSIS TECHNIQUES IN VIDEO GAMES

In this section, we address the specificities of UX eye tracking as part of the design process of a commercial video game title, which are applicable to the broad array of video games from high-quality, big-budget (i.e., "AAA title") games to social games.

We refer the reader to excellent books dedicated to research design, such as Creswell's work (2009) for refining a research question and employing mixed methods approaches, and to Duchowski's work (2007), which describes design considerations for studies with eye tracking.

Defining the Research Questions

Defining a research question is the first step toward designing a study and is extremely critical. The eye-tracking work within the gaming industry is part of the game development process; thus the eye-tracking findings need to inform game designers with actionable data.

The fast pace of the game industry requires a fast turnaround of results, for instance, delivering the study report within a few days. This fact underlies the need for clear-cut research questions.

Meeting with the key stakeholders should be part of defining the research question. As mentioned earlier in this chapter, common information that is informative to designers, producers, and other game team members include assessing:

- Whether players saw something
- When they saw it
- If there are patterns related to player gaze and behavior

These global questions can adopt numerous variations and can be shaped to the specific characteristics of the game to test.

Did the Player "See" a Design Element?

The ease and accuracy of answering the common question of whether players "see" a certain feature within the game can depend on several factors, but a key aspect is the nature of the feature. If the feature is part of a cutscene, overlay, or menu, then measurement is easier to automate given that the feature in question is likely to have a fixed screen location (or at least have a fixed screen location at a given point in time or after a specific user behavior). This allows UX researchers to define an AOI on the screen, and take advantage of various automated tools and features for tracking gaze within the area.

FIGURE 11.7   Battlefield 3. The overlays related to teammates (user's nickname in green font), enemy-held objective (letters in red), and user's team-held objective (letters in blue) are displayed on screen in a location relative to the user's character's point of view; if the character moves, the overlay location will change accordingly.

If the feature is an element within gameplay, and the user has the ability to manipulate the point of view (as in 3D games like first-person shooter games), it can be extremely difficult to manually assign AOIs using fixed screen locations. For example in Battlefield 3, as shown in Figure 11.7, the exact location of on-screen elements relevant to the user's objectives changes in relationship to the user's character and its placement in the game world. Analysis in these situations requires either custom codes/tools that can map gaze to dynamic screen elements or very time-consuming manual analysis of gaze data overlaid on the gameplay display.

When Did the Player "See" a Particular Design Element?
A key consideration of particular interest in games is the assumption of awareness. An eye tracker can record fixation or dwell time within an AOI (e.g., overlay of the scoreboard in a sports game), and the analysis would show whether the user indeed "saw" this feature. Knowing that a feature caught users' attention can be extremely valuable feedback for a designer.

However, some precautions should be taken with this finding: even if the user's gaze fell on the relevant AOI, it should not be interpreted that they understood the meaning of what they observed. Therefore, visual attention and cognitive processes have to be well distinguished from each other while defining the research question and study objective. It is useful to complement the eye-tracking data with qualitative data; for instance, once the eye-tracking data collection is complete, researchers may follow up with an interview in order to assess impressions and descriptive insights.

Similarly, if the eye tracker fails to record a fixation or dwell time within an AOI, it may not be safe to assume that the user was unaware of the feature. A user may be aware of an on-screen feature due to their peripheral vision. An experienced user may also predict or anticipate the location of an on-screen object based on its previous position, movement, or other cues within the environment. Thus, as with many metrics and measurements, care must be taken in defining measures and ensuring that what is measured can be translated into meaningful and accurate findings regarding the initial questions that prompted the study.

Are There Patterns Related to Players' Gaze and In-Game Behavior?

Once a research question has been defined and the eye-tracking study designed, UX researchers can focus on how to interpret eye-tracking data. As mentioned, different areas of the game have varying degrees of complexity in terms of analysis, and this complexity is due to the freedom of interactivity. However, note that grabbing the user's attention is not equivalent to cognitive processing, such as awareness and understanding.

Eye-tracking data analysis can reveal important information alone. For example, in a racing car game, players can drive at high speeds on challenging tracks, where the inclusion of visual cues support the driving experience. Assessing if users look at the cues can help UX designers determine the effectiveness of the design intention.

The next step in analysis is contextualizing the eye-tracking data with in-game behavior, which brings an interesting layer for more actionable data to improve the user experience. In racing car games, after tracking whether the player noticed the visual cue for an upcoming sharp turn, relating their follow-up behavior, such as repositioning and turning appropriately or crashing, can produce further information about the timing and interpretation of the relevant AOI, and, consequently, how it affects a user's overall experience of the game.

When playing video games, users mostly engage with visual assets moving on screen, for example, a soccer player running on the field. In this case, the common measurement "fixation" is not as representative of the game user experience. Smooth pursuit is more appropriate for eye tracking data of a moving target. Duchowski (2007) defined this concept as when the eyes match the velocity of the moving object. It differs from fixations: beyond the lack of movement of the target object, there are also distinctive miniature eye movements (e.g., drift, tremor, and microsaccade). This is exactly what happens in hockey games like NHL 13, where the characters and the puck are constantly moving on screen.

A suitable eye-tracking metric for video games is "glance duration," which is defined by the duration of the saccade for entering the AOI plus all the fixations and saccades within the AOI (SMI Vision, 2011). Measuring visual engagement with a game element includes all different eye movements involved in tracking the moving object.

Another relevant metric is time-to-first-fixation, which measures the time elapsed from the relevant AOI appearing on screen until the user fixates it for the first time. Game designers present information that has to be visually consumed in a timely manner; establishing what the time-to-first-fixation should be, in conjunction with the design team, can help to ground parameters for analysis.

Video games involve a series of decision processes on what actions will be taken to advance in the game; this applies to menu navigation, overlays, and gameplay. A useful analysis for understanding how users encounter information visually is an "AOI sequence," a time line with the order and the duration that each AOI is visited. For example, Figure 11.8 shows predefined AOIs for the Squad panel in FIFA Ultimate Team, and Figure 11.9 presents one user's AOI sequence of those predefined areas. This analysis and visualization can show a glimpse of how players process the information presented to them.

Interactivity, contextual information, and timing are defining aspects of the gaming user experience, and, consequently,

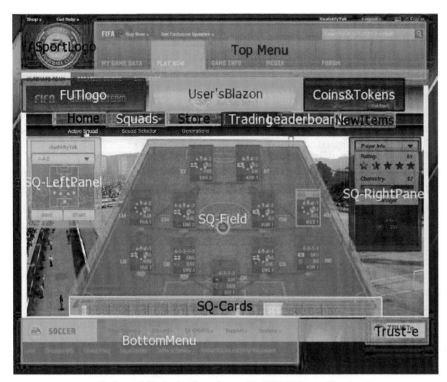

Defined AOIs in the Squad panel in FIFA Ultimate Team.

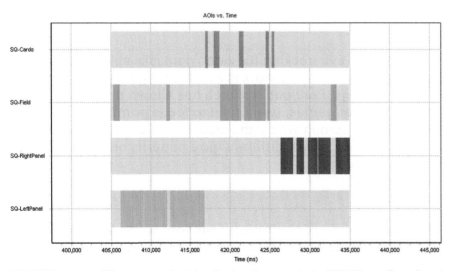

AOI sequence chart visualization of one user in the FIFA Ultimate Team Squad panel. Four AOIs are covered following a reading behavior (from left to right) with almost no backtracking.

analysis of eye-tracking data needs to reflect that essence. Metrics such as glance duration and AOI sequences are better aligned for analysis of the gaming experience, which should be combined with in-game events and overall time of the gaming session to better inform the analysis.

CONCLUSION

Eye tracking as an evaluation method of user experience in video games has gained significant attention during the last few years. Efforts from both industry professionals and academics have contributed to providing new value to the understanding of gaming user research and game design in general.

Eye tracking is an incredible tool. It instantly lets you see what the players are looking at. It shows you what players are looking at, what they notice, and more importantly what they miss. I can see eye tracking being used ubiquitously in our user testing. Having a general understanding of where a player is looking provides an invaluable level of understanding when it comes to all forms of user research.

Ian Livingston, User Research Project Manager, Ubisoft, Montreal, Canada

Nevertheless, eye tracking for video games is still under development, and more work is needed for generalizing the current findings. Previous research has shown that in first-person shooter games, users tend to focus primarily on the middle of the screen where the crosshair is displayed, whereas in sports video games, different gaze patterns arise based on users' skill levels.

The main strength of eye tracking has been access to an aspect of the player's experience that we can't get through any other medium.

Mike Ambinder, Experimental Psychologist, Valve, USA

Future research should focus on common distinguishable video game elements and take into account key guiding questions:

- Video game element groups:
  - Menu (list of options for playing the game)
  - Cutscenes (short movie clips supporting the narrative of the game)
  - Overlays (visual information that is part of the user interface while playing)
  - Gameplay (playing the game itself)
- Key guiding questions
  - Did players "see" a certain design element (or fail to see it)?
  - When did players "see" such a design element?
  - Are the patterns related to players' gaze and in-game behavior?

These areas set a strong framework for understanding user experience through eye tracking because each area has a different level of interactivity and consequent challenges.

More eye-tracking research in video games is needed for further specialization and for establishing general patterns across multiple game genres. This chapter covers the current general knowledge on video game eye tracking and a solid approach on how to deal with and understand eye-tracking data for video games. This is a promising, young niche for UX eye tracking research.

REFERENCES

Ambinder, M., 2011. Biofeedback in gameplay: how valve measures physiology to enhance gaming experience. In: Game Developers Conference, San Francisco, CA, UBM.

Barlet, M., 2008. AbleGamers speaks to PopCap Games Part I. AbleGamers. AbleGamers.com, Retrieved March 3, 2013.

Bernhaupt, R. (Ed.), 2010. Evaluating User Experience in Games: Concepts and Methods. Springer, London.

Creswell, J.W., 2009. Research Design: Qualitative, Quantitative, and Mixed Methods Approaches, third ed. Sage, Thousand Oaks, CA.

Duchowski, A.T., 2007. Eye Tracking Methodology. Theory and Practice, second ed. Springer, New York.

Entertainment Software Association, 2012. 2012 Essential Facts About the Computer and Video Games Industry—Sales, Demographic and Usage Data. Entertainment Software Association, 16.

Isbister, K., Schaffer, N., 2008. Game Usability: Advancing the Player Experience, first ed. Morgan Kaufmann, Burlington, MA.

Isokoski, P., Joos, M., Spakov, O., Martin, B., 2009. Gaze controlled games. Universal Access in the Information Society *8* (4), 323–337.

Rodriguez, A., Steiner, K., 2010. Exploring eye tracking for games user research: a case study of lessons learned. In: Internet User Experience 2010. Presented at the Internet User Experience 2010, Ann Arbor, Michigan.

SMI Vision, 2011. BeGaze Manual. SMI, Teltow, Germany.

Steiner, K., 2011. Human factors in the evaluation and testing of online games. In: Proctor, R. (Ed.), Handbook of Human Factors in Web Design. second ed. CRC Press, Boca Raton, FL, pp. 725–737.

Yuan, B., Folmer, E., Harris, F., 2011. Game accessibility: a survey. Universal Access in the Information Society *10* (1), 81–100.

Zammitto, V., 2011. The science of play testing: EA's methods for user. In: Game Developers Conference. UBM, San Francisco, CA.

Zammitto, V., 2012. Type of data and techniques in games user research. In: International Game Developers' Association, Perspectives, August issue. Retrieved March 3, 2013: igda.org.

IV

EYE TRACKING WITH UNIQUE POPULATIONS

12

OLDER ADULTS

Eugene Loos[1] and Jennifer Romano Bergstrom[2]
[1]University of Amsterdam, Amsterdam, The Netherlands
[2]Fors Marsh Group, Arlington, VA, USA

INTRODUCTION

In many countries, the population is aging at a rapid pace. According to the U.S. Census Bureau (2013), there were nearly 128 million people over the age of 75 in the world in 2000; this number rose to 155 million in 2010 and is expected to increase to 355 million in 2030 (see Figure 12.1). In contrast, while there may be more younger adults (under age 25) overall, their population remains relatively stable at around 3 billion. Older adults are also using the Internet at a faster rate than their younger counterparts (Figure 12.2; Romano, 2010).

While it is beneficial to many people that so much information is supplied in digital form, older adults have trouble using products with complex interfaces and excessive functionality, such as the Internet (Czaja & Lee, 2001, 2009; Pernice & Nielsen, 2002; Chadwick-Dias et al., 2003; Chisnell & Redish, 2004, 2012; Olson et al., 2011). As a result, they may end up frustrated when using the Internet and ultimately may use it with much less frequency compared to younger adults (Olson et al., 2011). Consequently, they risk being excluded from crucial information.

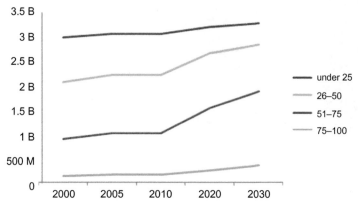

FIGURE 12.1   Estimated (2000–2010) and projected (2020–2030) world population, by age group (in millions and billions). Data from http://www.census.gov/population/international/data/idb/worldpop.php.

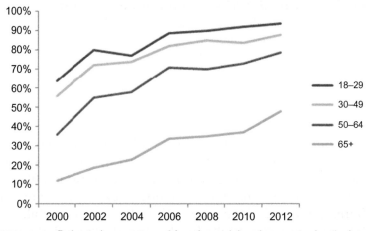

FIGURE 12.2   Estimated percentage of American adults who report using the Internet, by age group. Data from http://www.pewinternet.org/Static-Pages/Trend-Data-(Adults).aspx.

It is clear that if we wish to ensure that older adults have access to the same opportunities as younger adults, then enabling them to have easy access to online information is of prime importance (see Coleman et al., 2007 for a broader perspective on design for inclusivity). If we want to enable older adults to have access to online information, so they will not be excluded from society, then it is important to know to what extent they interact with online information differently than younger adults.

Eye tracking can help researchers to understand the difficulties older adults have when using websites, applications, mobile devices, and other technologies. Yet to date, there have been few studies that have examined age-related differences in eye tracking and the user experience (UX). In this chapter we will show how eye tracking can be used to gain insight into the user experience of older adults and we will provide examples of age-related differences in eye tracking and UX. We conclude with key considerations when conducting eye tracking with older adults.

> *Websites tend to be produced by young designers, who often assume that all users have perfect vision and motor control, and know everything about the Web. These assumptions rarely hold, even when the users are not seniors. However, as indicated by our usability metrics, seniors are more hurt by usability problems than younger users. Among the obvious physical attributes often affected by human aging processes are eyesight, precision of movement, and memory.*
>
> **Pernice & Nielsen, 2002, p.4**

As older adults increasingly make use of websites, it is important to know how age impacts the user experience. There are numerous well-known, age-related cognitive limitations that affect learning and that may influence Internet user experience, as shown in Table 12.1. Usability studies (e.g., Czaja & Lee, 2001, 2009;

Table 12.1 **The Impact of Age-Related Decline on UX**	
Age-related decline in...	...leads to UX issues, such as
Vision Normal aging of visual functions (Kline & Schieber, 1985; Corso, 1992; Bouma, 2000, p. 72; Schneider & Pichora-Fuller, 2000, pp. 168–178, 194–201; Czaja & Lee, 2009, p. 24)	■ Difficulties seeing and processing cluttered online content (Lunn & Harper, 2009) ■ Difficulties reading the screen (Charness et al., 1992; Charness, 2001, pp. 14–16; Echt, 2002, pp. 67–71)
Useful field of view Useful field of view (Ball et al., 1988)	■ Difficulties detecting items in the periphery of screens (Romano Bergstrom et al., under review)
Visual-motor coordination Movement control (Rogers & Fisk, 2000; Czaja & Lee, 2009, pp. 24–25)	■ Difficulties using a keyboard and mouse; selecting links and scrolling pages, especially when targets are small (Walker et al., 1996; Smith et al., 1999; Moffatt & McGrenere, 2007; Lunn & Harper, 2009) ■ Difficulties related to speed of behavior (Vercruyssen, 1997) ■ Difficulties using a mouse to position a cursor on a screen (Walker et al., 1997)
Hearing Age-related changes in the outer, middle, and inner ears (Schneider & Pichora-Fuller, 2000, pp. 159–168, 175–178, 186–194; Charness, 2001, pp. 16–18; Czaja & Lee, 2009, p. 24)	■ Difficulties in detecting high-frequency alerting sounds (beeps or pings) (Czaja & Lee, 2009, p. 24)

Hawthorn, 2003; Olmsted-Hawala et al., 2013; Romano Bergstrom et al., 2013) and gerontechnology research (e.g., Graafmans et al., 1998; Mendelson & Romano Bergstrom, 2013) clearly demonstrate that as people grow older, there is no escaping the fact that age-related limitations that are due to declining vision, hearing, cognition, and motor functions occur more and more. These declines inevitably influence their online experiences.

WEBSITE NAVIGATION AND SEARCH BEHAVIOR OF OLDER ADULTS

If we want to gain insight into the website navigation and search behavior of older adults, then it is important to compare their performance to younger and middle-age adults. Eye tracking enables us to qualitatively and quantitatively assess the differences in performance among user groups. It provides information about user behaviour above and beyond what users are able to tell us and what we observe in typical measures of performance. For example, in a recent study (Romano Bergstrom et al., under review), there were no age-related differences in usability metrics (i.e., accuracy, efficiency), but there were age-related differences in where participants looked on the website. Heat maps and gaze opacity maps demonstrated that older adults (mean age=67) looked at the peripheral left navigation, where important content was located, less often than both younger (mean age=22) and middle-age (mean age=44) adults, while they completed a website task (Figure 12.3). So while there was no difference in typical task performance metrics, there was in eye-tracking data, and this difference was discovered during the first 10 seconds of interaction, suggesting a difference in overall strategy. Another recent study (Hawkins et al., 2013) replicated these findings and found that younger adults (ages 18–29) looked at the top navigation more often than older adults (ages 50–69) on a cluttered home page, but there were no age-related differences for a less-cluttered landing page (Figure 12.4). This valuable information can inform UX designers of where older adults look on websites and can provide insight into differences in user performance and satisfaction.

Older adults generally take longer to make the first click (Olmsted-Hawala et al., 2013) and to complete web-based tasks (e.g., Pernice & Nielsen, 2002; Houtepen, 2007; Tullis, 2007;

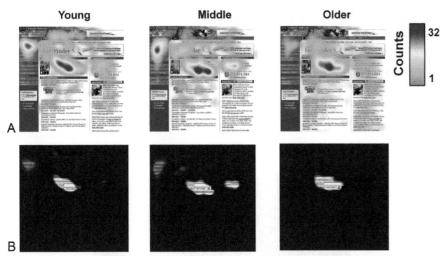

FIGURE 12.3   Mean fixation count (A) heat maps and (B) gaze opacity maps for each group: younger (left), middle-age (center), and older adults (right). Differences in eye movement are shown on the peripheral left navigation elements of the screen. A common area of fixation for all age groups was the center. (From Romano Bergstrom et al., under review.)

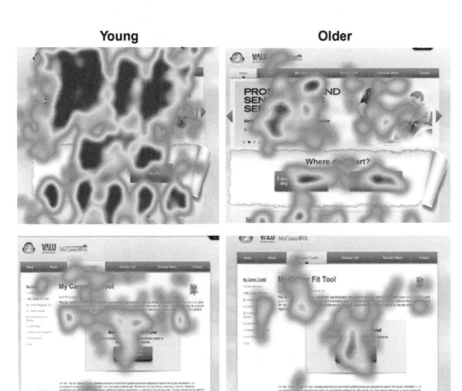

FIGURE 12.4   Mean fixation count heat maps for each group: Younger (left) and older adults (right) for the home page (top) and a landing page (bottom). On the cluttered home page, younger adults looked at the top navigation more often than older adults. There was no age-related difference in where people looked on a less-cluttered landing page. (From Hawkins et al., 2013.)

Loos, 2011; Loos & Mante-Meijer, 2012; Romano Bergstrom & Olmsted-Hawala, 2012; Romano Bergstrom et al., 2013). Loos & Mante-Meijer (2012) used eye tracking to gain insight into the navigation pattern of older and younger adults. Older (mean age=71) and younger adults (mean age=22) performed searches on a number of websites. The study focused on effectiveness (task successfully completed within 5 minutes),

FIGURE 12.5   Older participant using a laptop computer to look for information on a website.

FIGURE 12.6   Older participant using a tablet to look for information on a website.

Table 12.2 Mean Time to Complete Task by Young and Older Adults Across a Number of Usability Studies Where Efficiency Measures were Reported

Study Authors and Year	Sample Size and Age Range		Mean Time to Complete Task	
	Young	Older	Young	Older
Fukuda & Bubb (2003), input task*	13 (17–29)	14 (62–74)	10 seconds	14 seconds
Houtepen (2007)*	13 (18–25)	7 (50+)	2 minutes, 30 seconds	6 minutes, 00 seconds
Loos (2011)*	29 (~21)	29 (65+)	1 minute, .04 seconds	1 minutes, 51 seconds
Pernice & Nielsen (2002)*			7 minutes, 14 seconds	12 minutes, 33 seconds
Romano (2010)*	4 (23–31)	3 (51–59)	2 minutes, 10 seconds	3 minutes, 11 seconds
Romano Bergstrom & Olmsted-Hawala (2012)*	32 (~22)	32 (~68)	2 minutes, 30 seconds	3 minutes, 40 seconds
Romano Bergstrom et al. (2013), Study 1*	4 (23–31)	3 (51–59)	2 minutes, 10 seconds	3 minutes, 11 seconds
Romano Bergstrom et al. (2013), Study 2	3 (19–27)	3 (53–59)	2 minutes, 49 seconds	3 minutes, 27 seconds
Romano Bergstrom et al. (2013), Study 4	7 (19–27)	4 (65–75)	3 minutes, 31 seconds	3 minutes, 12 seconds
Romano Bergstrom et al. (2013), Study 5*	5 (20–29)	3 (52–57)	1 minute, 48 seconds	2 minutes, 46 seconds
Romano Bergstrom et al., under review	9 (20–25)	20 (62–72)	1 minute, 19 seconds	1 minute, 36 seconds
Tullis (2007)*	10 (20–39)	10 (50–69)	40 seconds per page	57 seconds per page

*Age-related difference in time to complete task.

efficiency (time needed to complete the search task), and the patterns of fixations. Consistent with previous research, younger adults successfully completed the search more often than the older group, and in most cases, the younger adults completed the task faster than older adults (1 minute 4 seconds vs 1 minute 51 seconds; Table 12.2).

The fact that most older adults need more time to accomplish their search tasks compared to younger adults is consistent with the decline in processing speed and reaction time that is associated with aging. However, older adults also may not be as comfortable using the Internet since they did not grow up using websites, as young adults presumably do. According to socialization theory, people are formed by the period in which they grow up, and socioeconomic and political circumstances and the technology available during their formative years (between the 15th and 25th year of life) shape their behavior (see Becker, 1992, p. 21; Peiser, 1999). Obviously, the introduction of a new technology can lead to the rise of a new "technology generation" (Sackmann & Weymann, 1994, pp. 41–43).

> *Successive cohorts grow up, each with their own specific constellation of available media, media competency, and media preferences. These early experiences with media could later lead to shared behavior patterns.* [translation] (Huysmans et al., 2004, p. 20).

Commenting on the relevance of socialization theory for media use, van der Goot (2009) argued:

> *Generations may very well develop specific patterns of media use when young and remain loyal to these patterns throughout the rest of their life* (Mares & Woodard, 2006; Hofmann & Schwender, 2007). [translation] (p. 255).

Prior experience with technology is a strong predictor of computer-related task performance (Czaja et al., 2001). As with many other tasks, as people become comfortable, they become better at doing something. In a recent study (Loos & Mante-Meijer, 2012), eye tracking showed that while younger adults looked at the right place where they were supposed to click in order to arrive at the web page containing the information they were looking for, more older adults than younger ones looked longer at the wrong place to click. However, when Internet experience was accounted for, the older adults who reported using the Internet daily looked less intensely at the wrong place compared to older adults who reported *not using the Internet daily* (Figure 12.7).

In another study that examined age-related differences in user experience, Docampo et al. (2001) confirmed that earlier experience with an interface enhances the user's effectiveness. They found that older adults with computer experience encountered fewer difficulties while using a videophone than older adults having less or no computer experience. Further, eye-tracking data demonstrated that novice older users made longer fixations overall than modestly experienced older adults. Computer experience proved to be a highly important factor in eye-movement behavior and performance.

Thus, it appears that daily Internet use may have greater impact on navigation patterns than age. This demonstrates that *age* may *not* be the explanatory variable for the navigation patterns previously found in website navigation and search

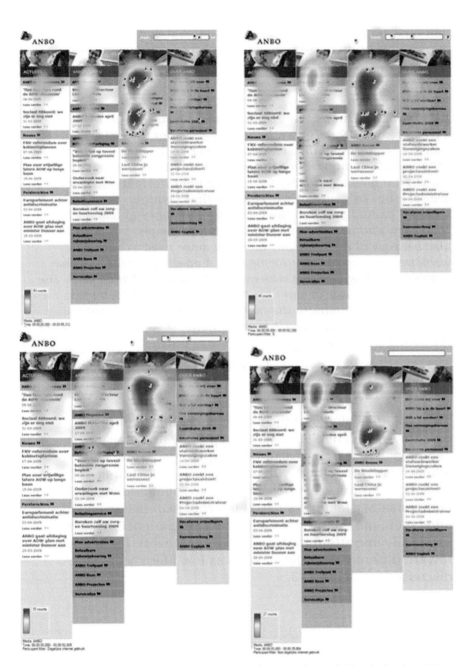

FIGURE 12.7   Mean fixation count heat maps for young (upper left) and all older adults (upper right), older adults who report using the Internet daily (lower left), and older adults who report not using the Internet daily (lower right). Older adults who report using the Internet daily have similar eye-tracking patterns (lower left) as younger adults (upper left). (From Loos & Mante-Meijer, 2012.)

behavior (e.g., Houtepen, 2007; Tullis, 2007). Rather, *Internet experience* appears to play a much more important role (see also Hill et al., 2011).

Different age groups absorb and process information in a completely different way, but also age is not the only decisive factor. Actually it is not age per se, but the amount of knowledge and practice the participants have on how to use digital media (websites) to gather the information they are seeking. In general, you can say that younger people are quicker, partially due to the fact that they move quicker with their eyes and process quicker than older people, but definitely also because of the fact that they are more used to using websites as a source of information. A challenge in that sense is to establish whether it was indeed physical age that made the participants slower or not able to find the right information on the Internet, or actually the fact that their knowledge of using a computer/websites to gather information was less than that of the younger group.

Luuk Houtepen, SThree GmbH, Germany

These studies highlight the importance of including demographic variables other than merely age in user experience research. It is not enough to learn that older adults have difficulties with an interface or that their eye-tracking patterns are different from younger adults. Other compensatory factors, such as Internet experience and education, may play a role in the user experience. This is especially important to consider when the interface is geared toward different audiences, such as low literacy users, as discussed in Chapter 13.

CONDUCTING UX RESEARCH WITH OLDER ADULTS

Older adults are a unique population, and conducting eye-tracking research with them can be tricky. These guidelines can be used when conducting UX and eye-tracking research with older adults.

1. Include Large Groups of Older and Younger Participants

The question of proper sample size often comes up with eye-tracking research. There is great debate in the field, with some arguing that eight participants per user group are sufficient (e.g., Wichansky, 2000; Goldberg & Wichansky, 2003, p. 512), while others believe that 30 participants are necessary (e.g., Pernice & Nielsen, 2002). While there is no magic number for proper sample size, it is often decided based on study objectives, time, and budget, as well as product and task complexity (e.g., completing paper forms). In reality, as UX researchers, we must keep in mind the client's objectives as well as the best study design. When using eye tracking, we have to consider our data collection process.

Many factors may play a role in the ability for a person's eyes to track well. For example, certain types of eye glasses (e.g., thick frames; bifocal lenses) impact the ability to track, and older adults are more likely to wear eye glasses. Facial structure also plays a role, and older adults' eyelids as well as the tissue around their eyes tend to sag. While many studies do not report how many participants must be dropped from data analysis due to lack of eye-tracking data, it has been our experience that older adults do not track as often or as well as younger and middle-age adults (e.g., Romano Bergstrom et al. [under review] reported that of eight participants who were excluded from analyses due to insufficient capture rate, seven were older adults). Thus, when working with different user groups, especially older adults, it is important to over-recruit participants to end up with enough usable data to make valid conclusions. Further, if you wish to compare older adults' data to other user groups, sufficient sample size is needed.

2. Collect Demographic Data

Individual differences increase as people age, and it is therefore important to focus not only on age, but also on other factors that may affect the user experience (e.g., Loos, 2011; Loos & Mante-Meijer, 2012). When conducting UX research with older users, be sure to collect data that include Internet experience, education, comfort using computers, and other variables that may affect performance. When analyzing results, it is important to understand the complete picture.

3. Slow Down

As we age, we slow down. Our reaction time and processing speed slow, and our memory declines. This is well-known, yet many UX researchers and session moderators forget this simple fact and treat older adults like young participants. This makes it difficult for the older participant to follow along and keep up. They may not tell the moderator that they would like something repeated because they do not want to appear slow. But it is our job to make them feel comfortable and welcome. This includes slowing down, pausing between sentences (e.g., during an introduction that explains the session), allowing breaks, and making sure our older participants understand the tasks and how they are helping us.

CONCLUSION

Older adults experience natural cognitive decline that may interfere with the user experience. UX researchers and designers must consider these needs and adapt. In some cases, "multi-modal redundancy," such as the use of both visual and auditory signs, may help older users (Wright, 2000, p. 86; Zajicek & Morissey, 2003; Blackler et al., 2006), whether in terms of presenting information during a usability study or in presenting information on a website or form. While some may fear that making user experiences easier for older adults might irritate younger and more experienced users, the opposite is true—rather than having an adverse effect on a site's usability, making it accessible to all tends to enhance it (Gregor et al., 2002; Johnson & Kent, 2007). Consider the experienced user who is under stress or who is ill—having a usable user interface makes the experience better for these individuals as well.

Manuals such as *Design for Inclusivity: A Practical Guide to Accessible, Innovative and User-Centred Design* by Coleman et al. (2007), *The Universal Access Handbook* edited by Stephanidis (2001), and *Human-Computer Interaction: Designing for Diverse Users and Domains* edited by Sears & Jacko (2009) advise us on how to achieve universal access in the information society from a design perspective.

In a society that is increasingly making information accessible online, it is crucial that the information is accessible for all. It is clear that examining the user experience for older adults is important. While there has been little empirical work in this area thus far, we can make the user experience more enjoyable and less stressful if we pay attention to all our users. While we know that factors such as age, Internet experience, and cognition all play unique roles in the UX, more work is needed to further understand the impact of each on interacting with computers and interfaces.

REFERENCES

Ball, K.K., Beard, B.L., Roenker, D.L., Miller, R.L., Griggs, D.S., 1988. Age and visual search: expanding the useful field of view. J. Opt. Soc. Am. 5, 2210–2219.

Becker, H.E. (Ed.), (1992). Dynamics of cohort and generation research. In: Proceedings of a symposium held on 12, 13 and 14 December 1991 at the University of Utrecht, the Netherlands. Thesis publishers, Amsterdam.

Blackler, A., Popovic, V., Mahar, D., 2006. Toward a design methodology for applying intuitive interaction. Paper presented at the WonderGround: 2006 Design Research Society International Conference, Lisbon, Portugal.

Bouma, H., 2000. Document and interface design for older citizens. In: Westendorp, P., Jansen, C., Punselie, R. (Eds.), Interface Design & Document Design. Rodopi, Amsterdam, pp. 67–80.

Chadwick-Dias, A., McNulty, M., Tullis, T.S., 2003. Web Usability and Age: How Design Changes Can Improve Performance. CUU'03, November 10–11, 2003, Vancouver, British Columbia, Canada. http://www.bentley.edu/events/agingbydesign2004/presentations/tedesco_chadwickdias_tullis_webusabilityandage.pdf.

Charness, N., 2001. Aging and communication: human factors issues. In: Charness, N., Parks, D.C., Sabel, B.A. (Eds.), Communication, Technology and Aging: Opportunities and Challenges for the Future. Springer, New York, pp. 1–29.

Charness, N., Schumann, C.E., Boritz, G.A., 1992. Training older adults in word processing: effects of age, experience, and interface. Presentation prepared for the Workshop on Aging and Disabilities in the Information Age, Johns Hopkins University, Baltimore, MD.

Chisnell, D., Redish, J., 2004. Designing Websites for Older Adults: A Review of Recent Research. AARP. Available at, http://www.aarp.org/olderwiserwired.

Chisnell, D., Redish, J., 2012. Modelling older adults for website design. In: Loos, E.F., Haddon, L., Mante-Meijer, E.A. (Eds.), Generational Use of New Media. Ashgate, Farnham, UK, pp. 107–128.

Coleman, R., Clarkson, J., Dong, H., Cassim, J., 2007. Design for Inclusivity. A Practical Guide to Accessible, Innovative and User-Centred Design. Gower, Aldershot, UK.

Corso, J.F., 1992. The functionality of aging sensory systems. In: Bouma, H., Graafmans, J.A.M. (Eds.), Gerontechnology. IOS Press, Amsterdam, pp. 51–78.

Czaja, S.J., Lee, C.C., 2001. The internet and older adults: design challenges and opportunities. In: Charness, N., Parks, D.C., Sabel, B.A. (Eds.), Communication, Technology and Aging: Opportunities and Challenges for the Future. Springer, New York, pp. 60–78.

Czaja, S.J., Lee, C.C., 2009. Information technology and older adults. In: Sears, A., Jacko, J.E. (Eds.), Human-Computer Interaction: Designing for Diverse Users and Domains. CRC Press, Boca Raton, FL, pp. 17–32.

Czaja, S.J., Charit, J., Ownby, R., Roth, D.L., Nair, S., 2001. Examining age differences in performance of a complex information search and retrieval task. Psychol. Aging 21, 333–352.

Docampo Rama, M., Ridder, H., Bouma, H., 2001. Technology generation and age in using layered user interfaces. Gerontechjournal 1 (1), 25–39.

Echt, K.V., 2002. Designing web-based health information for older adults: visual considerations and design directives. In: Morrell, R.W. (Ed.), Older Adults, Health Information, and the World Wide Web. Lawrence Erlbaum, Mahwah, NJ, pp. 61–87.

Fukuda, R., Bubb, H., 2003. PsychNology Journal 1 (3), 202–228.

Goldberg, J.H., Wichansky, A.M., 2003. Eye tracking in usability evaluation: a practitioner's guide. In: Hyönä, J., Radach, R., Deubel, H. (Eds.), The Mind's Eye: Cognitive and Applied Aspects of Eye Movement Research. North Holland, Amsterdam.

Graafmans, J., Taipale, V., Charness, N., 1998. Gerontechnology: A Sustainable Investment in the Future. IOS press, Amsterdam.

Gregor, P., Newell, A.F., Zajicek, M., 2002. Designing for dynamic diversity— interfaces for older people. Assets 2002, 151–156.

Hawkins, D., Strohl, J., Romano Bergstrom, J.C., 2013. Individual differences in eye movements during the visual search of websites. Poster presentation at the Human Computer Interaction International (HCII) Conference, Las Vegas, NV, July 2013.

Hawthorn, D., 2003. How universal is good design for older users? Conference paper, ACM SIGCAPH Computers and the Physically Handicapped, Proceedings of the 2003 conference on universal usability, issue 73–74.

Hill, R., Dickinson, A., Arnott, J., Gregor, P., McIver, L., 2011. Older Users' Eye Movements: Experience Counts. CHI 2011, May 7–12, Vancouver, British Columbia, Canada.

Hofmann, D., Schwender, C., 2007. Biographical functions of cinema and film preferences among older German adults. A representative quantitative survey. Communications 32, 473–491.

Houtepen, L., 2007. Op zoek naar Informatie. Onderzoek naar het vinden en beoordelen van informatie op de websites van de vijf grootste zorgverzekeraars [Unpublished Master thesis]. Utrecht University/Utrecht School of Governance, Utrecht.

Huysmans, F., de Haan, J., van den Broek, A., 2004. Achter de schermen: Een kwart eeuw lezen, luisteren, kijken en internetten. Sociaal en Cultureel Planbureau, The Hague.

Johnson, R., Kent, S., 2007. Designing universal access: web application for the elderly and disabled. Cognit. Tech. Work 9, 209–218.

Kline, D.W., Schieber, F.J., 1985. Vision and aging. In: Birren, J.E., Schaie, K.W. (Eds.), Handbook of the Psychology of Aging. Van Nostrand Reinhold, New York, pp. 296–331.

Loos, E.F., 2011. In search of information on websites: a question of age? In: Stephanidis, C. (Ed.), Universal Access in HCI, Part II, HCII 2011, LNCS 6766. Springer-Verlag, Berlin, pp. 196–204.

Loos, E.F., Mante-Meijer, E.A., 2012. Getting access to website health information. In: Loos, E.F., Haddon, L., Mante-Meijer, E.A. (Eds.), Generational Use of New Media. Ashgate, Farnham, UK, pp. 185–202.

Lunn, D., Harper, S., 2009. Senior Citizens and the Web. School of Computer Science, Manchester, UK.

Mares, M.L., Woodard, E., 2006. In search of the older audience: adult differences in television viewing. J. Broadcast. Electron. Media 50, 595–614.

Mendelson, J., Romano Bergstrom, J.C., 2013. Age differences in the knowledge and usage of QR codes. In: Proceedings from the Human Computer Interaction International Conference, Las Vegas, NV, July 2013.

Mofatt, K.A., McGrenere, J., 2007. Slipping and drifting: using older users to uncover pen-based target acquisition difficulties. In: ASSETS '07: Proceedings of the 9th International ACM SIGAACCESS Conference on Computers and Accessibility, 11–18. ACM, New York.

Olson, K.E., O'Brien, M., Rogers, W.A., Charness, N., 2011. Diffusion of technology: frequency of use for younger and older adults. Ageing Int. 36 (1), 123–145.

Olmsted-Hawala, E.L., Romano Bergstrom, J.C., Rogers, W., 2013. Age-related differences in search strategy and performance when using a data-rich web site. In: Proceedings from the Human Computer Interaction International Conference, Las Vegas, NV, July 2013.

Peiser, W., 1999. The television generation's relation to the mass media in Germany: accounting for the impact of private television. J. Broadcast. Electron. Media 43, 364–385.

Pernice, K., Nielsen, J., 2002. Web Usability for Senior Citizens. Design Guidelines Based on Usability Studies with People Age 65 and Older. Nielsen Norman Group, Fremont, CA.

Rogers, W.A., Fisk, A.D., 2000. Human factors, applied cognition and aging. In: Craik, F.I.M., Salthouse, T.A. (Eds.), The Handbook of Aging and Cognition. Lawrence Erlbaum, Mahwah, NJ, pp. 559–591.

Romano, J.C., 2010. Using eye tracking to examine age-related differences in web site performance. In: Proceedings of the Human Factors and Ergonomics Society 54th Annual Meeting, pp. 1360–1364.

Romano Bergstrom, J.C., Olmsted-Hawala, E.L., 2012. Effects of age and think-aloud protocol on eye-tracking data and usability measures. Poster presentation at Usability Professionals Association (UPA) Conference, Las Vegas, NV, June 2012.

Romano Bergstrom, J.C., Olmsted-Hawala, E.L., Jans, M.E., 2013. Age-related differences in eye tracking and usability performance: web site usability for older adults. Int. J. Hum. Comput. Interact. 29, 541–548.

Romano Bergstrom, J.C., Olmsted-Hawala, E.L., Bergstrom, H.C., under review. Older adults fail to see the peripheral parts of the display during a Web site search task.

Sackmann, R., Weymann, A., 1994. Die Technisierung des Alltags. Generationen und Technische Innovationen. Campus Verlag, Frankfurt, Germany.

Schneider, B.A., Pichora-Fuller, M.K., 2000. Implications of perceptual deterioration for cognitive aging research. In: Craik, F.I.M., Salthouse, T.A. (Eds.), The Handbook of Aging and Cognition. Lawrence Erlbaum, Mahwah, NJ, pp. 155–219.

Sears, A., Jacko, J.E. (Eds.), 2009. Human-Computer Interaction. Designing for Diverse Users and Domains. CRC Press, Boca Raton, FL.

Smith, M.W., Sharit, J., Czaja, S.J., 1999. Aging, motor control and the performance of computer mouse track. Hum. Factors 41 (3), 389–397.

Stephanidis, C. (Ed.), 2001. Universal Access in HCI: Towards an Information Society for All, Vol. 3. Lawrence Erlbaum, Mahwah, NJ.

Tullis, T.S., 2007. Older adults and the web: lessons learned from eye-tracking. In: Stephanidis, C. (Ed.), In Universal Access in Human-Computer Interaction. Coping with Diversity, HCI, LNCS 4554. Springer, Berlin, pp. 1030–1039.

van der Goot, M., 2009. Stand van de wetenschap. Televisiekijken in het leven van ouderen: een literatuuroverzicht. Tijdschrift voor Communicatiewetenschap 37 (3), 254–267.

Vercruyssen, M., 1997. Movement control and speed of behavior. In: Fisk, A.D., Rogers, W.A. (Eds.), Handbook of Human Factors and the Older Adult. Academic Press, San Diego CA, pp. 55–86.

Walker, N., Millians, J., Worden, A., 1996. Mouse accelerations and performance of older computer users. In: Proceedings of Human Factors and Ergonomics Society 40th Annual Meeting. Santa Monica, CA, pp. 151–154.

Walker, N., Philbin, D.A., Fisk, A.D., 1997. Age-related differences in movement control: adjusting submovement structure to optimize performance. J. Gerontol. B Psychol. Sci. Soc. Sci. 52B, P40–P52.

Wichansky, A.M., 2000. Usability testing in 2000 and beyond. Ergonomics 43 (7), 998–1006.

Wright, P., 2000. Supportive documentation for older people. In: Westendorp, P., Jansen, C., Punselie, R. (Eds.), Interface Design & Document Design. Rodopi, Amsterdam, pp. 81–100.

Zajicek, M., Morissey, W., 2003. Multimodality and interactional differences in older adults. In: Carbonell, N. (Ed.), Multimodality: A Step Towards Universal Access. Special issue of Universal Access in the Information Society, 2, pp. 125–133, 2.

Wichansky, A.M., 2000. Usability testing in 2000 and beyond. Ergonomics 43 (7), 998–1006.

Wright, P. 2000. Supportive documentation for older people. In Westendorp, P., Jansen, C., Punselie, R. (Eds.) Interface Design & Document Design. Rodopi, Amsterdam, pp. 81–100.

Zajicek, M., Morrissey, W. 2003. Multimodality and interactional differences in older adults. In: Carbonell, N. (Ed.), Multimodality: A Step Towards Universal Access. Special issue of Universal Access in the Information Society 2, pp. 125–133.?

13

LOW LITERACY USERS

Angela Colter[1] and Kathryn Summers[2]
[1]*Electronic Ink, Philadelphia, PA, USA*
[2]*University of Baltimore, Baltimore, MD, USA*

INTRODUCTION

If the interface you are testing is going to be used by the general public, it is likely that a significant part of your audience is going to have low literacy skills. Literacy affects almost all aspects of using the Web. For example, navigation (Chapter 6) is a very complicated literacy activity, since it requires reading a range of written labels, holding all of the labels in working memory, and then comparing the meaning of all the labels against each other and against your goal in order to identify the label that is most likely to lead to the desired content. Search (Chapter 2) is a complicated literacy activity because typing a search term successfully depends to some degree on spelling (some search engines help with spelling more successfully than others) and reading and comparing the results to identify the best option. Filling out a form online (Chapter 5) requires reading the instructions (which many people try to avoid, whether they have high or low literacy), reading the form field labels, and either spelling the answers to questions or reading and selecting from multiple-choice answers. For low literacy users, eye tracking can provide crucial information about which aspects of the interface are used, which are missed, and which are difficult to understand.

THE IMPACT OF LITERACY ON WEB USE

In order to fully appreciate the power of eye tracking for users with low literacy skills, it is important to understand what low literacy means, who it affects, and how it impacts Web use.

In the United States, literacy is defined by the National Literacy Act of 1991 as "an individual's ability to read, write and speak in English; compute and solve problems at levels of proficiency necessary to function on the job and in society; to achieve one's goals; and develop one's knowledge and potential (HR 751, 1991)." Low literacy, defined as below basic or basic literacy skills, affects nearly half of the adult population in the United States and the UK. In Germany, Canada, and Australia, over 40% of adults have low literacy skills. In Sweden, 25% have low literacy skills, and in Portugal, it is 80% (Organisation for Economic Co-operation and Development, 2000).

These are shocking numbers, but they do not mean that a large part of the population cannot read at all. Most can; they just don't do it very well. Low literacy means being weak in skills that contribute to literacy: skills such as word recognition, understanding sentence structure, being able to locate a piece of information in text, drawing inferences, applying the information read to the reader's own situation, and being able to use math to figure things out (White, 2003). As a result, those with low literacy skills may read slowly, with great effort, and come away with an incomplete or incorrect understanding of what they have read.

There are both market-driven and ethical reasons to design for those with low literacy skills. As creators of interfaces and the content those interfaces contain, we have a responsibility to ensure that anyone who wishes to can read and understand the materials we create. Accommodating low literacy is an accessibility issue no different than making sure people with low vision or blindness, hearing impairment, and motor or cognitive impairment can understand and use the information we publish.

It is estimated that 7–10% of the U.S. population has some sort of disability that can affect their use of the Web (Groves, 2011). With low literacy rates in many industrialized nations approaching 48% (OECD, 2000), it is critical to include this population if we wish to ensure access to all users. Even skilled readers may sometimes find reading more difficult when facing time pressure, fatigue, or stress. Fortunately, improving an interface for those who do not read well leads to increased usability and satisfaction for most users (Nielsen, 2005; Jarrett, 2012).

As mentioned in Chapter 7, when users look for specific content, they scan headings, bulleted lists, and link text to tell whether the content they are seeking is on the current page or whether they are better off looking elsewhere. From a cognitive perspective, reading involves both decoding and comprehension (Tunmer, 1986). First you "decode" the text on the page by associating the code (the words) with the concepts they represent. With familiar words, sight-word recognition happens immediately and without much effort, but unfamiliar words require the reader to consciously and deliberately figure out a word's meaning (Beck, 1995). After decoding the individual words, you move on to comprehension: figuring out what the writer was trying to communicate by putting those particular words together. Adults with low literacy skills can struggle with both word recognition and understanding what the words put together actually mean. For them, reading can be hard work. Holding the meaning of decoded words in memory and then comparing the meaning of one label or one passage to another is *really* hard work.

The Value of Eye Tracking When Designing for Low Literacy

Eye tracking can help reveal parts of an interface that present barriers to people with poor reading skills in a way that testing their understanding or asking them directly may not uncover. It is certainly possible to test a person's comprehension of what they just read by asking them questions about the content or having them paraphrase it. But asking them directly whether they had trouble reading is tricky. People with adequate reading skills might be able to tell you what parts they had trouble reading and why, but people who lack those skills might not even admit they had trouble reading. In fact, most adults who have very low levels of literacy describe themselves as being able to read "well" or "very well" (Kirsch, 2002). They might not be able to tell you why they had trouble or what it was about the material that they found difficult. They might assume, incorrectly, that they did understand what they read. Or they might simply wish to avoid the embarrassment of admitting that they had difficulty reading. People who are poor readers will often use strategies to avoid revealing their reading deficiencies, even to their family members (Parikh et al., 1996). Using eye tracking to observe how people read can provide clues to where they run into difficulties and save them from the uncomfortable task of explaining why the content is not working for them.

Eye tracking can also help reduce the cognitive effort required of your participant during a study. As discussed in Chapter 3, traditional usability tests often employ the "think-aloud" method, which asks participants to give a running commentary describing what they are doing and why. While this can be an effective method to gain insights about an interface's design, it has some disadvantages. For one thing, the think-aloud method places an additional burden on participants: not only do they have to attempt to complete tasks, but they also have to verbalize their thoughts. Having participants think aloud about what they are doing can also sometimes change what they do, thus potentially changing the very behavior that is being studied (Brinkman, 1992; Nagle & Zietlow, 2012). This method becomes an even bigger problem with participants who have cognitive impairments, such as those that often affect reading (Johnstone, 2006). In contrast, eye tracking can provide insight into a participant's experience without placing additional cognitive burden on them by having them think about (and possibly change) what they are doing. It can therefore be a particularly valuable choice for testing with people who have low literacy skills.

By understanding the reading process and observing a person's reading behaviors during an eye-tracking study, we can make inferences about the effort a reader is exerting. Here are some things to look for during eye-tracking studies that might indicate when a reader is having difficulty.

Reading Every Word: More Fixations and Longer Fixations on Text
Because people with low literacy skills can have a difficult time with both decoding and comprehension, reading can take a great deal of effort. It is common to see them fixate on nearly every word on the page to make sure that they do not miss the

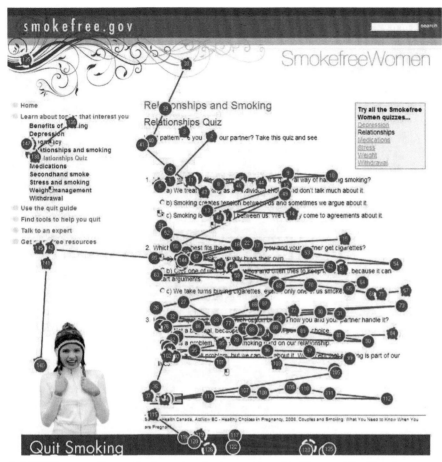

FIGURE 13.1   Gaze path of a reader who does not have low literacy skills skimming a page.

information they are looking for (Summers & Summers, 2004). This can mean that they are spending a lot of cognitive effort on word recognition with little left over to make sense of what the words actually mean (see Figures 13.1 and 13.2).

To save low literacy users from having to spend more effort on reading than necessary, make sure the content you provide is as clear and efficient as possible. Understand your users' needs when they come to your site and write to address those needs. Writing in an inverted-pyramid style—where the most important information to the reader is provided first followed by supporting material—is useful for any reader, but can be particularly helpful for those with low literacy skills (see more about the inverted pyramid in Chapter 7).

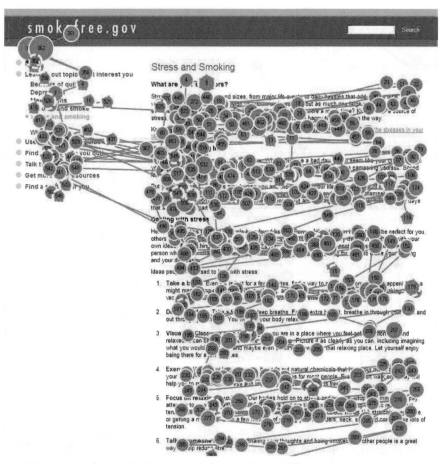

FIGURE 13.2   Gaze path of a reader who has low literacy skills plowing through every word.

Re-reading Words

Poor readers will often re-read sections of text and revisit interface elements in an effort to decode and comprehend. Despite having decoded each word on a page, they may still not understand what it means, and they will go back over a word, a phrase, a sentence, or even sometimes an entire paragraph to make sense of it. This may also happen when users are certain, or simply hope, that the information they are looking for must be in the section they just read. They may assume that the reason they did not find the answer was because they either did not notice it or did not understand what they read, so they read the passage again hoping to find whatever they missed the first time (see Figure 13.3).

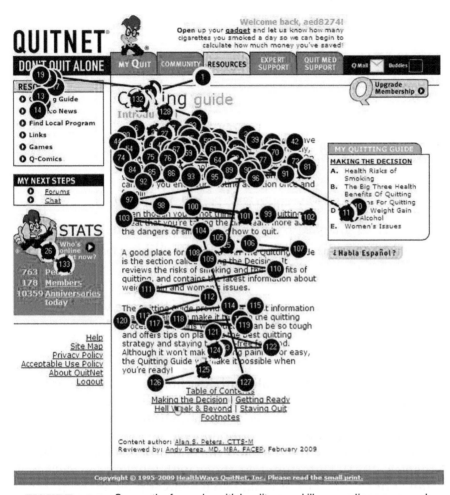

FIGURE 13.3 Gaze path of a reader with low literacy skills re-reading a paragraph.

Skipping Words or Sections

Because reading can require a great deal of cognitive effort for people with low literacy skills, they may attempt to do as little reading as possible or avoid reading altogether by skipping instructions on a form, hard words in a sentence, or even whole sections of dense text. It is common to see them skip over headings, sometimes landing right in the middle of a paragraph. As a result, they often miss the answer they were looking for or the cues that would tell them whether their question was likely to be addressed on the page or not (Summers & Summers, 2004, 2005; Summers et al., 2006). If eye tracking shows that participants with lower literacy skills are doing a lot of skipping

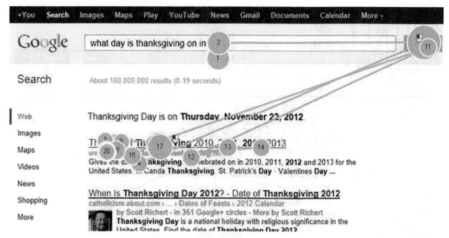

FIGURE 13.4   Gaze path of a participant searching for the date of Thanksgiving, skipping over the answer, and clicking a link to continue the search.

on your interface, you need to find ways to make your text *look* easier to read (Doak et al., 1996; Figure 13.4).

Satisficing

Another strategy that people with low literacy skills use to avoid reading is "satisficing." A combination of the words "satisfy" and "suffice," this is a decision-making strategy people employ to arrive at the best option available while reducing the cognitive burden of the decision-making process (Simon, 1956; Krosnick, 1991). Unfortunately, those with low literacy skills will often choose the very first plausible answer they encounter: not the best answer or even the right answer, but the one they first come across that could possibly qualify. You can identify this behavior in eye-tracking studies when participants are given a task or question to answer and you see them read until they find the first plausible answer, then they stop reading any further (Summers & Summers, 2005). In this situation, user experience (UX) designers must make sure that the first information users find is the most important and the easiest to understand (see Figures 13.5 and 13.6).

Getting Distracted

Perhaps one of the most useful applications of eye tracking to low literacy is witnessing which parts of an interface are distracting to a poor reader. The truth is, every element you

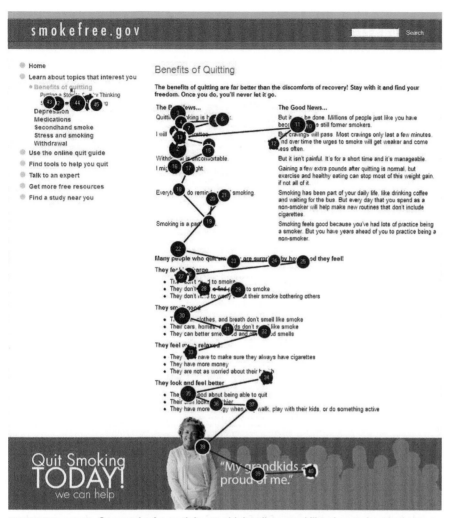

FIGURE 13.5   Gaze path of a participant with low literacy skills who reads only the text that looks easy to read, thus missing most of the valuable information on the page.

add to a page—an image, a word, or a text link, whether it moves or is static—competes for the reader's attention. But this competition for attention is particularly damaging for those who do not read well. Reading itself requires a lot of cognitive effort; additional elements in an interface that compete for the user's attention make the task even harder (Mayer, 2009). Of course, directing the reader's attention to a particular page element can be useful at times. Movement or changes in color can alert a user to new information that results from user input, such as an error message or form submission. Images and

FIGURE 13.6 Gaze path of a participant looking for the health dangers of smoking, and stopping before seeing information about children and second-hand smoke.

animations easily draw the users gaze and can do a better job explaining some types of information or processes than words alone (Mayer, 2009). But too much extraneous information and too many attention-getting elements can make the difference between task success and failure for those with poor reading skills. Eye tracking can help to identify when and how interface elements attract attention. We can use this information to ensure we are supporting task success rather than impeding it (see Figures 13.7–13.9).

Determining a Participant's Literacy Level
Since you cannot simply ask your participants what their literacy level is—they likely do not know—you will have to confirm by testing.

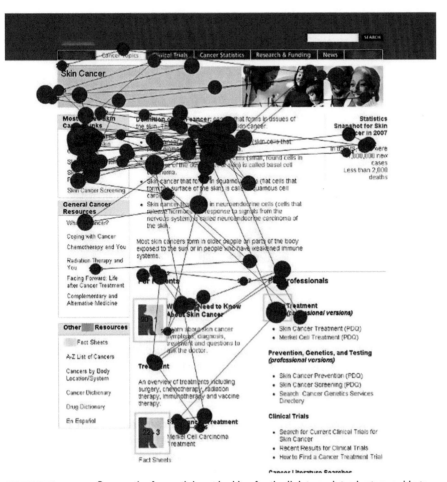

FIGURE 13.7 Gaze path of a participant looking for the link to an introductory guide to skin cancer on a multi-column page of resources.

People who are older, less educated, who have low income, have a chronic health condition, or have been incarcerated are more likely to have low literacy skills (Kirsch, 2002). While someone who did not finish high school is more likely to have low literacy skills than someone who did, you cannot rely on number of years of school attended to accurately predict literacy level. Having these characteristics makes it more likely that a person has low literacy skills, but participants must be assessed in person to verify their literacy levels.

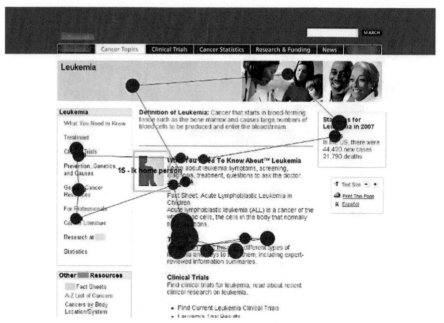

FIGURE 13.8   Gaze path of a participant finding the link to an introductory guide to skin cancer on a single-column page of the same resources. Note that the cognitive effort of finding the target content is much reduced by the simpler layout.

> *Because identifying people with low literacy skills can be so difficult, a study sought to identify if there were any questions a participant could answer about themselves that accurately predicted low literacy (Wallace et al., 2006). One question was able to predict low literacy with a high degree of certainty: "How confident are you filling out medical forms by yourself?" Answering "somewhat," "a little bit" or "not at all" predicts low literacy 83% of the time. If respondents answer "extremely" or "quite a lot," they're more likely to have high literacy skills.*

There are many methods available to assess a person's literacy level, but all must be done in person. Several of the methods, like the Wide Range Achievement Test (WRAT), can take 35–45 minutes to administer and score. By that time, your participants may have spent a great deal of cognitive effort on your literacy assessment test before they have even started your UX study. Better solutions for user research are assessments that take less than five minutes, like the Slossen Oral Reading Test (SORT) or the Rapid Assessment of Adult Literacy in Medicine (REALM; See Figure 13.10; Davis et al., 1991).

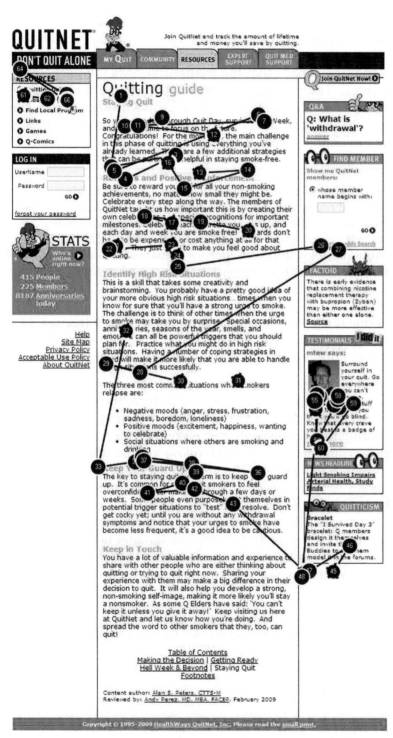

FIGURE 13.9 Gaze plot of a participant failing to process main content and getting pulled off-task by visual elements on the sidebars.

REALM is a word recognition test that physicians use to determine whether their patients have low literacy skills and therefore may need additional help with instructions. It is a list of 66 medical words that the moderator asks the participant to read aloud. The number of words the participant pronounces correctly accurately reflects that person's literacy level.[1] The test takes only 2–3 minutes to administer and score, making it ideal for use in usability test recruitment.

> *The REALM (Rapid Estimate of Adult Literacy in Medicine) is a word recognition test that uses common words to assess a patient's literacy level. It takes about three minutes to administer and score the 66-word instrument. The REALM is commonly used in health literacy research and can be useful for identifying usability test participants with low literacy skills.*

Working with Participants Who Have Low Literacy Skills

There are some special considerations to keep in mind when including adults with low literacy skills in eye-tracking studies:

- Low literacy sometimes correlates with low income, which means these participants may also have uncorrected vision issues or damaged glasses. Consider having a small collection of drugstore reading glasses on hand for participant use.
- Be sensitive to the fact that reading may be difficult and even physically exhausting. The attention span of people with low literacy skills begins to wane much earlier than other participants. Try to keep sessions as brief as you can, and consider providing short breaks. Make sure that your most critical tasks are first in the session, in case there is no time for later tasks.
- Don't ever mention that you are talking to them because they have low literacy skills. If anyone asks why you have asked them

---

[1] The readability of text and a person's literacy skills used to be measured in terms of American grade level, and this is the scale used by the REALM. While text readability is still rated in terms of grade level, literacy skills are measured in terms of competency level. The National Adult Literacy Survey (NALS), for example, rates literacy on a scale of 0–500, with 0–225 considered functionally illiterate and 226–275 considered low literate. This makes it somewhat difficult to match up how well a person reads with the estimated grade level the text is written. While those who do usability studies involving low literacy sometimes compare NALS low literacy levels to an equivalent grade level (Doak et al., 1996; Summers & Summers, 2005), the creators of the NALS do not correlate their literacy levels to grade level this way and object to such characterizations (Riffenburg, 2009).

RAPID ESTIMATE OF ADULT LITERACY IN MEDICINE
(REALM)©

Terry Davis, PhD • Michael Crouch, MD • Sandy Long, PhD

Reading Level _____

Patient Name/
Subject # _____ Date of Birth _____

Grade Completed _____

Date _____ Clinic _____ Examiner _____

List 1		List 2		List 3	
fat	_____	fatigue	_____	allergic	_____
flu	_____	pelvic	_____	menstrual	_____
pill	_____	jaundice	_____	testicle	_____
dose	_____	infection	_____	colitis	_____
eye	_____	exercise	_____	emergency	_____
stress	_____	behavior	_____	medication	_____
smear	_____	prescription	_____	occupation	_____
nerves	_____	notify	_____	sexually	_____
germs	_____	gallbladder	_____	alcoholism	_____
meals	_____	calories	_____	irritation	_____
disease	_____	depression	_____	constipation	_____
cancer	_____	miscarriage	_____	gonorrhea	_____
caffeine	_____	pregnancy	_____	inflammatory	_____
attack	_____	arthritis	_____	diabetes	_____
kidney	_____	nutrition	_____	hepatitis	_____
hormones	_____	menopause	_____	antibiotics	_____
herpes	_____	appendix	_____	diagnosis	_____
seizure	_____	abnormal	_____	potassium	_____
bowel	_____	syphilis	_____	anemia	_____
asthma	_____	hemorrhoids	_____	obesity	_____
rectal	_____	nausea	_____	osteoporosis	_____
incest	_____	directed	_____	impetigo	_____

SCORE

List 1 _____
List 2 _____
List 3 _____
Raw Score _____

FIGURE 13.10 The 66-word REALM is a word recognition test used to estimate a person's literacy level. Used with permission of Terry Davis, Louisiana State University. To order the manual containing the REALM word list, examiner sheets, and instructions for how to administer and score it, email Terry Davis, PhD, at tdavis1@lsuhsc.edu or visit http://www.lsuhscshreveport.edu/HealthLiteracy/HealthLiteracyInfo.aspx.

to participate, answer that you want to make sure the interface you are testing is easy for people to use—which is the truth.
- Try to reduce how much participants actually have to read. Cutting out reading that is not related to the actual task means less work for participants and less chance that they will tire of reading before they have even begun. It also gives you the opportunity to make sure they have understood the task you have asked them to attempt. Go over consent forms verbally.
- As you would with any participant, show them respect.

CONCLUSION

Low literacy is an enormous problem in many societies. As we put more information and services online, it will continue to be important to make sure that members of our target audiences can read, understand, and act on the information they find.

Addressing the demands of low literacy can be a frustrating problem, one that is seemingly unsolvable. But there are ways to design information that make it easier for people with low literacy skills to get what they need—or at the very least, remove some of the barriers they encounter. The first step is to include people with low literacy skills in UX studies, especially when designing critical information, such as government services and healthcare. Efforts to design for this population can be even more effective if we make their struggles to find and comprehend information visible through the use of eye tracking. Eye tracking can open a window into their experience and increase our empathy for these users and the challenges they encounter online.

REFERENCES

Beck, I.L., 1995. The role of decoding in learning to read. American Educator 19 (2), 21–25.

Brinkman, J., 1992. Methodological problems when determining verbal protocol accuracy empirically. In: Proceedings from Second Workshop of Cognitive Processes in Complex Tasks '91, Eindhoven University of Technology, 52.

Davis, T., Crouch, M., Long, S., Jackson, R., Bates, P., George, R., et al., 1991. Rapid assessment of literacy levels of adult primary care patients. Fam. Med. 23 (6), 433–435.

Doak, C., Doak, L., Root, J., 1996. Teaching Patients with Low Literacy Skills, second ed. J.B. Lippincott Company, Philadelphia.

Groves, K., 2011. Website accessibility and buying power of persons with disabilities. Retrieved from, http://www.karlgroves.com/2011/10/21/buying-power-of-persons-with-disabilities/.

HR 751, 1991. National Literacy Act of 1991.

Jarrett, C., 2012. Buttons on forms and surveys: a look at some research. Presentation at the Information Design Association conference, Greenwich, UK, http://www.slideshare.net/cjforms/buttons-on-forms-and-surveys-a-look-at-some-research-2012.

Johnstone, C.J.-M., 2006. Using the Think Aloud Method (Cognitive Labs) to Evaulate Test Design for Students with Disabilities and English Language Learners. University of Minnesota, National Center on Educational Outcomes, Minneapolis, MN, University of Minnesota.

Kirsch, I., 2002. Adult literacy in America: A First Look at the Results of the National Adult Literacy Survey. National Center for Education Statistics U.S. Department of Education, Washington, DC.

Krosnick, J.A., 1991. Response strategies for coping with the cognitive demands of attitude measures in surveys. Appl. Cognit. Psychol. 5 (3), 213–236.

Mayer, R., 2009. Multimedia Learning, second ed. Cambridge University Press, Cambridge, UK.

Nagle, M., Zietlow, E., 2012. An Exploratory Comparison of Two Website Usability Testing Methods: Concurrent Think-Aloud and Eye-Tracking with Retrospective Think-Aloud. Unpublished Masters Thesis. University of Baltimore.

Nielsen, J., 2005. Lower-literacy users: writing for a broad consumer audience. Retrieved April 23, 2013, from Alertbox, http://www.nngroup.com/articles/writing-for-lower-literacy-users/.

OECD, 2000. Literacy in the Information Age: Final Report of the International Adult Literacy Survey. Organization for Economic Co-operation and Development, Paris.

Organisation for Economic Co-operation and Development, 2000. Literacy in the Information Age: Final Report of the International Adult Literacy Survey. OECD Publishing, Paris.

Parikh, N.S., Parker, R.M., Nurss, J.R., 1996. Shame and health literacy: the unspoken connection. Patient Educ. Couns. 27 (1), 33–39.

Riffenburg, A., 2009. Phone conversation. (A. Colter, Interviewer).

Simon, H., 1956. Rational choice and the structure of the environment. Psychol. Rev. 129–138.

Summers, K., Summers, M., 2004. Making the web friendlier for lower-literacy users. Intercom 51 (6), 19–21.

Summers, K., Summers, M., 2005. Reading and navigational strategies of web users with lower literacy skills. Proc. Am. Soc. Info. Sci. Tech. 42 (1).

Summers, K., Langford, J., Wu, J., Abela, C., Souza, R., 2006. Designing web-based forms for users with lower literacy skills. Proc. Am. Soc. Info. Sci. Tech. 43 (1), 1–12.

Tunmer, P.B., 1986. Decoding, reading, and reading disability. Remedial and Special Education 7 (1), 6–10.

Wallace, L.S., Rogers, E.S., Roskos, S.E., Holiday, D.B., Weiss, B.D., 2006. Screening items to identify patients with limited health literacy skills. J. Gen. Intern. Med. 21 (8), 874–877.

White, S.A., 2003. Framework for the 2003 National Assessment of Adult Literacy (NCES 2005-531). U.S. Department of Education, Washington, DC.

V

CONCLUSION

14

THE FUTURE OF EYE TRACKING AND USER EXPERIENCE

Andrew Schall[1] and Jennifer Romano Bergstrom[2]
[1]Spark Experience, Bethesda, MD, USA
[2]Fors Marsh Group, Arlington, VA, USA

It might be difficult for those in the field of user experience (UX) design to imagine what we will be doing in the next decade. Many of us have become comfortable as UX practitioners with our existing methodologies and have been able to refine our processes over the last two decades. New game-changing capabilities are on their way that may redefine how we conduct our research. So, where will we be in 2020 (see Figure 14.1)?

INTEGRATING EYE TRACKING INTO USER-CENTERED DESIGN METHODOLOGY

In the past, user research was considered a luxury and an optional component of digital product design. Over time, product managers found ways to successfully integrate user-centered design into most projects. To do this, the process needed to be more agile and compatible with often hectic development cycles.

FIGURE 14.1   What will the future hold? La Sortie de l'opéra en l'an, 2000.

Eye tracking has always been seen as the ultimate in luxury in both time and money. Few user research labs had eye trackers, and many of those who did had few opportunities to use them. The management and design teams also tended to see limited value from eye-tracking studies; the perceived benefit was often that they would receive pretty pictures (i.e., heat maps) with little interpretation beyond where users did or did not look (Figure 14.2).

FIGURE 14.2   Heat maps have often been used as pretty pictures without much substance to them.

While still in its infancy, eye tracking has made its way into user research in recent years.

We are slowly seeing the emergence of eye-tracking research that can scale to quick turnaround studies with smaller sample sizes to larger scale studies that provide deeper insights into user behavior. Education continues with product design teams regarding limitations and opportunities for small-scale qualitative eye-tracking studies. These studies have emerged as a compromise of sorts that allow eye tracking to fit into tight development time lines but can be highly focused to certain interface components rather than a holistic view of the entire product experience.

Larger eye-tracking studies are now supported, mostly by larger corporations, to help understand users as part of a comprehensive metrics program. Companies are beginning to understand the value in using eye-tracking insights as part of a continual improvement process where small, iterative changes can be made to improve the user experience.

Continued Improvements to Eye-Tracking Technology

Current uses of eye tracking are often limited to a lab environment where we set up an artificial situation for study participants. Yet still, eye tracking has come a long way and is now easy to use and not very intrusive. We can now conduct studies in which participants are hardly aware of the eye tracker at all. We suspect that the technology will continue to improve and will be less and less of an obstacle to collect eye-tracking data (Figure 14.3).

FIGURE 14.3   The SMI RED-m eye tracker, a new generation of compact eye trackers. (Courtesy of SensoMotoric Instruments Inc.)

As discussed in Chapter 10, new eye trackers, such as the Tobii X2 (Figures 14.4 and 14.5), allow for true plug and play

FIGURE 14.4   A Tobii X2 can be combined with a mobile stand for mobile device testing.

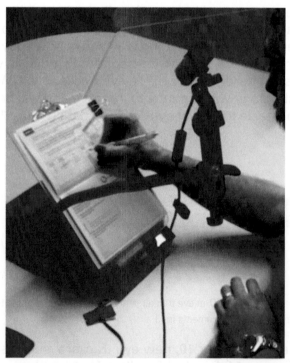

FIGURE 14.5   A Tobii X2 can be combined with a mobile stand for print material testing.

capability. These near pocket-sized models can be connected to most computers with a single connector, such as a USB cable. These "mini" eye trackers are also incredibly versatile in the possible types of testing configurations including laptops, desktop displays, mobile devices, and even print materials.

The usability of eye-tracking software has improved almost as well as the hardware. The current version of most eye-tracking software is considerably easier to use and is more stable, with fewer crashes. There has also been a concerted effort to make the software hardware agnostic allowing researchers to mix and match configurations that best meet their study needs. Eye-tracking manufacturers have vastly improved the ability to track individuals with different physical attributes in a variety of environmental conditions. This has helped to drastically reduce the number of individuals that cannot be tracked and has reduced the need to over-recruit participants.

The current trajectory of software and hardware improvements will likely lead to near effortless abilities to collect eye-tracking data by 2020. This will make eye tracking accessible to a wider range of professionals and will help improve the turnaround time of results.

While software and hardware continue to improve, UX researchers must also improve their study techniques and interpretation of eye-tracking findings. This is arguably more important than the improvement in technology; a poorly conducted study and misused eye-tracking data can only harm the field. In the future, advances in artificial intelligence will help by leading to low-level results that are analyzed and processed by computers, allowing UX researcher to focus less on interpreting individual fixation patterns and descriptive statistics and more on strategic implications.

THE FUTURE OF THE EYE-TRACKING TECHNOLOGY

As discussed in Chapter 4, physiological response measurements coupled with eye tracking have entered the UX field. These techniques are in their infancy for UX researchers, but we expect these technologies to continue to improve and be as easy to use as modern eye trackers. By 2020, companies large and small will be more aggressive in seeking new ways to engage their users, and it will be common for marketers and UX practitioners to use eye tracking with electroencephalography or electrodermal activity to assess the user experience. Competition in the digital advertising space will go beyond traditional website banner ads and click-through rates. While much of the rich user experience still involves traditional links, innovative products are emerging that allow UX researchers new opportunities.

Current eye-tracking technology allows UX researchers to track users' eyes through untethered headset units, such as the Tobii Glasses. These eye trackers allow users complete freedom of movement and can track everything the user looks at from mobile devices to the menu in their local café. By allowing users to freely move about their environment, we are able to observe more natural behaviors compared to when participants sit in front of an eye tracker in a lab. Marketers are now able to overlay eye-tracking data with shopping shelves to assess what people look at while they shop (Glazer, 2012), and Google has recently patented a process for measuring pay-per-gaze as a way to measure the effectiveness of advertising. The patent describes a process in which a head-mounted gaze-tracking device can identify ads that a user looks at (Figure 14.6). These data can be used to understand what types of advertisements people attend to and in what situations people pay attention to them (Bilton, 2013). Advertisements will likely continue to be a revenue source for both digital and offline content in the future. Eye tracking will help designers to understand a user's level of engagement with ads by fixation counts and duration in the context of the user's actions.

Others are creating technology whereby the eyes control the device. Taking advantage of built-in webcam technology, manufacturers are introducing eye-tracking capabilities into mobile devices. A *Wall Street Journal* article published in May of 2013 broke the news that Amazon has been developing a new mobile phone that would include retina-tracking technology that will allow users to navigate through content by simply using their eyes (Bensinger, 2013). Software already exists that allows users to merely look at the corner of an iPad to turn the page of an eBook, or look at the corner of a television screen to change the station (McKenzie, 2012; Objective Asia, 2013). This modern technology enables accessibility for disabled people who cannot interact with technology with their hands. The smartwatch (Figure 14.7) has recently been patented, which uses eye trackers to decide what content to display on a tiny watch interface (Schenck, 2013), and other researchers are using eye tracking

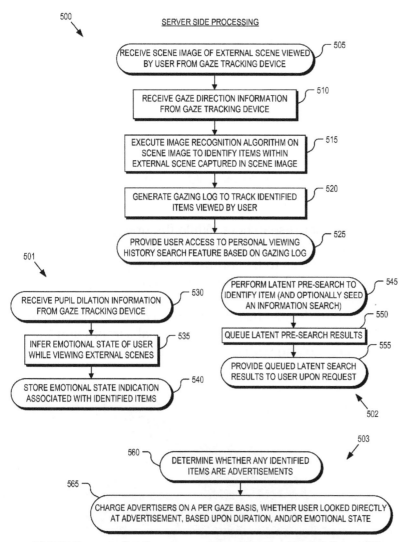

FIGURE 14.6   Google pay-per-gaze workflow from the U.S. Patent Office.

to diagnose Alzheimer's disease, schizophrenia, and memory disorders (Jutras et al., 2013; Newbern, 2013). Thus, we are now at a time when eye tracking is used not only to evaluate products but to interact with them and to diagnose disorders.

As eye-tracking technology continues to become miniaturized and cost less, we will see many more devices with this capability built in. Google Glass presents numerous opportunities for interaction

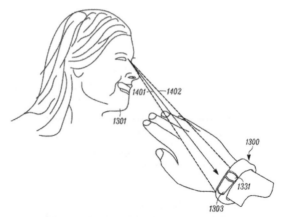

FIGURE 14.7   Eyes can control the smartwatch. (From: http://pocketnow.com/2013/08/30/motorola-smartwatch.)

designers and user researchers. While the first generation of this technology will be somewhat limited, by 2020, we can expect these types of devices to be commonplace. Eye tracking is likely to become an integral part of head-mounted displays where most user interactions will take place with eye movements. In addition to being an input device, user researchers can see through the eyes of their users with the existing external camera and track where they are looking with a camera facing the eye (Figure 14.8).

FIGURE 14.8   Generation 1 Google Glass headset.

Ubiquitous Eye Tracking

We are entering a brave new world for eye tracking. New technologies are emerging that will allow UX researchers to track users' eyes anywhere and everywhere. Obviously this will come with significant concerns about privacy and the ability for the user to control when they are being tracked.

While webcam-based eye tracking has emerged, there are still significant limitations to using this technology. Bojko (2013) identified several concerns about this methodology related to accuracy:

> Webcam eye tracking has much lower accuracy than real eye trackers. While a typical remote eye tracker (e.g., Tobii T60) has accuracy of 0.5 degrees of visual angle, a webcam will produce accuracy of 2–5 degrees, provided that the participant is NOT MOVING. To give you an idea of what that means, five degrees correspond to 2.5 inches (6 cm) on a computer monitor (assuming viewing distance of 27 inches), so the actual gaze location could be anywhere within a radius of 2.5 inches from the gaze location recorded with a webcam. I don't know about you but I wouldn't be comfortable with that level of inaccuracy in my studies.

As both the quality of webcams increases and the algorithms used for tracking the movement of the eyes improves, we can expect to see more of this type of eye tracking used in the future.

A short distance in the future will be a time of ubiquitous eye tracking with the ability to track a user's eyes on nearly every device they use. For UX researchers, this opens up enormous opportunities for large-scale quantitative eye-tracking studies. In addition to reaching broad audience groups currently not practical with today's technology, we will also have true freedom to collect eye-tracking data in the user's natural environment.

TAKING THE NEXT STEP

This book has presented an overview of how eye tracking is currently used by industry professionals to assess and improve the user experience of websites, forms, surveys, and games, both on desktop and mobile devices. The case studies and topics of this book illustrate the wide range of applications of eye tracking in user experience design. It is by no means an exhaustive assembly of all possible uses for eye tracking and interactive media. Many of the applications referenced in this book are still in their infancy and further research is required to better understand these areas. Our goal is to empower and inspire those who conduct UX research to integrate and see the value that eye tracking provides.

REFERENCES

Bilton, N., 2013. How pay-per-gaze advertising could work with Google glass. [online] Available at: http://bits.blogs.nytimes.com/2013/08/20/google-patents-real-world-pay-per-gaze-advertising/ (accessed: 01.09.13).

Bensinger, G., 2013. Amazon developing smartphone with 3-D screen. [online] Available at: http://online.wsj.com/article/SB1000142412788732474410457847308137337170.html (accessed 01.09.13).

Bojko, A., 2013. Rosenfeld Media—eye tracking the user experience: the truth about webcam eye tracking. [online] Available at: http://rosenfeldmedia.com/books/eye-tracking/blog/the_truth_about_webcam_eye_tra/ (accessed 01.09.13).

Glazer, E., 2012. The eyes have it: marketers now track shoppers' retina. [online] Available at: http://online.wsj.com/news/articles/SB10001424052702303644004577520760230459438 (accessed 14.08.13).

Jutras, M.J., Fries, P., Buffalo, E.A., 2013. Oscillatory activity in the monkey hippocampus during visual exploration and memory formation. Proc. Natl. Acad. Sci. U. S. A. Early Edition. http://www.pnas.org/content/early/2013/07/17/1302351110.

McKenzie, H., 2012. Three guys in a garage are turning your eyes into powerful remote controls. [online] Available at: http://pandodaily.com/2012/10/05/three-guys-in-a-garage-are-turning-your-eyes-into-powerful-remote-controls/ (accessed 12.10.13).

Newbern, L., 2013. Eye movement rhythm important to eye-tracking diagnoses. [online] Available at: http://news.emory.edu/stories/2013/07/yerkes_theta_saccades/campus.html (accessed 14.08.13).

Objective Asia, 2013. The other side of eye tracking. [online] Available at: http://eyetracking.com.sg/2013/08/28/the-other-side-of-eye-tracking/ (accessed 01.09.13).

Schenck, S., 2013. Motorola patents multi-display, eye-tracking smartwatch. [online] Available at: http://pocketnow.com/2013/08/30/motorola-smartwatch (accessed 01.09.13).

GLOSSARY

Areas of Interest (AOIs) Regions of a display that researchers define and classify by shape—quantitative data can be calculated for these regions.

Attention distribution The percentage of total visual attention allocated to a set of webpage features.

Attentional salience The power of visual elements to attract low-level, generally automatic visual attention.

Banner blindness Unintentionally not "seeing" ads or information that look like advertisements.

Breadcrumbs A navigation utility designed to let users know where they are within the site and how to get back up to higher levels within the information architecture.

Bricklet A small window to aid navigation on a web page.

Capture rate Percentage of eye-tracking data sampling based on length of recording. The capture rate is affected by calibration, time spent looking on the screen, and visual acuity. The higher the percentage, the more eye-tracking data present in the recording.

Card sort A research method used to understand how end users expect items (e.g., menu items) to be organized and the labels that should be used for each category of an information architecture.

Cognitive interview A method of interviewing users to obtain feedback about how they understand text and terminology and how they determine responses to (survey) questions.

Corneal reflection A method used by modern eye trackers to detect and track the location of the eye as it moves. It uses a light source to illuminate the eye, which then causes a reflection that is detected by a high-resolution camera.

Cutscene Scripted short movies displayed during non-interactive moments in video games.

Drift Slow and small difference between the user's gaze on fixated visual target and the true location of the target.

Dwell time Total time the gaze is within an area of interest, including all fixations and saccades.

Electrodermal Activity (EDA) Measures the electrical conductance of the skin. There are several names for it, including: electrodermal response (EDR), galvanic skin response (GSR), psychogalvanic reflex (PGR), skin conductance response (SCR), and skin conductance level (SCL).

Electroencephalography (EEG) Records electrical activity of the brain by placing electrodes on the scalp.

Element viewing The percentage or number of participants that view a given web page feature during a given task.

Eye gaze The location of an individual's eyes at a given point in time.

Eye tracker A device that measures eye positions and movements to understand where an individual is looking.

Fixation The pause of the eye movement on a specific area of the visual field.

Fixation count The number of times the eye gaze pauses in a specific spot (e.g., within an area of interest).

Foveal A region of human visual perception that is highly detailed and provides complete clarity about what a person is looking at.

Front loading Starting a piece of content with information-rich words.

Gaze angle The direction of gaze relative to the head.

Gaze opacity map An inverse map of compiled fixation data. The opposite of a heat map, it is best used to highlight areas on the interface that received fewer fixations. It is also known as a Spotlight map.

Gaze plot A visual representation of fixations and saccades—circles represent fixations; often the sizes of circles represent duration.

Gerontechnology   The intersection of gerontology and technology, often with the aim of improving the functioning of older people in daily life through the use of technology.

Gestalt principles   In visual perception, the regions of the visual field where portions are perceived as grouped or joined together and are thus segregated from the rest of the visual field.

GSR   Galvanic skin response (*see Electrodermal activity*)

Heat map   A visualization that uses different colors to show fixation count or duration.

I-TRAC   Five steps in the process of preparing eye tracking data for analysis: identify, trim, remove, aggregate and code.

Information Architecture (IA)   The combination of organization and labeling of navigation systems.

Information foraging   A theory that humans search for information in much the same way that our ancestors searched for food. We constantly assess whether the information we could potentially gain is worth the energy we would expend to gather that information, or whether it would be potentially more efficient to move to a different source of information.

Information scent   Words and phrases that are more likely to capture our attention because they match our intent.

Likert scale   A psychometric scale for questionnaires named after its inventor, psychologist Rensis Likert. It is used for scaling responses in survey research (rating scales).

Low literacy   Having limited ability to use printed and written information successfully.

Macro negative space   The space between blocks of content (e.g., gutters between columns of text).

Mental model   The mental constructs people have of themselves, others, the environment, and the things with which they interact. Mental models are constructed based on prior experiences, and they shape expectations for future experiences.

Micro negative space   The space within a block of content (e.g., the spacing between lines).

Microsaccade   Quick, short saccade to maintain fixation on a visual target.

Multimodal redundancy   Using a variety of senses (e.g., visual and auditory) to help older people with age-related functional limitations to access digital information.

Overlay	Each visual element that is part of the user interface when playing video games.
Paper prototype	A paper model of an interface that allows a product to be evaluated with users before being completely developed. Also referred to in low-fidelity testing in which there is limited functionality and navigational capabilities.
Parafoveal	A region of transition within human visual perception in which the image becomes gradually less focused as a person moves from the fovea into the peripheral area.
PDP	Acronym for Product Description Page. A web page devoted to imagery, pricing and information regarding a specific product.
Perceptual flow	The most common order in which elements of a web page are viewed for the first time.
Peripheral	The largest region of human visual perception. It has very poor acuity and is optimized to pick up movements and contrasts.
Plain language	Communication your audience can understand the first time they read it.
Pupillometry	The measurement of changes in pupil diameter.
Rapid Assessment of Adult Literacy in Medicine (REALM)	A word recognition test that uses common words to assess a patient's literacy level. It takes about three minutes to administer and score. Commonly used in health literacy research.
Regressive saccades	Rapid eye movements that are backtracked such that a user looks back at content previously seen; can be indicative of confusion or uncertainty.
Retrospective Think Aloud (RTA)	After a usability task is completed, the participant is asked to recall what they had been thinking as they worked on the task. This is typically done as the participant watches a video replay of their task. When used in conjunction with eye tracking, the participant is often shown a video replay of their eye movements and asked what they had been thinking.
Saccades	Rapid movements of the eye from one fixation to another.
Satisfice	A decision-making strategy of choosing an option that is "good enough" rather than spending cognitive effort on finding the best possible choice, combined form of "satisfy" and "suffice."
Scanability	The ease that something (e.g., a screen) can be visually covered and understood.

Scene camera	Capture videos of the scenes, so researchers can calculate where users are looking, and then overlap eye movements onto the scenes for visualization. Used in mobile eye-tracking research.
SERP	Search Engine Result Pages.
Smooth pursuit	Eye movement that closely tracks a moving object by steadily matching its velocity.
Think aloud	Participant in a usability study is asked to think out loud as they work on the usability task so that there is a running commentary of what they are thinking and feeling, moment by moment. The UX team is able to get a better understanding of what is happening to participants and the process they are going through as they work on a task.
Tree test	A research method for validating the intuitiveness of an information architecture by having participants perform tasks using the menu structure.
Tremor	Small oscillation of the eye during fixation.
Usability test	Technique in user-centered design to evaluate a product by testing it with actual end users. Typical measures are accuracy, efficiency, and user satisfaction.
Visual affordance	Design cues that suggest how to interact with an object.
Visual hierarchy	A visual order for guiding users in viewing a web page. This order is designed by manipulating the attributes (e.g., size, location) of perceptual elements (e.g., text, image) on the page.
Wide Range Achievement Test (WRAT)	A norm-referenced test that measures the basic academic skills, including word reading and sentence comprehension.

INDEX

Note: Page numbers followed by *f* indicate figures, *b* indicate boxes, *t* indicate tables, *np* indicate footnotes, and *ge* indicate glossary.